The Politics of the Peace Corps and VISTA

The
POLITICS
of the
PEACE
CORPS
&VISTA

T . ZANE REEVES

•

THE UNIVERSITY OF ALABAMA PRESS

Tuscaloosa and London

Library of Congress Cataloging-in-Publication Data

Reeves, T. Zane.
The politics of the Peace Corps and VISTA.

Bibliography: p.
Includes index.
1. Peace Corps (U.S.) 2. Volunteers in
Service to America. I. Title.
HC60.5.R45 1988   361.2'6   86-19194
ISBN 0-8173-0323-5

British Library Cataloguing-in-Publication Data is available.

To my parents
Randall and Tomazine Reeves
who inspired their eleven children
to see what lies on the other side
of the mountain.

Contents

Acknowledgments

Of course it is impossible to acknowledge all those individuals who have influenced the writing of this book. Some might wish not to be mentioned or acknowledged. After all, this book is neither an apologia nor a defense of the Peace Corps or VISTA. It is critical but from one who is deeply fond of both organizations. Although this work proposed to be a policy analysis, it is even more a labor of love that began when a young, idealistic volunteer joined the Peace Corps following its creator's tragic assassination.

To remember all those whose influence has shaped my thoughts and research is truly a humbling experience. Three groups of individuals must be readily acknowledged: volunteers, family, and professional colleagues. First, there were the Peace Corps volunteers who, together, experienced training at the Experiment-in-International-Living and finally served in Brazil. As volunteers during the early 1960s, we stayed up countless late evenings in an undying effort to understand our new and exciting environment: Don Batchelder, our leader; Willy and Sue Schuerer; Ann and Tom Ventre; Art and Marge Morin; Dave and Joan Drenth; and, of course, Betty Shackleford. We and others were Brazil-17.

And there were the other volunteers, the ones without the glamour of service in exotic lands. The VISTA volunteers and the University Year for ACTION (UYA) students faced frustration and hardship far closer to home. My sister, Melody, and David Dotson gave me insights into VISTA volunteerism that most of my fellow Peace Corps volunteers would never appreciate. I learned much as a fledgling director of VISTA's UYA program in inner-city Los Angeles. "My" volunteers were a pretty cool bunch: Steve Bennett, Kenna Gose, Jane Hamilton, Mike Pleassance, Jane McDonald, Alison Gilbert, and Teddie Randall.

My family's contribution is strongest but less tangible. My parents blessed me by choosing me to be the oldest of their eleven children. I will always be appreciative to them and to my brothers and sisters who were always there when I needed them the most. Also, I owe a special debt to my son and daughter, Bradley and Renata, who helped me finally come of age as a single parent during their teenage years.

Nor could this book have reached printed form without the patience of Malcolm MacDonald at The University of Alabama Press. In particular, Roy Grisham, Jr., did a masterful editing job. I also suspect that an author may be only as good as his or her research assistants. In that respect I "lucked out" by getting Roy Turpen and Scott Nystrom to do endless library "grunt" work. To Cheryl Hayes I owe a special debt for her editing and research skills.

Finally, my theoretical mentors were both unmerciful and encouraging. I will always be in the debt of Bill Lammers, of the University of Southern California. Charles Goodsell, at Virginia Tech, forced me to forge a stronger theoretical model of the inner workings of political ideology and organizational culture.

To these folks and many more, I owe so much.

T. Zane Reeves
Albuquerque, New Mexico

The Politics of the Peace Corps and VISTA

One

Organizational Culture and Ideology

Since the inception of the Peace Corps and VISTA (Volunteers In Service To America) in the 1960s an intense conflict has raged within the two agencies. For almost twenty-five years at the Peace Corps and twenty years at VISTA, two warring camps have vied for ideological supremacy: on one side, presidentially appointed administrators in both agencies; on the other, career employees and former volunteers. Both groups fought via the avenue of administrative discretion—for example, ultimate choices reached through decision-making freedom. Although, on occasion, there have been instances of illegal pressure and political hardball, by and large, each side has attempted to undermine the other through discretionary administrative tactics. This book is an analysis of that struggle.

Typically, political appointees in the two agencies work hard to reshape existing organizational goals and values to conform with their own ideological worldviews. Not surprisingly, political appointees are resisted, often with equal fervor, by career government employees, volunteers, and former volunteers in the Peace Corps and VISTA. They are adamantly opposed to the imposition by exempt (noncivil service) employees of new or conflicting value systems ("ideologies") from the political arena. Thus, organizational culture and political ideology have continually been at odds, and they remain so during the Reagan administration.[1] It should be noted that this conflict is not a struggle between Democrats and Republicans; rather, a particular ideological viewpoint is enforced within each party when it is in control of the presidency. These ideologies differ markedly in the underlying assumptions regarding poverty, its causes and cures, and the proper role of agency volunteers. Ideology, as interpreted by political appointees, career employees, volunteers, and former volunteers, has played a major role in shaping agency goals, objectives, and project selection during this turbulent period.

Organizational conflict began during the Kennedy and Johnson administrations, when civil service employees were socialized by a dominant *activist* ideological framework. "Activists" are defined as those individuals with a strong commitment to encourage direct political action in solving the problems of the poor.[2] Although they supported direct intervention by the federal government in fighting local pockets of poverty, activists did not seek a political restructuring of society. As David Pass observes, and volunteer attitudinal surveys substantiate, VISTA volunteers saw themselves as political resources available to the poor.[3] Both Peace Corps and VISTA volunteers, as educated and aware individuals, believed they had a moral imperative to help the less fortunate.[4]

One might reasonably wonder why activist values were so attractive to the policymakers who designed the Peace Corps and VISTA. In part, the attractiveness of these values may be attributable to what Anthony Downs calls an ideological life cycle that many public agencies experience.[5] Over an agency's lifetime, the agency usually moves through certain stages of ideological change, with each stage becoming progressively more conservative. Initially, bureaucracies are dominated by advocates or zealots who promote the agency's social mission over the self-interest of individuals.

In the early stages of agency evolution, this evangelical phenomenon is often particularly true in such agencies as VISTA or Peace Corps, which utilize altruistically committed volunteers.[6] As true believers, these short-term volunteers frequently are motivated by psychological gratification rather than monetary reward. Further, as full-time volunteers, they become intensely involved and committed to the agency's social mission.

Thus Peace Corps and VISTA were developed by policymakers with strong activist values. Peace Corps was designed in 1960–61 by a special task force of activist thinkers headed by President Kennedy's brother-in-law, Sargent Shriver. Four years later, Shriver headed another task force, one that outlined the War on Poverty, including VISTA. Both programs were formulated and administered by men who held strongly activist views.

Activist values, along with a secularized missionary identity, were accepted by Peace Corps and VISTA employees, both career staff and volunteers, who were given a special sense of mission and duty toward the poor.[7] Volunteers were knights sent forth with a noble cause: fight poverty at home and abroad. They were socialized through an activist set of values, beliefs, and norms of behavior. From the moment of their inception in the 1960s, Peace Corps and VISTA were endowed with a rare organizational factor among governmental bureaucracies—an identifiable organizational culture. In this particular case, it was a coherent activist culture.

Corporate and Noncorporate Cultures

Peace Corps and VISTA were born with what can be viewed as the governmental equivalent of a corporate culture.[8] Operationally, *organizational culture,* in both private and public agencies, may be defined as shared philosophy, ideology, values, beliefs, expectations, and norms. These attributes usually are not written down or formalized; they are learned as part of being inducted, or socialized, into the organization.[9] From the perspective of dynamics, an organization's culture is the "invisible force behind the tangibles and observable in any organization, a social energy that moves people into action"; thus its culture is to the organization what personality is to the individual—a "hidden . . . unifying theme that provides meaning, direction, and mobilization."[10]

Activist cultures at the Peace Corps and VISTA were enhanced by the charisma of a martyred president, by exotic portrayals of young Americans helping poor villagers abroad and the once invisible poor in the United States. VISTA and Peace Corps projects were designed by activists who believed sincerely that poverty could be eradicated by direct intervention. They were "poverty warriors" who accepted the activist culture and its challenges.[11]

To claim that any governmental agency might possess an organizational culture, much less a strong one, must strike many as implausible. Admittedly, governmental cultures do not always resemble their corporate counterparts. No doubt, many observers and citizens agree with the authors of *Corporate Cultures* that governmental organizations might, at best, be categorized as simply *process* cultures, "because no single transaction breaks [them] . . . financial stakes are low. Decisions are low risk and without much feedback. Employees who protect the status quo are 'heroes' in this clique."[12] To describe all governmental organizations thus is a mistake, however, even though it reinforces a commonly held and, perhaps, self-serving stereotype of public organizations as dehumanizing bureaucracies.[13]

Organizational cultures are indeed found in every organization, be it public, private, or not-for-profit; but there the similarity ends. The characteristics of organizational cultures vary greatly. More careful scrutiny points to a small number of governmental organizations whose performance neither fits the bureaucratic mold nor exhibits a process culture at work. Those governmental organizations with strong prevailing cultures and a clear sense of mission have organizational cultures that deserve closer analysis.

Certain government cultures are similar to corporate cultures, especially in the conditions surrounding their creation. In particular, some government and corporate cultures are marked by a commitment to excellence. They are distinguished from other organizations by: a shared set of simply stated values; the influence of a strong, often charismatic leader at their inception; a clear sense of organizational purpose; a proclivity to take action; strong interaction with consumers or clients; and the ability to encourage creativity among employees.[14]

When judged by these criteria, certain governmental and corporate organizations, in their formative stages, are guided by what are often referred to as "commitment cultures." Government agencies such as the Tennessee Valley Authority (TVA), the Federal Bureau of Investigation (FBI), and the National Aeronautics and Space Administration (NASA) are examples of working commitment cultures that come readily to mind. As is true of corporate-commitment cultures, the cultures of these agencies were forged by strong leaders, such men as David Lilienthal, James Webb, and J. Edgar Hoover.[15] They, in turn, often were backed by such strong presidents as Franklin Roosevelt, John Kennedy, and Lyndon Johnson. Only Hoover could effectively dominate an organizational culture with no or little presidential support.

These government organizations were effective largely because of clearly defined missions, action orientations, and high employee morale. In each case a commitment culture permeated the agency, a culture that was understood and that motivated career employees at all levels. Because of the culture's strength, there was no counterculture and no confusion of mission. TVA, the FBI, and NASA were unusually rare among bureaucratic organizations. The disastrous Challenger shuttle program at NASA in 1986 tragically demonstrated how quickly an organizational culture can be destroyed. To this selective list of government organizations with commitment cultures can be added several voluntary-action and antipoverty programs created during the New Frontier and the Great Society. The Peace Corps and its later domestic cousin, VISTA, are notable examples. The Peace Corps, initially a campaign promise of Senator Kennedy's in the 1960s, was heralded as the epitome of idealistic commitment for young Americans who wished to serve overseas. VISTA subsequently was subsummed under Lyndon Johnson's War on Poverty as a kind of domestic Peace Corps for voluntary service to the poor at home.

At this point, the reader might with some justification ponder the fact that few commitment cultures have emerged within government bureaucracies. Why don't more government agencies strive for commitment and clarity of purpose? First, unlike their counterparts in the corporate world, government cultures rarely are given sufficient time and the proper nurture to flourish, especially in the United States, with its seeming revolving-door system of appointments. Depending on electoral currents, those politicians and their appointees who first shape and mold an agency's culture are soon replaced by a new, often ideologically hostile administration. This kaleidoscopic world ensures a "government of strangers."[16] New presidential appointees, often holding ideological beliefs significantly contrary to a prevailing organizational culture, assume power but usually within less than two years are replaced yet again.

Second, commitment cultures in government probably are more numerous than is commonly thought, but they are concentrated in smaller organizations with a more easily identifiable sense of purpose. Undoubtedly, a number of state and local governments develop and encourage commitment cultures. It is equally evident that several public universities with national reputations for excellence operate within organizational cultures that emphasize commitment and clarity of mission. The same can be said of elite military units and numerous other publicly funded programs.

Commitment cultures, in both private and public sectors, which survive over a period of time, do so because they are passed on and enriched by successive generations of organizational leaders. In the public sector, however, enrichment of organizational culture and its accompanying behavior norms are blocked by the electoral process. The election of a new president or governor signals the arrival of another group of agency administrators. Fresh from the campaign trail, they usually are intent on implanting a new ideology or a presidential mandate. There is little perceived benefit in perpetuating organizational values and programs initiated by political enemies.

The Peace Corps and VISTA are unfortunate examples of conflict between organizational culture and political ideology. Whereas an activist culture originally was set in place during the Kennedy and Johnson administrations, Richard Nixon's narrow victory in 1968 over Hubert Humphrey ushered in an ideology with opposing values. President Nixon, as would later presidents Ford and Reagan, appointed administrators to those agencies who can only be categorized as ideological conservatives. These appointees did not disagree with the legislatively mandated goal of alleviating poverty; they were simply "less impressed with the severity of social problems than with the danger of injurious side effects from the proposed solutions."[17] Conservatives distrusted federal agencies and their career civil servants and instead looked to local initiatives, especially those in the private sector, for solutions to the poverty problem. Republican conservatives rejected the activist notion of outside antipoverty volunteers and supported local volunteerism that would demonstrate an achievement ethic or role model intended to motivate the poor.

Throughout six administrations, presidential appointees attempted to change and redirect governmental programs to conform with their own ideological views of poverty. Program goals and organizational culture supported during the Kennedy and Johnson presidencies were attacked by presidential appointees in each succeeding administration. Nowhere was the confusion more evident than in VISTA and Peace Corps, with their strong missionary cultures. Ever since their optimistic beginnings— the Peace Corps in 1961 and VISTA in 1964—intense ideological conflict had reigned. An ideological chasm developed between activists and conservatives, between political appointees and career employees, volunteers as well as former volunteers.

Bridging the Ideology Gap

Conservative appointees during the Nixon administration intended to use their administrative powers to the fullest in redirecting the Peace Corps, VISTA, and other War on Poverty programs. They soon learned, however, that organizational cultures, once in place, are not easily destroyed, or even displaced. Administrative discretion is not the sole domain of political appointees; career administrators in government organizations, particularly those with strong missionary cultures, do not drop overnight their cultural values, roles, and behavior norms. They held intense activist values regarding poverty and the role of volunteers in breaking the cycle of poverty. During the New Frontier and the Great Society, activist administrators waged the "just war" in their agencies. They were not prepared to abandon principle just because Richard Nixon had slipped by a narrow victory into the White House.

Conflict thus ensued between Nixon appointees and career civil servants. Nowhere was the conflict more intense than at Peace Corps and VISTA. On one side, activist career employees and former volunteers fought to protect activist values and programs; while on the other, conservative appointees to both agencies sought to introduce conservative values and ideology. Surprisingly, ideological conflict and confusion did not subside with the election of Jimmy Carter. As will become evident, the struggle between political appointees and career employees intensified in certain areas.

Regardless of their political party, presidential appointees were faced with administering agencies staffed by long-term career employees. As young adults, many had joined the VISTA, Peace Corps, and War on Poverty programs in the 1960s. As organizational zealots, many held to the activist culture of that era. Periodically they were joined by former VISTA and Peace Corps volunteers with even stronger activist convictions.

Their antagonists were political appointees, sometimes by conservatives such as Nixon, Ford, and Reagan; at other times, by Jimmy Carter. In any case, political appointees almost invariably were campaign loyalists whose appointments were seen as the just rewards of victory. Presidential appointees from both parties tended to be ideologues or true believers, more likely than the average voter or even the candidates themselves to have narrow ideological views. It is no secret that presidential campaigns, with their emphasis on winner-take-all and middle-of-the-road strategies, lead to shallow discussion of issues by candidates (even when the candidates are Walter Mondale and Ronald Reagan).[18]

As indicated, the ideological struggle is not between Democrats and Republicans or even solely between activists and conservatives. From 1977 to 1981, Democrats were once again in control of the executive branch, yet conflict in the Peace Corps was perhaps the most bitter in its history. Although career Peace Corps administrators and most of the former volunteers adhered to the agency's original activist values, Carter's political appointees did not. Under the ACTION director, former New Left activist Sam Brown, a new ideology was imposed—radical activism. During the Carter administration, organizational conflict was no longer between Nixon-Ford conservatives and activist civil servants. Radical activists stressed political priorities over neutrality in Peace Corps involvement overseas. It was an ideological tenet that traditional activists at the Peace Corps would find abhorrent.

In assessing the organizational struggles at the Peace Corps and VISTA between appointees and administrators, several factors must be noted at the outset. First, political appointees are often reluctant to define limits on their own powers of administrative discretion. The prospect of organizational culture or tradition is seen as an obstacle to effective decision-making, not aid for motivating employees. Second, perhaps due to their recent, still euphoric campaign successes, partisan appointees often see their own authority as a direct extension of the President's. The winning team (we) has an electoral mandate from the people to bring about change, to shake up the status quo (them). Third, political appointees frequently are shocked to find that their directives are not always carried out promptly or that their priorities are not widely accepted in the organization. Perhaps political appointees feel that government workers will obey as willingly as campaign workers. Obviously, that is hardly the case, especially in cases where employees believe in a different organizational culture or value system. Even in government agencies with no commitment cultures, civil service employees still control the information, proposals for policy formation, and knowledge for assessing project feasibility.[19] Even among governmental bureaucracies in Downs' final stage of conservatism, "a gap does exist in communication between political appointees and career executives."[20]

This fundamental war in the bureaucracy between politics and administration has long been recognized. The conflict was not new in the Nixon administration, and it remains active in the 1980s.[21] Max Weber, among others, recognized the natural divergence between political and bureaucratic objectives, noting that a politician's calling is to advocate issue positions, while the administrator acts from a conflicting principle—professional responsibility: "The honor of the civil servant is vested in his ability to execute conscientiously the order of superior authorities. Without this moral discipline and self-denial, in the highest sense of the term, the whole apparatus would fall into pieces."[22] Although Weber was able theoretically to envision an organizational environment in which politicians make policy and bureaucrats administer programs, is such an environment truly possible? As the Centennial Agendas Projects asked of the American Society for Public Administration, can we realistically achieve a "deeper and more genuine partnership between elected officials and career managers?"[23]

From a more contemporary vantage point, Donald Devine, President Reagan's former director of the Office of Personnel Management (OPM), defends the predominant role of politics in administrative decision-making: "There is a public administration view that you should remove politics from government. I think that's kind of a dream. Politics doesn't, of necessity, mean partisanship or arbitrariness; it simply means that there must be response to what the elected officials of the government want."[24] Devine raises two key questions: First, to what extent can the gap between politics and administration, between political appointees and career employees, be bridged? No doubt, a certain tension will always exist; as Douglas Yates argues, "the structure of public bureaucracies is characterized by interest group behavior, fragmentation, and conflict and cooperation."[25] Although I have, by design, placed appointees and careerists together, need they be enemies, especially to the degree they were in conflict in the Peace Corps and VISTA?

Second, how much administrative discretion should be given political appointees, to enable them to change the minds (and hearts) of nonexempt employees? As indicated, few appointees remain in their positions for even half a presidential term, creating a "government of strangers."[26] Many career employees at ACTION, the umbrella agency for VISTA and Peace Corps after 1971, originally accepted the activist values of the New Frontier and Great Society; they believed in, and were willing to defend, these ideals against conservative newcomers. Resentment harbored by many employees with activist values was vividly expressed on the morning after President Ford's electoral defeat. ACTION employees placed a sign in the agency's headquarters office that read: "We won!"[27]

Is it possible that "the working relationship between career government executives and appointed managers is one that must be reinvented with every change of administration?"[28] From city halls to the federal bureaucracy, change in elected administrations produces some discontinuity. At the very best, career employees are faced with "the periodic appearance of a new boss whose selection was not based on any expertise in subjects within that organizational jurisdiction and who provided no careful preparation for the position he or she was to assume. The department or agency finds itself with a new leader who, at the outset at least, is not equipped to lead."[29] If the political appointee arrives convinced that an organization's culture is unacceptable, the inevitable result is a royal brouhaha.

Nor has there been notable success in efforts to legislate peace between appointees and career executives in federal service. The politics-administration saga did not end with the Civil Service Reform Act of 1978 (CSRA), a law intended, among other things, to make federal civil servants more accountable to their political superiors. Evidence exists suggesting that CSRA has served as the vehicle for even greater politicization of the federal bureaucracy, one waged ferociously during the Reagan presidency.[30] In his book *The Administrative Presidency,* Richard Nathan notes that unusual reliance was placed by the Reagan cabinet and subcabinet appointees on training and indoctrination activities, with the intention of insulating political appointees and maintaining ideological purity.[31]

By appointing political managers to top administrative positions while guaranteeing job security for career employees, the United States has ensured roles for both political and administrative discretion in the implementation of policy. Administrative discretion allows bureaucratic resistance to even overwhelming electoral "mandates," as occurred in the presidential elections of 1964, 1972, 1980, and 1984 (although the precise nature of the mandate may be unclear). Only a few ideologues on the political far right seek unlimited political discretion, so that civil servants are merely neutral tools for carrying out policies made elsewhere. "Career staff will supply information, but they should never become involved in the formulation of agenda-related policy objectives."[32] Clearly, the proper constitutional, ethical, and political limits of administrative decision-making remain an important agenda item for continued debate and discussion.

No doubt, administrative discretion can be abused by both political appointees and career employees; both can wage ideological warfare from positions of organizational or partisan political strength. As Chester Barnard observes, the true role of an administrator is to shape and manage an agency's values or culture.[33] Effective leaders are value-shapers concerned with the informal human dynamics of an organization. They stand in sharp contrast to iconoclastic administrators who *manipulate* through relatively effective short-term rewards and punishment. They know the limits and responsibilities of administrative discretion. As leaders, they understand the potential value and symbolism that lies within a culture possessing a strong commitment. Their ideological baggage is left on the proverbial doorstep.

In most of the circumstances described in this book, political appointees of various political persuasions did not totally succeed in their efforts to redirect organizational values or cultures. Like presidential panjandrums, they believed that an organizational culture could be undone with a stroke of the administrative pen. Consequently, commitment cultures that originally prevailed at VISTA and the Peace Corps in the 1960s were replaced by ideological warfare between career employees and political appointees—*conflict that occurred regardless of which party was in power.* The result was, and is, organizational confusion and ideological dominance over culture.

Perhaps it is unrealistic to expect either political appointees or career employees voluntarily to diminish their own power. Activist versus conservative, radical activist versus activist, as well as countless other ideological permutations, will continue to influence policymaking decisions and organizational cultures. It is inherent in the combined political-administrative bureaucracy. In most governmental agencies, a strong cultural and ideological conflict is, by design, prescribed. At best, it is an uneasy symbiosis.[34] At worst, it is the style of organizational warfare that has existed at the Peace Corps and VISTA since the 1960s. It is a "how not to" that demands attention. In essence, our task is to explore ways of making political appointees less disruptive (even to make them take advantage of their insights) while developing strong commitment cultures in government organizations.

Two

An
Activist
Peace Corps and VISTA

To many observers, the Peace Corps—and, to a lesser extent, the Alliance for Progress—symbolize the finest expression of John F. Kennedy's presidency.[1] In a similar vein, the War on Poverty (which included VISTA) represented the noblest accomplishment of Lyndon Johnson's one-term administration. Created four years after the establishment of the Peace Corps, VISTA, dubbed the "domestic Peace Corps," was an opportunity for young Americans to achieve at home what they had achieved overseas. During the Nixon administration both programs were combined—but not disbanded—within the newly created ACTION agency. As we saw in Chapter 1, the Peace Corps and VISTA were concrete examples of activist policymaking assumptions regarding poverty and the poor.

The Peace Corps and VISTA were the only government programs that relied on a unique strategy for fighting poverty, both in the United States and abroad: use of the full-time volunteer. The role of the volunteer was central to the projects of both VISTA and the Peace Corps. Although the goals of voluntary action varied significantly, depending on whether activist, conservative, or radical-activist appointees were in control, full-time volunteers remained the focal point of VISTA and the Peace Corps. While other antipoverty and government programs for the poor utilized paid, full-time employees and part-time volunteers, the Peace Corps and VISTA relied on full-time volunteers.

VISTA and Peace Corps volunteers were expected to work toward the same result: liberation of the poor from poverty. Antipoverty volunteers in both programs were required to serve full-time; live in the poverty community, in order to be accepted by the poor; live at a poverty level on a minimal cost-of-living stipend; and be a change-agent resource for the community. Thus antipoverty and Peace Corps programming was intended to change the lot of the poor via a strategy of planned social intervention. The catalyst for change was the full-time volunteer.

For more than two decades, and during the administrations of six presidents, antipoverty volunteers waged a war on poverty at home and in Third World countries. During this period, the original goals of both programs were revised or eliminated, depending on the particular values or political ideologies of the appointees in power. For activist, radical activist, and conservative ideologues, the Peace Corps and VISTA provided a means of acting on their contrasting beliefs regarding the causes of poverty, the cures for poverty, the appropriate program objectives, and the requisite volunteer skills and characteristics.

In VISTA and the Peace Corps, the volunteer's role was subject to ongoing debate between political appointees holding a particular ideology, and career civil servants and returned volunteers holding an organizational culture. As we have seen, both the Peace Corps and VISTA began with cultures of strong commitment and relied on voluntary action programs. Unfortunately, both factors lend themselves to ideological battle and thus are excellent case studies for examining ideological struggle with organizational administration.

Liberating the Poor:
Activist and Conservative Values

Although the Peace Corps predated VISTA by some four years, both programs share an underlying value system in their activist assumptions about poverty and its causes. Created later, VISTA was actually a resurrection of the abortive National Service Program during the Kennedy administration. Both VISTA and the Peace Corps assume an antipoverty view of poverty that was expressed in other War on Poverty programs as well; but only the Peace Corps and VISTA employed the full-time volunteer as a specific antipoverty strategy.

As defined by most dictionaries, *antipoverty* did not appear before the early 1960s. As a concept, the term is used to state what one is against—poverty—not how the goal is to be accomplished, or even if the elimination of poverty is possible. Neither does the term suggest how it differs from numerous other government efforts to help low-income citizens: welfare, compensatory education, and work training.

As formulated during the New Frontier and Great Society, the unique nature and essence of antipoverty programs centered on a strategy of planned intervention designed to break the cycle of poverty.[2] It was assumed that only direct intervention could alter the environmental forces that kept the poor destitute. Unlike general welfare, social services, or public jobs programs for the poor, the antipoverty program used planned intervention to attack the root causes of poverty. In the case of VISTA and Peace Corps, full-time volunteers largely from nonpoverty backgrounds would be at the front line of intervention.[3]

Clearly, antipoverty policies reflect activist values and assumptions. Activists, as well as the later radical activists of the Carter presidency, believe that poverty is caused by structural economic problems inherent in capitalism. In their view, the poor are exploited by capitalists whose interests, in turn, are protected by an activist political system. The poor are powerless pawns and will never escape unless outside catalysts intervene to help them organize themselves. Otherwise, they would not be able to end the vicious cycle of poverty that supposedly is passed on from generation to generation.[4] Activists assume that a redistribution of political and economic power should occur so the poor can control their own destinies. Full-time volunteers would serve as resources in planning social change; after all, they understand how the economic and political system functions. As children of the establishment, Peace Corps and VISTA volunteers could lead the way in liberating the poor.

Conservatives take a wholly different view of poverty and the poor. They are convinced that in general poverty is caused by low individual self-esteem and low achievement goals. Both anti-poverty programs and their underlying activist values are mistaken. Conservatives believe that governmental programs must be founded on an ethic of individual achievement. The poor should be encouraged to join David McClelland's "Achieving Society."[5] Rather than train volunteers as community organizers and mobilize them to change the system, volunteers should function as role models for the poor. The poor need to be instilled with optimism and hope, not turned into angry revolutionaries.

The historical roots of this philosophical cleavage between activist and conservative value systems are deep and are beyond the scope of this book. Simply put, the debate centers on the appropriate strategies for human liberation from **any** social problem, in this case, poverty. Theorists and practitioners alike differ profoundly about how to free the poor from poverty. Even such historical luminaries as Karl Marx and Sigmund Freud disagreed sharply on this issue.[6]

Basically, activist values stress social problems as the product of environmental distortion. Human liberation occurs essentially because of outside intervention. After all, no one wants to be poor; given the chance, anyone would choose to escape poverty.[7] Thus it must be that external constraints force poor people to remain poor. Conversely, conservatives see human liberation as more a process of internal direction: virtually anything can be achieved if only the individual believes it possible. Accordingly, if one feels that poverty is caused, say, by political injustice or economic enslavement, liberation is achievable by anti-poverty programs or by some other planned-intervention strategy or strategies. If one feels, however, that poverty is a sickness perpetuated by distorted expectations, then liberation is possible only by accepting an "achievement attitude," a conviction that the escape from poverty lies within the soul.

Activists and conservatives alike have proclaimed their common goal of liberating the poor from poverty, but they try to accomplish this task via quite different routes. Perhaps the gap between conservative and activist values was best summed up by a community-action worker in the 1960s: "How do you fight poverty? Do you walk up to it, grab it by the throat, kick it in the ass, and say, 'Get the hell out of my life'? Or do you sit down with it, study on it, and quiet-like chew away at it till it's all gone? I know which way is most fun, but which way works longest and best?"[8]

Basic differences between activist and conservative values should not suggest a single or a common ideology in either group. Policymakers and presidential appointees in the Carter administration differed widely from their Johnson and Kennedy counterparts, especially in their differences as to how far the federal government should go in changing the poverty environment. Radical activists during the Carter administration distrusted Washington's commitment to redistributing political and economic power at the local level. They were grass-roots community organizers who believed that poor people, if they are to bring about real change, must be taught to organize themselves independent of federal programs.

The radical activists who dictated VISTA and Peace Corps programming under Carter were opposed to reliance on outside volunteers whose views they considered "pornographic."[9] Radical activists, however, were content to wait until the Republican retreat from the White House in 1977 to apply their ideology to the Peace Corps and VISTA organizational cultures begun during the New Frontier of John F. Kennedy.

The New Frontier Discovers Poverty

No one questions that the strategy of using volunteers to fight poverty originally was conceived of during John F. Kennedy's brief term in office. Determining how large a role Kennedy played in what came to be called the War on Poverty and in the formulation of a voluntary-action policy requires detective work as well as the thankless task of demythologizing the Kennedy mystique.

Analysis of Kennedy's presidency continues in the 1980s, further complicating the task of separating fact from the tale of Camelot revisited.[10] Nor will a comprehensive probe of Kennedy's self-proclaimed New Frontier be undertaken in this book. Rather, its dual focus is to understand the role played by activist values in two New Frontier initiatives calling for voluntary action programs: the Peace Corps and VISTA (as it emerged from the stillborn National Service Corps). The initiatives originally were intended as patriotic, public service outlets for volunteerism rather than as antipoverty crusades. Both VISTA and the Peace Corps were launched as expressions of activist values. Through a full-time voluntary commitment, young, idealistic college graduates could make a difference in the lives of the less fortunate.

An Activist Corps of Peace

"How many of you, who are going to be medical doctors, are willing to spend your days in Ghana? [How many of you who are going to be] technicians or engineers are willing to do so?"[11] With these eloquent phrases President Kennedy introduced the first Peace Corps volunteers in September 1961. Many participants in the hurriedly organized Peace Corps envisioned a noble place in history for the program: "Two or three generations hence, when historians look back upon our century, they will find much to praise and [much to] blame. Among those features of American life in the sixties that will stand the test of time most adequately, the Peace Corps will, I think, rank high."[12] Perhaps more than any other New Frontier initiative, the Peace Corps symbolized the Camelot quality of John F. Kennedy's presidency. The Peace Corps supposedly would enhance world peace by "eliminating the root cause of war: poverty, ignorance, hunger, despair."[13]

The Peace Corps initially was formulated as an instrument of U.S. foreign policy in combatting communism. Its creation predates later antipoverty programs, such as VISTA, and even the perception among most Americans that widespread poverty exists. The Corps was not designed as an overseas antipoverty program; it was to be a weapon in the Cold War arsenal, one President Kennedy hoped would demonstrate to the world that "a new generation of Americans has taken over this country . . . young Americans [who will] serve the cause of freedom as servants of peace around the world, working for freedom as the communists work for their system."[14] Kennedy felt that the Peace Corps would mobilize popular idealism among the young in a fashion similar to Fidel Castro's youth mobilization efforts in Cuba.

Although the Peace Corps will long be identified with President Kennedy, the concept of voluntary service abroad had been discussed for some time before he became president. During his Democratic-primary struggles with Senator Kennedy, Senator Hubert Humphrey spoke several times of a Peace Corps and a Youth Peace Corps. "It was to be another dimension of American aid to the less fortunate," he said; "personal aid in the form of training and education."[15] In June 1960, Senator Humphrey introduced a bill in Congress that proposed voluntary action opportunities overseas for young men. Conceptually, the Peace Corps was closely linked to Franklin Roosevelt's Civilian Conservation Corps (CCC) of 1933. Like the CCC, the Peace Corps and the unsuccessful National Service Program were intended to provide voluntary service opportunities for American youth. Unlike the CCC, however, the Peace Corps would offer service opportunities to the children of mostly affluent Americans. Because of its direct activist values—that volunteers should intervene directly in the cycle of poverty—the Peace Corps drew sharp criticism from conservatives. Former President Eisenhower called it a "juvenile experiment," and Richard Nixon accused Kennedy of proposing "to send as America's representatives to other nations young men [whom] he calls volunteers but who in truth in many instances would be trying to escape the draft."[16]

Critics of the Peace Corps, however, could not offer a more symbolically effective antidote to the image at the time, that of the Ugly American. Nor was there any denying that the Peace Corps proved immensely popular with many university students. "The New Frontier gospel of criticism and hope stirred the finest instincts of the young; it restored a sense of innovation and adventure to the republic. . . . The Peace Corps was the most dramatic form of the new idealism."[17] As Margaret Mead reflected, the immediate popularity of the Peace Corps was due to its image as an "ethical enterprise, a way for an excessively fortunate country to share its optimism and generosity."[18]

From its inception, the Peace Corps had numerous ingredients for developing a commitment culture. Kennedy and his aides recognized the Corps' important symbolic value. One of these aides, Richard Neustadt, thought that the Peace Corps and Food for Peace "had more political potential" than other New Frontier programs and that they should be kept under the president's personal control.[19] Kennedy's advisers opposed merging the Peace Corps with other foreign-aid programs. Arthur Schlesinger urged Kennedy not to allow the Peace Corps to lose its semiautonomous status; "nothing could take the heart out of a new idea more speedily than an old bureaucracy [because the] Peace Corps had to retain its own identity and élan."[20]

Undoubtedly, the key to early formation of a commitment culture was Sargent Shriver. Although many believed that Shriver had been selected on the basis of his family ties to the President, he "surprised many observers by the quality of his leadership and [the] shrewdness of his political judgment."[21] R. Sargent Shriver, Jr., assistant general manager of the Merchandise Mart and president of Chicago's board of education, chose his staff with an eye to projecting a unified organizational culture and public image. One exasperated volunteer lamented later: "It wasn't Kennedy's Peace Corps. . . . It was Shriver's Peace Corps."[22] The charges of his critics notwithstanding, Shriver wanted to project an image that epitomized the New Frontier itself: bright, realistic, liberal, tough, task-oriented— as well as attractive, young, and athletic.

To promote this image on Capitol Hill and in the media, Shriver hired Bill Moyers, a protégé of Lyndon Johnson. He also recruited several young journalists from various newspapers. As a result, the Peace Corps benefited from a barrage of publicity, one that helped create the desired Peace Corps mystique. Twenty-five years later, Moyers, a seasoned reporter, reflected nostalgically on that mystique: "I was present at the creation, when the bright flame of conviction took hold in the imagination of the country and the Peace Corps became a promise fulfilled."[23]

The mystique was transformed into an organizational culture that became an inspiration for Peace Corps staffers and administrators alike. Shriver set the tone by accepting his position for the nominal salary of one dollar a year. Belief in the Corps' mission, as well as acceptance of its missionary culture, motivated many Peace Corps employees to work in highly unbureaucratic ways. Because of the agency's rapid start-up in 1961, numerous employees who volunteered for employment in the Peace Corps actually were on leave from other agencies. They served as true believers in the mystique of the Corps:

> . . . many of these people worked in good faith for weeks without seeing a check as one evidence of their commitment to the Peace Corps. In effect, they were the first volunteers.

> . . . many of the non-government people took leaves of absence to help set up the Peace Corps.

> . . . there was no guarantee that a permanent agency would be set up, but this didn't seem to deter people who left their other jobs to join the staff.

> The pace at [the] Peace Corps is such that there are almost as many people working in the evenings and on weekends as during "normal hours." The five-day, forty-hour week doesn't exist for the staff anymore than it does for the volunteers in the field.[24]

Early Peace Corps employees were hardly functionaries operating under the influence of a "process" organizational culture; they were committed volunteers with a clear vision of the Corps' mission.

Finally, the Peace Corps' commitment-organizational culture was encouraged by the in-up-out principle that it followed, which emphasized an action orientation and a responsiveness to self-sacrifice. From the outset, the Peace Corps followed the principle: "returned volunteers and other qualified persons move into the staff structure, move up rapidly if they merit promotion, and then mandatorily move out to permit room for newer persons."[25] The idea Shriver promoted was ensuring that the Peace Corps remained permanently responsive to new ideas, particularly from volunteers in the field. No Peace Corps staff member above grade GS-9 would be employed longer than five years.

From 1961 to 1968, the Peace Corps' organizational culture was one of intense activism. Full-time volunteers serving as change agents in communities throughout the Third World believed in the Corps' mission and their activist role in that mission. They resolutely believed that poverty, disease, and ignorance could be ended, that planned social intervention, combined with Yankee ingenuity, could make a difference, that unjust economic and political exploitation kept the poor oppressed. These volunteers could show the poor how to change the system—or so the commitment-organizational culture held. The troublesome war in Vietnam, however, and the ascendancy of Richard Nixon, forced a reassessment of the culture.

Meanwhile, the nation was discovering that poverty was not found only in the Third World. In the early 1960s, the "invisible poor" in the United States emerged as a national problem. As they had done with the Peace Corps overseas, activist policymakers now created a federal program for young Americans who wished to volunteer their services in fighting poverty at home.

A Domestic Peace Corps

Unlike poverty in Third World countries, domestic poverty in the United States generally was invisible to most Americans. It was not until December 1962 that President Kennedy publicly discussed poverty in the United States. The American public became aware of poverty through a source often maligned: the media. Of particular importance in raising poverty as a domestic issue were the books and articles of Michael Harrington, Dwight McDonald, Leon Keyserling, Harry Caudill, and Homer Bigart.[26] Thus poverty was perceived from an activist perspective as an economic and political injustice intolerable in the richest nation on earth. Liberal, activist thinkers raised the poverty issue to the level of consciousness enjoyed by the elite. The emergency of poverty on the agenda of national issues occurred as a result of an unanticipated event, or "circumstantial reactors" (for example, the intensive media attention given to the problem in 1962–63).[27] Poverty could no longer be ignored.

Some writers conjecture that candidate Jack Kennedy became aware of poverty through "glimpses of the sagging shacks and ravaged bodies in the forgotten hollows of West Virginia during his 1960 primary campaign."[28] Despite reports that poverty had had a deep personal impact on Kennedy, such apparently was not the case.[29] Key biographical accounts by White, Sorensen, Salinger, and Schlesinger do not corroborate a relationship between the West Virginia primary and the subsequent War on Poverty.[30]

Again, domestic poverty in 1960–61 was virtually invisible to most citizens. An overview of the major indexes to magazines, newspapers, and journals in the years 1960–61 reveals not a single entry under "poverty," "antipoverty," or "Appalachia."[31] It is extremely unlikely that Senator Kennedy's understanding of poverty was so far ahead of the emergence of the poverty issue three to four years later; rather, it is more reasonable to assume that President Kennedy's innovative Peace Corps and the attempted National Service Corps reflected a "pre-poverty" policy aimed solely at encouraging volunteerism among Americans. With the formulation of the Great Society's War on Poverty in 1964, VISTA was legitimized as the bona fide voluntary service program at home and the Peace Corps as a "practical way to [meet] the needs of those living in the deepest poverty around the world."[32] Both the Peace Corps and VISTA relied on non-poverty volunteers, generally from middle-class backgrounds, to spread the activists' antipoverty message.

President Kennedy's response to the undeniable poverty issue at home was, in part, to establish a presidential study group on a national service program in late 1962, with the mandate to propose a feasible program for attacking poverty in the United States through voluntary service. Significantly, the group included several members of the Shriver task force that designed the War on Poverty two years later: Sargent Shriver, Richard Boone, and Robert Kennedy. On January 14, 1963, the study group submitted its report to the President. It included a recommendation for a National Service Corps (NSC) that would "act as the vehicle through which local communities can be shown new ways and means of helping themselves. National Service Corpsmen, working *full-time,* will by their example and inspiration motivate many other citizens to give part-time service in their own communities."[33] The NSC was to work with and under the supervision of local community groups, with an emphasis on helping the poor directly.

It was the study group's view that volunteerism, particularly among retired citizens, was essential to NSC's success:

> A vast manpower and womanpower resource, with wisdom, skill, and experience, exists in our elderly population. . . . Older people can bring to the Corps their wisdom, skill and maturity. Among the men and women aged 60 and over, who will soon retire and [who] are active in the labor force, are: 126,000 schoolteachers, 36,000 lawyers, 3,000 dietitians and nutritionists. . . . There is a large [reservoir] of talent and experience among those retired people, who could make a major contribution to the Corps and . . . inspire other older people to find a useful role in the community.[34]

Shriver believed that a "substantial number of older people" who were unacceptable for Peace Corps service would apply to the proposed NSC. Apparently, older people, those deemed unsuitable for the rigors of living abroad or for learning a foreign language, still could volunteer to fight poverty in the United States.[35]

As the domestic counterpart to Peace Corps, the NSC would prepare its volunteers to support a wide variety of voluntary action projects, including tutoring, literacy teaching, helping juvenile delinquents, clearing vacant lots, and assisting the physically handicapped and the elderly. Essentially, NSC volunteers would serve in whatever capacity was needed. Like volunteers in the Peace Corps, they would be guests in a local community. They would also avoid conflict by avoiding controversial issues. Just as Peace Corps volunteers were not allowed to organize birth-control clinics in Latin America, NSC workers would not help integrate those areas of the United States still segregated in 1963.

Although the National Volunteer Service Act was defeated in Congress, due to fear of promoting integration and political activities, the NSC was revived within the Economic Opportunity Act of 1964 as the Volunteers In Service To America (VISTA). Senate and House hearings clearly indicate that VISTA was envisioned as a reformulated National Service Corps.[36] Essentially, their programmatic goals were identical, but the NSC would, like the Peace Corps, have functioned autonomously, whereas VISTA was answerable to the Office of Economic Opportunity (OEO). This meant that VISTA volunteers frequently were directed in the field by locally constituted Community Action Programs (CAP).

VISTA emerged phoenix-like from the ashes of Kennedy's National Service Corps. Meant to be far more than a conduit for middle-class volunteerism, VISTA would provide the shock troops for the fight against poverty. Because of its domestic role in fighting poverty, VISTA generated a more consistent conflict than its more glamorous cousin, the Peace Corps.

The Stage Is Set for Activism

In the early 1960s, the Kennedy presidency found conditions ripe for implementing activist values in policymaking. The nation had been awakened, largely by the media and the intelligentsia, to the contradiction evident in poverty amid abundance in America. Poverty was now firmly on the national agenda for action. Autonomous, staunchly apolitical, and highly popular, the Peace Corps demonstrated as well the viability of solving problems through full-time volunteerism overseas. Although the NSC was defeated in Congress, a "domestic Peace Corps" concept awaited resurrection when needed. Thus President Kennedy's role in antipoverty policymaking was that of a legitimizer, a creative symbol. He had "become a model, a paragon, a creative symbol to many people, able to evoke feelings, provide meanings, and control and direct behavior."[37] All the legitimizing symbolism was present in "JFK"—his appeal to youth, his charismatic oratory, and, later, the pathos of martyrdom. The "myth of JFK's heroic qualities" was solidified by his tragic death. Lyndon Johnson was determined to shake the symbolic "ghost of Jack Kennedy" while simultaneously utilizing Kennedy symbols to legitimize his own activist policies. The War on Poverty was LBJ's opportunity to make poverty "the right issue for the right man at the right time."[38]

VISTA's Shock Troops in the War on Poverty

Despite its lineage from the unsuccessful National Service Corps, VISTA must be understood as a product of the War on Poverty as much as one of the New Frontier. It combined the New Frontier's emphasis on voluntary service for youth with the antipoverty goals of the Great Society. As the domestic Peace Corps, the autonomous NSC was to have been oriented toward community-service projects, whereas VISTA, as directed by the Office of Economic Opportunity (OEO), provided full-time volunteers for the front lines of the War on Poverty. Along with other antipoverty programs such as the Job Corps, Head Start, and Legal Services, VISTA lent support to community-action agencies. The thrust of antipoverty was to mobilize poor people for direct social action; considerations of voluntary service in VISTA were of secondary importance to activist policymakers.

Formulating an Activist War on Poverty

Perhaps no other major social policy developed in a political milieu as unusual as that of the War on Poverty. Symbolically, President Kennedy's brother-in-law was selected to head a task force that possessed a mandate to formulate a war on poverty, thus linking the Kennedy charisma to whatever policy was forthcoming. As head of earlier task forces that produced the Peace Corps and the National Service Program, Sargent Shriver proved the ideal symbolic leader. In his first State of the Union address, President Johnson repeatedly invoked Kennedy's name as he asked "citizens of the richest . . . nation in the history of the world to wage unconditional war against poverty."[39] A metaphorical war on poverty would link Johnson's pragmatism with Kennedy's magnetism.

Influenced by the absence of the usual checks and balances in
the political process, policy formulation of the War on Poverty
moved rapidly. Shriver's task force was unhindered by inter-
agency jurisdictional quarrels or congressional committee
trade-offs. President Johnson's landslide victory over the conservative Barry Goldwater combined with a lingering national
remorse over Kennedy's assassination to produce a political consensus; there would be no significant opposition to any programs formulated by Mr. Shriver's sequestered task force. One
observer mused: "It is doubtful that any single piece of legislation of similar importance and scope had [in a quarter of a
century] moved so rapidly and easily through Congress."[40] In
effect, the Shriver task force, during its design of a grand war on
poverty, was not restrained by political expediency or value conflict. It was free to plan for the total elimination of poverty in the
United States.[41] The task force worked, knowing that the President would support and Congress ultimately pass whatever reasonable antipoverty policy it might submit. It was indeed a rare
opportunity to create activist programs for planned social intervention.

As social activists, task-force members were motivated by
heady idealistic purposes in their quest of eradicating poverty in
America. Interestingly, with the exception of Bill Moyers, who
had helped Shriver put the Peace Corps together, the Shriver
task force did not consist primarily of Johnson advisers. By
background and loyalty, they were Kennedy people. As John
Donovan notes, they were a "team of Eastern, liberal intellec-
tual-politicians who were personally acceptable to Sargent
Shriver."[42] On loan from their respective agencies and academic
institutions, they were people of demonstrated creativity, intelligence, and administrative abilities: Patrick Moynihan, Harold
Horowitz, James Sundquist, Hyman Bookbinder, Adam Yarmolinsky, Christopher Weeks, Frank Mankiewicz, Paul Jacobs,
Michael Harrington. (Incidentally, none were women, minorities, or poor; they were all activists who wished to plan for the
demise of poverty, though none had experienced it firsthand.)

Thus the Shriver task force was generally representative of a
liberal-intellectual orientation toward poverty and the poor. In
1964, its activist enthusiasm for restructuring social and eco-

nomic institutions prevailed as a perspective widely shared among liberals and intellectuals. The intelligentsia took credit for discovering the "invisible poor" and for raising Appalachia into the national consciousness. Authors and social critics such as Barbara Tuchman, Robert Heilbroner, Norman Podhoretz, and Richard Rovere urged President Johnson to offer new leadership in changing "materialistic commercialism" to "moral values, to a new found concern with poverty and ignorance."[43] "It's all here," one Johnson staffer said in describing the President's enthusiastic embrace of Barbara Ward's *The Rich Nations and the Poor Nations;* "the whole challenge—lifting people out of poverty and ignorance."[44] Lyndon Johnson was converted to the activists' cause.

To activists, a truly great society seemed one in which continued toleration of poverty amid national affluence was unconscionable. A new national program to combat poverty was needed, and activists were ready with their newly conceived antipoverty programs. Unlike maintenance-oriented welfare and unemployment programs, antipoverty policy would "take action through the national political and governmental process."[45] Ironically, once Lyndon Johnson grasped the activists' vision, he went beyond even their own plans. Merle Miller wrote: "The whole idea of declaring a big war on poverty and ending it for all time—all the rhetoric appealed to him very much. In fact, I think he built the rhetoric far beyond that which had been planned by his advisors." He added that Johnson's massive War on Poverty also dwarfed anything envisioned by Kennedy's New Frontier.[46]

The War on Poverty programs were designed with the following activist assumptions in mind:

The eradication (elimination) of poverty is the ultimate goal of governmental programs for the poor.

Effective antipoverty programs can best be designed by federal antipoverty agencies in consultation with elected representatives of the poverty community. State and local politicians should be excluded from direct policy-making because of their generally conservative bias against the poor.

As a change of strategy, antipoverty programs should utilize "community organization or development" techniques in breaking the cycle of poverty. Social or human services projects not directly concerned with economic deprivation should be avoided as poverty projects.

Program implementation [is to be] spearheaded by full-time, nonpoverty volunteers who [will be] brought in as community organizers, or change agents.

Most important, liberation from poverty is considered possible only when external barriers (economic and political) [have been] removed. Following this, attitudinal and pathological "problems" of the poor can be addressed.

The entire national War on Poverty was to be directed and coordinated by the Office of Economic Opportunity. Not surprisingly, Sargent Shriver left the Peace Corps to become OEO's first director.

VISTA was but one of OEO's multipronged weapons in combating poverty. Activist values formed the core of organizational cultures in a variety of OEO-directed programs. For example:

Community Action Program (CAP). Antipoverty administrators considered CAP the heart of the entire War on Poverty effort. Local CAP organizations operated as umbrella agencies for a host of antipoverty efforts, which were to be determined by the poor themselves through their specially elected "representatives." The OEO phrase "maximum feasible participation of the poor" expressed the belief held by War on Poverty formulators that the poor themselves should decide their own destiny by acting as policymakers at the local level. Critics such as Daniel Patrick Moynihan later charged CAP agencies with creating a "maximum feasible misunderstanding."[47]

Head Start. Intended to compensate for educational and cultural disadvantages suffered by children from poor families. Despite early program-evaluation problems, Head Start survived and is currently funded.

Job Corps. Set up centers and camps, somewhat removed from ghettos and poor neighborhoods, in which poor youths could be taught rudimentary skills and receive job training. Despite cutbacks and controversy, the Job Corps exists today.

Foster Grandparents. Set up to recruit the aging poor to work with handicapped children in residential-care facilities, usually for twenty hours a week at minimum wage. Possibly the most popular program among conservatives, Foster Grandparents has been actively supported by Betty Ford and Nancy Reagan.

Upward Bound. Enrolls high school students from poor families in a year-round, summer-intensive program designed to upgrade the educational skills necessary to achieve a higher education. It is no longer funded.

Legal Services. Employs "volunteer" lawyers to represent the poor as individual clients and as a group in class-action suits. Reconstituted as a quasi-public corporation, Legal Services has withstood unending attacks by its conservative critics, including Ronald Reagan, who feuded with California Rural Legal Aid while he was governor. Despite its enemies, Legal Services, too, is currently funded.

These antipoverty programs, along with VISTA, have relied on a variety of lawyers, social workers, and other professionals to accomplish their objectives, usually as VISTA volunteers delegated to local community-action agencies. Although part-time and community volunteers also served in CAP programs, full-time VISTA volunteers formed a dedicated cadre of antipoverty shock troops in implementing the activist policy. These VISTA volunteers were the storefront organizers. Like the Peace Corps volunteers in whose more glamorous shadow they were doomed to live, VISTA volunteers usually were college or professional-school graduates and not from poverty or minority backgrounds.[48] Typically volunteers would take a year off between graduation and beginning their careers to volunteer for VISTA service. They served as architects, planners, nurses, and community organizers in poverty-stricken communities throughout the United States. Their common bond was a belief that poverty's vicious cycle could be broken, that change was possible.

Organizational Culture and Public Attitudes

Activist policymakers in the Democratic administrations of John Kennedy and Lyndon Johnson had been given an exceptional opportunity—to construct and implement programs that reflected their own worldviews. They successfully initiated programs with commitment cultures at Peace Corps, VISTA, and other War on Poverty programs. Unfortunately for the activists, their view of poverty and the plight of the poor was not a dominant one, nor was it one widely shared by the public.

One might speculate how a War on Poverty might have been put together if Richard Nixon or Ronald Reagan had been president at the time, or what might have happened if conservatives such as William Buckley, Edward Banfield, George Gilder, or even George Will had been asked to head a task force to recommend a national policy on poverty. Although conservatives did not start the Peace Corps or such antipoverty programs as VISTA, they soon inherited them.

Why, then, is the public not particularly sympathetic to the plight of the poor, as some have alleged?[49] Perhaps it is because middle-class values and attitudes toward poverty were shaped largely by the Great Depression and by work values developed over decades if not generations. During the period when activist antipoverty programs were being created, most Americans did not consider the poor as helpless victims of their environment, but rather as people not properly motivated to work.[50] In a national survey done by the Gallup organization in 1981, 80 percent of Americans expressed a belief that the poor suffered from individual character flaws and that poverty was an inescapable fact of life in American society.[51]

Interestingly, two decades after the War on Poverty was inaugurated, public opinion seemingly is even more sympathetic to conservative values than to activist ones. Although the work force has changed dramatically since the early 1960s, Horatio Alger is still alive and well, as evidenced by the following responses to the Gallup poll of 1981.[52] The survey revealed:

Question: Do you think it's possible nowadays for someone in this country to start poor and become rich by working hard?

Possible through other means	2%
Not possible	29
Possible	69

Question: Some people say that other people get ahead by their own hard work; others say that lucky breaks or help from other people are more important. Which do you think is more important?

Luck or help	11%
Both equal	20
Hard work	69

Perhaps a majority of those interviewed believed that since the cycle of poverty had not trapped them the trap must not exist.

Opposition to activist notions concerning the poor and poverty is deeply ingrained in American Protestantism in its various manifestations.[53] To many people, Judeo-Christian tradition reinforces a belief in the inevitability of poverty. There seems to be little doubt in the Reverend Billy Graham's mind concerning the means by which the poor can escape poverty:

> If you gave every person in the world today one million dollars and a Cadillac automobile, or a Chrysler Imperial or Lincoln Continental . . . it wouldn't bring him happiness. Jesus said, "Man shall not live by bread alone."[54]

Of course, few if any religious groups use biblical justification to openly attack the poor. Instead, the Bible is used as a basis for explaining the individual's obligation to shape his or her own destiny. As Max Weber's study of Protestantism and capitalism underscores, individuals who accept the Protestant work ethic can also determine their own economic futures as well.[55]

The debate over how to liberate the poor from their misery extended into Kennedy's inner circle. During an informal seminar in Robert F. Kennedy's home, George F. Kennan expressed the view that "nothing could be done about poverty since, as the Bible said, the poor would be with us always. [Walter] Heller strenuously objected [to this view] and was joined in the ensuing debate by Robert Kennedy and Harrington against Kennan, Supreme Court Justice Potter Stewart, and Randolph Churchill, son of the former prime minister."[56]

It was an argument heard in many households throughout the country during the 1960s as activist thinkers brought up New Frontier and Great Society programs to mount an attack on poverty. Conservatives, and even the majority of Americans, were not sympathetic. Some even went so far as to agree with "Jesus Christ Superstar":

> Surely you're not saying we have the resources
> To save the poor from their lot?
> There will be poor always, pathetically struggling
> Look at the good things you've got.[57]

To many Americans, the values of entrepreneurial capitalism and self-achievement, as a cure for poverty, appealed far more than did activist intervention.

Ambivalent or openly hostile attitudes toward activist intervention on behalf of the poor were later expressed in the form of "workfare" welfare proposed by the Nixon administration. These proposals, as well as attacks on activist initiatives to fight poverty, were dismissed by activists as "merely efforts to ensure [the] survival of the fattest" by conservative ideologues.[58]

Nor did activist policymakers accept the thesis that priorities in antipoverty programs should be set according to mass public opinion. After all, as Hitler, Huey Long, and mob rule have demonstrated, mass decision-making has its dark side. Sometimes, Thomas Dye and L. Harmon Dye argue, the public has to be led by elites who know better what lies in the public's best interest.[59] Justice is not always reached at the ballot box on such issues as racism, oppression, and poverty. Support of the downtrodden was a symbolic commitment no less than a morally right crusade. Planned intervention by VISTA and Peace Corps volunteers to fight poverty was a moral imperative regardless of mass public opinion.

Finally, activist-designed programs, such as Peace Corps and VISTA, were formulated by individuals with little experiential knowledge of poverty in the United States or of conditions in developing countries. After all, until they were discovered by reporters and writers for the media in the early 1960s, the poor had remained largely invisible to most of society. Peace Corps volunteers were in the field within six months of President Kennedy's executive order on March 1, 1961. Even supporters of the Peace Corps understood that it was an "overseas cultural gamble" to hope that the Peace Corps would "recruit, train, program, supervise, and counsel massive numbers of volunteers to participate in a complex variety of programs in a large number of alien cultures around the world."[60] *The Wall Street Journal* was skeptical: "What person can really believe that Africa aflame with violence will have its fires quenched because some Harvard boy or Vassar girl lives in a mud hut and speaks Swahili?"[61]

Nor was there much experience with poverty communities among those who created antipoverty programs. David Gottlieb describes a war on poverty plotted by men who hardly knew the poor but who dreamed of reshaping the lives of the poor. He describes an extensive debate in 1965 among staffers at a Job Corps center in anticipation of the arrival of the first group: "When the first thirty boys arrive, should we give them cigarettes or should we give them milk and cookies? Are they adults or are they children? . . . Then the bus pulled up and these kids started getting off, and it became very clear that lower-income kids were a side of the moon we had never seen before."[62]

Hubert Humphrey, the consummate antipoverty warrior, described the "surprising things" he had witnessed at a Chicago Job Corps center:

> Young adults were being trained in personal grooming, how to use the public washroom neatly, how to punch a time clock. One might ask: How could they *not* know these things? There are people in America who do not have money for food, much less soap. Routine cleanliness is almost irrelevant in lives in which hot water for a bath is unavailable.

> It was a shock to visit [a] Job Corps camp and see adults who had been through some years of our public education system stare at a blackboard where a teacher was writing "cat" or helping them write their own names. In another room, men were learning to tell time. What are you to make of the strange apparatus of a time clock if you can't tell time?[63]

For many policy formulators in Washington, the poor were a theoretical abstraction—exotic when in foreign lands, invisible at home.

Hyman H. Bookbinder—another OEO administrator, who later administered programs he had developed while on the Shriver task force—felt that antipoverty policymakers fell prey to simple solutions regarding the nature of poverty. "We didn't fully realize what kind of poor we were dealing with," he wrote. "It wasn't like it was in the 1930's when all you had to do was improve the economy and people went back to work. Here we were faced with large numbers of blacks and others in the cities where there were deep maladies."[64] Nor were the administrators of antipoverty programs prepared for the peculiar needs of the rural poor, the elderly, poor American Indians on reservations, or the large number of poor, single heads of household. On the one hand, poverty could no longer linger as a policy abstraction, while, on the other, it offered no simple solutions to activist designers.

To compound matters, VISTA, like the Peace Corps, hastily put its projects together. The emphasis was on getting volunteers to work as soon as possible. Again, within a few months of passage of the Economic Opportunity Act of 1964, VISTA had placed volunteers in the field. Consequently, the results were predictable. "The training center in Oregon was sending trainees all over the country, including to Florida, and the training operation in Florida was sending trainees all over the country, including to Oregon. We had precisely that happen several times."[65]

As a result VISTA quickly set up four organizational divisions: recruitment and selection; rural projects; urban projects; and training and support. Unfortunately for organizational planning and coordination, no effort was made to divide the country geographically into regions, with the result that it became difficult to coordinate recruitment and training of volunteers with appropriate placement.

At the same time, there was no appropriate mechanism for training VISTA volunteers. VISTA quickly contracted (through noncompetitive bidding) with numerous training institutes and universities to remedy this defect.[66] At one time in 1966 there were nineteen different training centers operating in the Midwest alone. This confusing situation was made worse by VISTA's mandate to develop projects on Indian reservations, for migrant laborers, at Job Corps centers, and in mental health clinics. During its first year of operation, however, VISTA managed to train and place approximately 2,500 volunteers.

Despite its organizational snafus, VISTA was judged a success. Its designers hailed it as a "bridge between middle-class America and the poor."[67] As an assistant director of OEO proclaimed, "The volunteers live among the poor twenty-four hours a day, helping them in innumerable ways." Furthermore, they have a "special compassion for the poor [which] means that they can perform assignments for which it is not possible to hire an employee."[68] VISTA volunteers generally saw their one-year term of service as rewarding; almost 34 percent reenlisted for additional time.[69] VISTA epitomized the activist commitment to breaking the cycle of poverty through voluntary service.

Despite the strong organizational cultures that came into being with the advent of the Peace Corps and VISTA, by the midpoint of Lyndon Johnson's presidency both programs were under attack. In an environment of competing ideologies and mixed public opinion, counterattack by conservatives was inevitable. Conservative criticism came at first from hostile members of Congress and then later from Richard Nixon's appointees to the Peace Corps and to VISTA. In both cases, however, the activist organizational culture proved remarkably resilient to ideological assault.

The Conservative Counterreaction

Conservatives, excluded from establishing the Peace Corps and the War on Poverty, did not long remain passive. "Thus the War on Poverty reached that point where the normal process of congressional review began to tighten legislative control of administrative action, while at the same time, those forces within the executive branch which seek 'coordination,' 'clear-cut policies,' and sound administrative practices were spinning their web of detailed procedures and restrictions."[70] Less than two years after the grand beginning, the War on Poverty foundered under heavy attack by conservative critics from within both political parties.

Undoubtedly the most controversial feature of the anti-poverty program was the Community Action Programs (CAP), which supposedly would allow the poor to design their own programs as well as set funding priorities. In the view of War on Poverty policymakers, the poor knew their own needs. In addition, policymakers felt that CAP would give the poor needed decision-making experience.[71] Community control through CAP was intended to be a "revolutionary concept in American government,"[72] a means of redistributing economic and political power in the United States. By 1967, more than 87 percent of VISTA volunteers were assigned to local CAP projects and other related OEO projects.[73]

State and local political elites were less than excited about the VISTA and CAP effort to shake things up. Specifically, they were not enthusiastic about "organizing rent strikes, picketing welfare agencies, and the like."[74] Mayors, city councils, and local business people often were faced with the prospect of organized pressure by VISTA volunteers working under the auspices of local CAP agencies and, not surprisingly, thought that the taxpayer's dollar could be spent more wisely.

The counterreaction by conservatives was swift and predictable. Opposition in the House of Representatives, based in part on evaluation of various OEO programs, focused on the OEO's 1967 budget request. The House Committee on Education and Labor that had earlier held hearings on the Economic Opportunity Act of 1964 now recommended a shift away from VISTA's controversial community organizing programs to programs that were less inflammatory, such as Head Start and adult employment programs.[75] "Maximum feasible participation of the poor," reinterpreted as a maximum of one-third participation on CAP boards, diluted the power of the poor.[76] Senator Dirksen, Republican from Illinois, succeeded in getting OEO appropriations cut to the House level, and Senator Byrd, Democrat from Virginia, inserted a motion to deny CAP funds to known "rioters" and "subversives."[77]

The final amendments to OEO's 1967 budget were a clear victory for conservative lawmakers opposed to activist community-action projects. Following a resolution by the U.S. Conference of Mayors, hostile to community organizing projects, Congress passed the Green amendment, dubbed by its critics "the bosses and boll weevil amendment." It allowed local governments veto power of and control over all CAP agencies and VISTA projects within their jurisdictions.[78] Henceforth, VISTA volunteers could not be sent into any state without prior approval of the governor and the OEO regional director.

Clearly, the heat was on VISTA to discontinue those community-organizing efforts that were considered radical. Joseph Califano recalls that President Johnson was besieged by congressmen complaining about VISTA activities, because volunteers "were organizing political actions against incumbent mayors, incumbent school board members. We put out I don't know how many directives to Shriver to stop that."[79] Ironically, during the policy debate conducted by the Shriver task force in 1964, "the possibility of major conflict between [the] politicians in city hall was simply not one that anyone worried about."[80] It was an oversight that had come back to haunt VISTA and the OEO.

Less than two years after their inception, the War on Poverty and VISTA were in trouble. Most observers anticipated the ignominious demise of the two programs as a consequence of Nixon's election in 1968. But that did not occur. Only with Gerald Ford's assumption of the presidency was the OEO fully dismantled. Such antipoverty programs as VISTA, Head Start, the Job Corps, and even Legal Services continue to this day. VISTA and the Peace Corps did not end with Richard Nixon or even Ronald Reagan in the White House; but, over two decades, activist goals and the values of organizational cultures were reshaped according to the ideological values of political appointees by presidents from both political parties.

Activist Values as Organizational Culture

"Most accounts of the War on Poverty's birth make it seem inevitable, but historical research highlights the role of chance."[81]

Perhaps, as Machiavelli claims of great events, it was a combination of chance *(fortuna)* and seizing the moment *(virtu).*[82] Kennedy's assassination provided the opportunity, and Johnson took the initiative, to create radically innovative programs aimed at eradicating poverty.

President Kennedy was assassinated before he could push his own plans for youth, human services, and employment. To some extent, his fame rests on the Peace Corps and his support of the National Service Corps concept; yet it appears uncertain that Kennedy would have implemented other antipoverty efforts. Instead, Lyndon Johnson recognized that the time had come to place a war on poverty on the national policy agenda. Linkage to a martyred president gave him a symbolic cause, a claim to the presidency in his own right.[83] He now had a ready-made policy issue.

Symbolically, President Johnson's decision to characterize the antipoverty effort as a "war" was crucial. By doing so, Johnson imparted important policy significance to both employees and volunteers. By calling for "total victory," he exhibited confidence that the War on Poverty was winnable. The enemy was defined as the enslaving cycle of poverty rather than the shortcomings of individuals. As David Zarefsky points out, the symbolic discourse Johnson employed to describe the War on Poverty was crucial in shaping the context within which people view the social world.[84] VISTA and Peace Corps volunteers and employees incorporated the symbolism of warfare in their thinking. As organizations, the Peace Corps and VISTA accepted victory over poverty as their mission.

Despite his interest in the poverty issue, Lyndon Johnson cared little for programmatic design; that he left to Sargent Shriver's task force. Shriver had "created" and led the Peace Corps; he could now lead the War on Poverty. Consequently, the activist task force proposed nothing less than the eradication of poverty in the United States. Rather than expand jobs or welfare programs, it formulated bold, experimental solutions designed to break the intergenerational transmission of poverty. In VISTA, full-time volunteers would be a catalyst, a twenty-four-hour-a-day resource for community-action efforts. Like their

Peace Corps counterparts fighting poverty throughout the world, they would fight it throughout the United States.

From the beginning, President Johnson realized that programs like VISTA would shake up local government, but "I decided that some shaking up might be needed to get a bold new program moving. I thought that local governments had to be challenged to be awakened."[85] Unlike activist thinkers on the Shriver task force, Johnson envisioned political benefits as well. "But inevitably the VISTA people are going to see that in order to do something, people are going to have to vote."[86] Just as Franklin Roosevelt had seen the New Deal's political payoff as one of mobilizing new participants in the political process, so Lyndon Johnson anticipated a War on Poverty that would bring the alienated poor into the Democratic party.

Ironically, Richard Nixon could not win either of Lyndon Johnson's wars, the one on poverty or the one in Vietnam. As we have seen, most Kennedy and Johnson programs were not terminated by Nixon. Even though the Peace Corps and VISTA came under sharp congressional criticism, both programs have endured—this even after Nixon derided VISTA as a Madison Avenue stunt and the Peace Corps as a haven for draft dodgers.

Why were VISTA and the Peace Corps not destroyed by the conservatives? An interesting phenomenon occurred: Rather than terminating activist programs, conservatives (and, later, radical activists) reshaped most of the programs to reflect their own ideologies. Political appointees to these programs defined their mission as one of changing activist values imbedded within prevailing organizational cultures. In most cases, organizational cultures were severely weakened rather than destroyed.

On closer examination, we can see that the antipoverty programs that persisted through five administrations were those most plagued by ideological debate. In other words, each succeeding wave of presidential appointees attempted to restructure the Peace Corps and VISTA in light of strongly held activist, radical activist, or conservative values. Those programs that were malleable to different ideological worldviews were spared; others were not. Thus Republican conservatives during the Nixon, Ford, and Reagan administrations attempted to mold the Job Corps, VISTA, the Peace Corps, and Head Start to conform to their ideological values. Radical activists in the Carter administration did the same. Throughout, organizations with strong organizational cultures and high employee morale would decline further, sinking into a morass of conflict and confusion.

Three

Richard Nixon's War on Poverty

The grand design of the Nixon administration did not include a well-conceptualized policy toward either the War on Poverty or the Peace Corps. True, during the 1960 presidential campaign, Nixon attacked Kennedy's proposed volunteer Peace Corps as "superficial," as "conceived solely for campaign purposes," asserting that it would become a haven for draft dodgers and other youthful malcontents.[1] When he assumed office nine years later, the Peace Corps had already passed its peak enrollment (15,500 volunteers) and its highest budgetary appropriation ($114 million). By the end of the decade, Nixon's comments on the Peace Corps had become decidedly more favorable.

Such War on Poverty programs as Legal Services, VISTA, and Head Start were not issues during the 1968 presidential campaign, despite Hubert Humphrey's active role in developing the programs. Even though candidate Nixon declared several times that, if elected, he would eliminate the Job Corps as an economically wasteful program, it survives today.[2] Nixon undoubtedly had little sympathy for activist values or Great Society programs, *yet not a single antipoverty program was abolished during his term in office.* As he would do concerning so many other decisions, ranging from recognition of the People's Republic of China to his protection of Legal Services, Richard Nixon displayed a clear preference for pragmatism over ideology.

Initially, the Nixon White House was more interested in the self-proclaimed "great goals of New Federalism": welfare reform, revenue-sharing, governmental reorganization, peace-time prosperity, the natural environment, and health care.[3] Recalcitrant congresses did succeed in frustrating most New Federalism goals during Nixon's first term, while the Watergate scandal stymied his second-term priorities. The White House approached antipoverty program reform as an afterthought of organizational reform, as a task delegated to more ideology-minded political appointees to those agencies. In setting his policy priorities, the President, in an attempt to produce what he considered greater efficiency and cost-effectiveness, was deeply concerned with reorganizing the federal bureaucracy.

Executive reorganization of existing agencies and the simultaneous creation of new federal agencies are characteristic of all contemporary presidents. Well over a hundred "presidential reorganization plans" have been submitted to Congress since the Reorganization Act of 1949, and more than eighty have been implemented. Bipartisan acceptance of the President's right to reorganize the bureaucracy is routinely accepted. Later on, President Carter mounted his own reorganization in the form of the Civil Service Reform Act of 1978, which, among other things, abolished the Civil Service Commission and created the Office of Personnel Management. Yet Richard Nixon's presidency marks the apex to date of executive reorganization efforts.

Reorganization of antipoverty agencies and the Peace Corps needs to be appreciated from the overall perspective of federal restructuring. Merger of the Peace Corps and VISTA into the newly created ACTION agency in 1971 is but a minor reorganization against a backdrop of the massive changes that occurred during the Nixon presidency. Perhaps the most far-reaching and enduring agency to evolve from Nixon's reorganization measures is the Office of Management and Budgeting (OMB), formerly the Bureau of the Budget. More comprehensive in policymaking scope than its predecessor, OMB represents a "basic change in concept and emphasis."[4] Of particular relevance to the Peace Corps and VISTA, OMB was charged with conducting a systematic analysis of all programs from within the executive office. It became the President's watchdog and the evaluator of program performance in the White House, as well as OEO's and the Peace Corps' new master.

OMB's role in assessing the performance of OEO and the Peace Corps was virtually unchallenged, in fact, except by an occasional Congressional committee. The agency's emphasis was on greater efficiency through governmental reorganization. During President Nixon's first term in office, 1969–73, reorganizational issues were stressed over ideological concerns. Only after the electoral landslide of 1972 did conservative appointees at OEO, the Peace Corps, and VISTA begin seriously to attack the activist cultures in those agencies. Ideological attacks were carried out during Nixon's second term and the Ford administration by such conservative appointees as Michael Balzano, ACTION's director, and Howard Phillips, director-designate of OEO. Political appointees, rather than the President or his top aides, were given administrative discretion sufficient for them to restructure activist cultures and programs at both VISTA and the Peace Corps.

Presidential Reorganization and Conservative Ideology

Activist values held by an entrenched bureaucracy were of secondary importance to a president concerned more immediately with consolidating his power through reorganization. Consequently, Nixon's tenure in the White House, albeit shortened, can be viewed as consisting of two stages of policymaking concerning VISTA and the Peace Corps. During the first three years of the Nixon administration, executive office programs were thoroughly assessed by OMB and the General Accounting Office (GAO). In the latter part of Nixon's term (1972–74), perhaps because of the consuming fire of Watergate, political appointees at VISTA and the Peace Corps became more discreet in redirecting their agency cultures toward conservative values.

Reassessing the War on Poverty

Even though he had criticized the Job Corps and Community Action programs during the campaign of 1968, President Nixon took no immediate steps to phase out antipoverty programs or to cap the growing antiwar sentiment among Peace Corps volunteers; rather, he ordered that programs inherited from his Democratic predecessors be reevaluated for continued support. It was, in fact, a period of reassessment by the President of who should coordinate national antipoverty and voluntary-action efforts.

Initially, Nixon directed the Urban Affairs Council to evaluate programs within OEO. "At my direction, the Urban Affairs Council has been conducting an intensive study of the nation's anti-poverty programs, of the way in which the anti-poverty effort is organized and administered, and of ways in which it might be more effective. That study is continuing."[5] In order to give the Urban Affairs Council time to submit antipoverty recommendations, the President requested and received a one-year extension of appropriations for OEO.

Interestingly, antipoverty assessment was entrusted to the Urban Affairs Council rather than OEO, although OEO submitted to the President a request for a Phase I four-year plan (1968–72) to fight poverty.[6] OEO's plan included the goal of ending poverty in the United States by 1976 (in time for the bicentennial celebration). OEO's plan originally was prepared for President Johnson, who had reacted by classifying it "administrative confidential," thus protecting the plan from public scrutiny.[7]

The Urban Affairs Council was unable to assess antipoverty programs, however, in part because its members were key federal administrators with major responsibilities elsewhere. For example, the Council for Rural Affairs, appointed by the President, had virtually the same members on its council.[8] In June 1969 the President asked the Urban Affairs Council to study the nation's hunger problem and report on it. Meanwhile, the Economic Opportunity Council, with a major function to advise the OEO director "with respect to policy matters," found itself ignored.[9]

Part of the reluctance to evaluate OEO programs probably stemmed from difficulty in evaluating the nonquantitative nature of most antipoverty projects, especially those at VISTA. For instance, how does one evaluate the success of VISTA volunteers whose handbook includes the objective: "Through their understanding, sensitivity, patience, and dedication, they will help inspire those who are now isolated to participate in community life. Their ultimate objective is to stimulate initiative and self-confidence, and to replace despair with hope"?[10]

When asked to measure its contribution to the poor during the 1960s, VISTA consistently presented anecdotal success stories rather than measurable proofs.[11] Such stories, while they made great human interest stories in the press, were hardly convincing to OMB or GAO.

An independent evaluation by the General Accounting Office found it difficult to evaluate OEO programs on the basis of measurable indexes: "This has been a difficult and unprecedented review for the General Accounting Office, dealing as it does with a relatively new program, and dealing as it does with many types of programs which were difficult to measure in any quantitative way."[12] GAO urged the President to delegate OEO-evaluation functions to OMB or another agency, which could mandate quantitative measures of success.

Meanwhile, the Economic Opportunity Act in 1969 required each executive office agency to implement its own systematic evaluation of all program activities. This task was assigned to OEO's restructured Office of Planning, Research, and Evaluation (OPRE). Not coincidentally, OPRE's staff included several recent political appointees whose conservative leanings were in tune with those of OEO's director, Donald Rumsfeld. By mid-1970, OPRE had concluded program evaluations of Community Action, Family Planning Services, Comprehensive Health Centers, Day-Care Services, Migrant Services, Legal Services, the Job Corps, and VISTA. Not surprisingly, the evaluation studies ranged from negative to mixed in their conclusions.[13]

The evaluation of VISTA was undoubtedly the most controversial, especially to the staff and former volunteers, whose irritation was aggravated by conservative appointees at OPRE who undertook the study "out of an expressed concern . . . that a number of VISTA volunteers were engaged in inappropriate activities of a social or political nature that were leading to consequences which were deleterious to the effective achievement of the goals of the projects to which they were assigned, to the goals of VISTA and the Office of Economic Opportunity."[14] In other words, conservative appointees at OPRE were convinced that VISTA projects were proposing political organization for the poor rather than self-help programs for them.

Even VISTA's activist defenders admit that individual VISTA volunteers occasionally ventured into political or social activities that were perhaps questionable. "Many VISTA members are young and idealistic, and one reason they joined the Corps was to take part in eliminating injustice. At times the only way to accomplish this was by defying a local or state law, and many did not flinch when this appeared to be necessary. Mistakes and errors of judgment no doubt were made." As the assistant director of OEO confessed, volunteer mistakes and errors of judgment "kept life lively in the Office of Economic Opportunity."[15] The assistant director might have added that these mistakes contributed to the subsequent dismantlement of OEO.

OPRE's study of VISTA volunteers revealed an activist culture at VISTA that confirmed conservatives' worst fears. The study indicated that, for most volunteers, a year's service in VISTA was a *significant politicizing experience*.[16] Specifically, the VISTA experience radicalized a third of the volunteers politically and moved most of them toward a more leftist social and political orientation. According to Gottlieb, nearly half of those VISTA volunteers under age thirty became more suspicious of government and of social-action programs.

Not only did the volunteers' experiences in poor communities prove radicalizing, so did VISTA's own training program for volunteers. According to the VISTA evaluation, most volunteers initially were politicized by the agency itself. The study concluded that VISTA training "speeded up the volunteer's politicization process" by teaching political values that were *even more radical* than those generally held by poor people or college students.[17] Further, the study observed that VISTA's indoctrination of trainees with radical values probably intensified during 1970–71.[18]

That most VISTA volunteers were radicalized by their training does not mean that all VISTA training programs were intentionally radicalizing. As Michael P. Balzano, Jr., a former OPRE staffer, points out, training goals and objectives varied considerably throughout VISTA's many decentralized training centers.[19] Most centers, however, were similar to the University of Maryland center, which stressed four activist themes to its VISTA trainees during the 1960s:

> In the scheme of social change, the volunteers are not a part of the establishment and operate outside of it, if not against it.
> Middle-class Negroes are allies of the white middle class and thus [are] equally opposed to the advancement of poor Negroes.
> The morality of tactics, which can be used to bring about change in the status quo, [is] relative to the situation.
> Social change, of necessity, involves conflict.[20]

The activist values taught VISTA volunteers were anathema to VISTA's presidentially appointed administrators.

From the conservatives' perspective, their study of VISTA and other OEO programs called for policymaking and programming reorientation. Dismantling OEO programs would be strongly resisted by congressional and clientele support groups, such as the Friends of VISTA. Narrowly elected in 1968, Nixon hardly needed a costly fight over OEO. Although OEO itself was abolished after Nixon's landslide victory in 1972, the timing in 1971 did not lend itself to terminating VISTA. Instead, such OEO programs as VISTA, the Job Corps, Head Start, Legal Services, and Foster Grandparents were removed from OEO's jurisdiction and delegated to other departments. Supposedly this would leave OEO free to focus on poverty research and program development and evaluation. Since 1969, President Nixon had emphasized that OEO, with no administrative responsibility for antipoverty programs, could do important research on poverty. "OEO is to be the cutting edge by means of which [the] government moves into unexplored areas; the experimental temper is vital to its success. It should be free to take creative risks . . . set up . . . demonstration projects and carefully test their effectiveness and systematically assess the results."[21]

Delegation of antipoverty programs to other agencies theoretically would allow an unencumbered OEO to function as an administrative watchdog over its former wards. "Any delegation agreements for anti-poverty programs should be drafted to require OEO to set up guidelines, dispense funds and monitor performance in such a way as to ensure that a department operating a delegated program keeps its focus on the needs of the poor."[22] OEO was, in fact, reduced administratively to a powerless report-producing agency.

Even before OPRE's evaluations were complete, OEO programs were transferred to federal departments. Head Start was delegated to Health, Education and Welfare (HEW), along with Health Services and Foster Grandparents. The Job Corps moved to the Department of Labor, and Legal Services was reconstituted as an independent corporation.[23] Later, the Peace Corps and VISTA were placed in ACTION, the newly created agency for voluntary action. By mid-1971, OEO's line programs had been parceled out, leaving it without an operational base.

Transfers occurred even though, according to the Economic Opportunity Act of 1964, only programs of proven success could be delegated out of OEO. OEO's conservative critics, however, believed that such programs as VISTA and the Job Corps would retain their activist prejudices if allowed to remain within the OEO fold. By transferring them out of OEO, the programs could be redirected and improved. For example, Head Start was delegated to HEW, to "strengthen it by association with a wide range of early development programs within the department."[24] Conservatives were also aware of the political benefits of reorganization. As one observer noted of the Job Corps' move to Labor: "Job Corps would lose its freedom of action and would become easier to control. The purpose was thus to bury it bureaucratically so that it would lose its vitality and initiative."[25] A similar fate awaited the Peace Corps and VISTA in the new ACTION agency.

By the same token, conservatives were skeptical of what antipoverty programs claimed to have accomplished. Conservative appointees charged that special programs for the poor had raised expectations needlessly while failing to reduce poverty in the United States.[26] To these appointees, drastic action must be taken that would change the organizational cultures in antipoverty programs. Only if agency volunteers and staff carried an achievement ethic to the poor would there be any hope of liberating the poor from poverty. In their assessment, VISTA had done more harm than good for the poor.

The Not So Tranquil Peace Corps

Perhaps no government program had ever received the favorable (and at times lavish) praise that initially was bestowed on the Peace Corps. On its twentieth anniversary, in 1980, Secretary of State Muskie credited the Peace Corps with having awakened "the energy, the dedication, the faith in our purpose, the confidence of success. It was a powerful vision that enlisted the commitment of thousands—a vision of poverty eased, of hunger tamed, of disease alleviated, of human potential more fully realized."[27] Even conservatives such as Senator Goldwater proclaimed his admiration for the Peace Corps' vision.

Although President Nixon no longer was openly critical of the Peace Corps, clearly the once nobly portrayed Corps was in the throes of an organizational identity crisis. By 1968, a former Peace Corps trainer was describing the agency's problem in the following terms:

> Today, the bright promise of the Peace Corps is badly corroded; the ringing phrases which introduced it have a distinctly hollow sound. . . . The Peace Corps has been ejected from Pakistan, Guinea, Mauritania and Gabon. Demands for its ouster are proliferating, and its future is doubtful in several nations including Turkey where there were 590 Peace Corps volunteers in 1965 and are now only 220. In the United States applications have declined precipitously.[28]

What had changed since the early 1960s, when the Peace Corps, inundated with highly qualified applicants, shocked the Washington establishment by returning its unspent annual appropriation to the federal treasury? The most visible dilemma concerned the Corps' famed neutrality as an instrument of official U.S. foreign policy.

The Vietnam War inevitably forced Peace Corps volunteers and its politically appointed administrators into a political confrontation. In the final years of Johnson's presidency, the Peace

Corps was helpless to stem the rising tide of volunteer discontent with the U.S. role in the war in Vietnam.[29]

Consider the protests that occurred during the year preceding Nixon's narrow presidential-election victory in 1968:

> Eight Peace Corps volunteers from Ecuador wrote an "indictment of [the] Peace Corps" that was published in several U.S. newspapers. It criticized the agency as "arrogant and colonialist in the same way as the government of which it is a part."[30]

> Nine hundred members of the Committee of Returned Volunteers signed a letter to President Johnson stating that the Vietnam War had made them unwilling agents of the U.S. imperialism.[31]

> In October, 1967, twenty-four volunteers in Brazil wrote to the *New York Times* protesting that "there is an inherent contradiction in representing a government which is engaging in a war while serving that government in the Peace Corps."[32]

> In September, 1967, 659 Peace Corps volunteers criticized [the] Peace Corps' acquiescence [in] the war as, at best, a poignant gesture: a worse than cruel hoax.[33]

The Vietnam War produced an unavoidable struggle between Corps volunteers and the agency's top political appointees.

The Peace Corps—though for entirely different reasons than its domestic counterpart, VISTA—had been thoroughly politicized. It is important to note that the Peace Corps had been torn apart by the Vietnam issue even before Nixon assumed office in 1969. Highly visible protests by scores of former Peace Corps volunteers against the war, however, did little to endear the Corps to conservative Republicans, nor did the enthusiastic participation by numerous former volunteers in the 1968 Democratic primary campaigns of senators Eugene McCarthy and Robert Kennedy.[34] By 1972, Frank Mankiewicz, himself a former Peace Corps staffer, was openly alluding to the "secret weapon of 20 to 30 thousand returned Peace Corps volunteers in the Democratic arsenal."[35]

Attacks on the Peace Corps were not restricted to supporters of the Vietnam War. Others, such as Representative Otto Passman (Democrat) of Louisiana, vociferously attacked the Peace

Corps because of alleged poor program design and mismanagement. Specifically, the Peace Corps was criticized in four areas:

Peace Corps accomplishments were difficult to quantify.

Fourteen countries terminated Peace Corps projects even though none of these countries ended AID technical assistance programs.

Terminations in certain countries were due to poor conduct on the part of some Peace Corps volunteers.

The agency was not successful in spending all its budget allocations from Congress.[36]

Not surprisingly, supporters of the Peace Corps in Congress and elsewhere dismissed these charges as a scurrilous "insult" to the Corps' humanitarian efforts.[37] Defensive reactions by Peace Corps' defenders, however, could not hide the serious internal ideological polarization within the agency. In retrospect, it was unrealistic to expect the Peace Corps to remain placid and untouched by the growing antiwar movement. According to the organizational culture of the Peace Corps, volunteers were neutral and should not be advocates of U.S. foreign policy. Volunteers prided themselves on being independent thinkers, unlike the AID or embassy people with whom they were sometimes associated. The unpopular war in Vietnam, however, severely tested this independence (and neutrality). With the intensifying war there surfaced a conflict between an organizational culture forged in a pre-Vietnam era and the ideological realities of wartime.

Because of the type of volunteer the Peace Corps and VISTA attracted, the agencies were in part ideological lightning rods. During the 1960s and early 1970s, they recruited predominantly young, well-educated volunteers. Although the Peace Corps and VISTA ostensibly solicited applications from individuals of all ages and occupations, their main recruiting effort was focused on college campuses. Ironically, recruiting materials urged college students to seek fundamental social and economic changes at home and abroad through Peace Corps or VISTA.[38]

At the same time, Peace Corps and VISTA administrators, as political appointees by the current administration in Washington, were unsympathetic to volunteer actions that might prove embarrassing.

Regardless of whether Peace Corps volunteers were stationed in rural or urban areas, official communication with them often was erratic at best. The official explanation of events in Vietnam came primarily through the Voice of America, the British Broadcasting Corporation, and Radio Moscow. On many occasions, the communication problem was compounded by a daily environment of hostility, suspicion, and loneliness. Many volunteers became disillusioned and politically radicalized by their encounters with entrenched local elites. Given this situation, it appeared that few Peace Corps volunteers could or would explain their country's involvement in Vietnam.

Both VISTA and the Peace Corps had developed strongly activist cultures before Nixon took office. Both accepted a worldview in which external political and economic forces shaped people's lives, at home and in Southeast Asia. In their training, activists were taught that the powerless must be organized to resist these forces. By the time of Richard Nixon's reelection campaign, presidential appointees at VISTA and the Peace Corps were ready to change this; erroneous activist values must go, to be replaced by a conservative ideology. Neither activist employees nor volunteers could have anticipated the intense organizational conflict that lay ahead.

A Conservative Plan of ACTION

As we have seen, much of President Nixon's first term in office focused on a policy of program reassessment and reorganization, after which it became clear to conservatives that such programs as VISTA and the Peace Corps must discard their activist cultures. Unlike the OEO programs delegated to old-line departments for administration, a different fate awaited VISTA and the Peace Corps. Along with several other old and newly created programs, they were combined in the ACTION agency.

Under President Nixon's Reorganization Plan No. 1, of 1971, programs involving 20,000 volunteers, 1,600 employees, and an annual budget of $140 million (FY 1972) were consolidated in ACTION, the voluntary action agency.[39] Yet the surprise creation of ACTION raised two questions. Why was it created at all, especially within the executive branch? Specifically, why were Foster Grandparents, the Peace Corps, and VISTA merged? Certainly Foster Grandparents and VISTA could be delegated, as were other OEO programs, to HEW or HUD. The Peace Corps clearly had no desire to lose its semi-autonomous status or to combine with VISTA. Apparently, ACTION was a shotgun wedding for all involved.

The creation of ACTION fulfilled two goals of the administration: increased effectiveness through reorganization, and conservative redirection of organizational values. Retrospective assessment, in light of Watergate and other nefarious activities directed at career employees during Nixon's final years in office, indicates that organizational efficiency was a secondary motive for creating ACTION. Instilling conservative ideology in AC-TION programs became the primary goal.

Specifically, the creation of ACTION was prompted in large part by conservative policymakers wishing to accomplish four political objectives: (1) end VISTA's community-organizing activities; (2) set up conservative alternatives to VISTA, using budgetary funds allocated to VISTA; (3) defuse the expression of antiwar statements by Peace Corps volunteers; and (4) stop community-organizing activities by the Peace Corps. In a larger sense, ACTION's genesis in 1971 reflects a conservative strategy of destroying activist cultures at the Peace Corps and VISTA and replacing them with conservative ideological values.

Predictably, the creation of ACTION by executive order was opposed by eighty-seven organizations, including every organized group of volunteers and former volunteers from the Peace Corps and VISTA.[40] They submitted, to no avail, voluminous testimony claiming that the consolidation of the Peace Corps and VISTA in ACTION was politically motivated and destructive of the distinctive identity of both programs. The protests were ineffective; ACTION, authorized by executive order, answered only to the White House.

It wasn't until July 1973, two years after executive authorization of ACTION, that the Senate passed an authorization bill for the agency. Thus, for two years ACTION operated "without benefit of authorizing legislation. It had to look to four different pieces of legislation for authorization of appropriations. ACTION had been responsible to more than 15 committees and sub-committees of Congress."[41] The Nixon administration defended the creation of ACTION on the same grounds it defended other presidential reorganization plans: to do so would yield greater financial savings, greater managerial efficiency, and consolidation around common functional or agency goals.[42]

In soliciting congressional support for his new voluntary action agency, President Nixon chose not to criticize activist values or programs. Instead, he promised that ACTION would "build on what we've learned."[43] He could have added that conservatives had "learned" that activist values and community-organizing projects at VISTA and the Peace Corps were, in their view, a mistaken framework for policymaking. It was hoped that consolidation of ACTION would allow conservative appointees to have better control of two voluntary action agencies, agencies that were an embarrassing legacy of activist idealism.

Purging VISTA of Community Organizing

To conservatives, the community-organizing projects of the Peace Corps and VISTA symbolized the bankruptcy of activist values. At best, the community-organizing approach was naïve liberalism; at worst, it was a sinister concoction of activists intent on revolutionizing the masses. VISTA's own recruiting literature, rewritten in 1971 to convey a conservative perspective, faults VISTA's reliance on community organizing in the 1960s: "The concept of community development—helping groups of poor people help themselves—was an ideal theory, but [it] turned out to be vague in practice. [It] proved to be futile when . . . volunteers didn't know what the poor needed or wanted. They'd get groups of people to come to meetings, then wonder, 'What did we organize them for?'"[44] Community organizing as an inappropriate approach was made even more harmful by VISTA volunteers who supposedly were poorly trained and who generally served less than twelve months in a poor community.

VISTA's community-development approach, like that of the Peace Corps, was based on the concept of full-time volunteers living in a poor community as a means of gaining the confidence of poor people. First, once the volunteer was accepted by the community, he or she ascertained what were its felt needs in such areas as health care, economic development, and education. Second, the volunteer was taught to learn who were "key influentials" in the community and to gain their confidence and trust. The volunteer would then be in a position to serve as a resource to the community and its leaders, so that strategies of social action could be devised. Third, the Peace Corps or VISTA volunteer would help carry out social action. In this way, activists thought that the cycle of poverty could finally be broken through "empowerment to people—so that they take direct action on their own behalf."[45]

Conservatives disagree, claiming that community-organizing projects failed because felt needs were not derived from the poor community, but rather, in too many instances, reflected the volunteer's own activist preferences. Community development as practiced by VISTA mistakenly "stressed the impact of VISTA service on the volunteer, with programs developed and monitored by the VISTA staff and volunteers themselves, rather than by community groups."[46]

Community action by the activists was no longer tolerable to conservatively oriented administrators at ACTION. They did not agree with the activist view that the world is divided between good and evil, between "huge corporations, mass media and 'benevolent' government" on one side and poor people on the other. Nor did they accept the community-organizing view that the "profit line is the bottom line for institutions" or that the haves and have nots are engaged in a "war of values."[47]

Conservative appointees at ACTION imposed evaluation guidelines by which VISTA's community-organizing projects were to be evaluated. Local sponsoring agencies, under the oversight of local governments, would monitor VISTA projects closely. Because few community-action projects could posit measurable objectives, under these criteria, more than a hundred

VISTA projects were cancelled immediately and most of the others were redesigned.[48]

A related problem stemmed from sharp divergence between conservative appointees and activist staffers regarding the proper role of volunteers as community organizers. Michael Balzano, OEO senior staff member during the first Nixon term, concluded that community organizing was generally a façade for political organizing: "The only problem with the so-called relevant activities, such as politically organizing the poor under the guise of community organization, is that such activities were never proposed to Congress and would never be sanctioned by that body. *There is nothing wrong with organizing the poor politically. It may be a worthwhile activity which should be carried out. But that is not a VISTA function.*"[49] Nixon conservatives at OEO and ACTION believed that volunteers who politically organized the poor were undermining what they considered the agency's service orientation.

As might be expected, the open hostility of ideological conservatives toward community-organizing projects at VISTA provoked career employees, volunteers, and groups of former volunteers to counterreact. They expressed deep concern that the agency survive, with at least a semblance of activist values intact. Contrary to their worst fears, President Nixon did not abolish VISTA or other OEO-administered programs; the Peace Corps and VISTA were allowed to live. Through executive reorganization within a new White House agency, VISTA and the Peace Corps supposedly emerged reborn in a conservative image. Their activist cultures would be remade. New conservative programs for voluntary service would be tested. Conservative-designed programs, as a counterbalance to alleged VISTA excesses in community action, would validate conservative values by motivating the poor to achieve liberation through their own efforts.

Conservative Alternatives to VISTA

In 1971 conservatives moved quickly to demonstrate that voluntary action programs in the United States need not be based on activist values of planned social intervention. Shortly after its creation, ACTION launched the University Year for ACTION (UYA) program. Formulated by ACTION's Office of Policy and Program Development (OPPD), UYA was viewed as a forerunner of conservative initiatives in voluntary action policymaking.[50] As a side benefit, UYA was financed as a demonstration project through VISTA's operating budget.

UYA's goals were to be accomplished by mobilizing untapped resources in traditional VISTA programs—students in universities near poverty communities. As planned by its conservative designers, UYA volunteers would be uniquely qualified to address poverty issues by: providing effective manpower to work on poverty problems, decentralizing the administration of voluntcer programs through educational institutions, allowing students to combine community service and academic study, and encouraging university assistance to local poverty communities.[51]

Unlike traditional VISTA volunteers, who had no immediate access to university resources near poverty communities, UYA volunteers were college students. As university students (many of them were residents of poverty communities), supposedly they could mobilize student leaders and other, similar university resources in the fight against poverty.[52] In addition, UYA volunteers were achievement role models par excellence. As it was in the case of VISTA, UYA's raison d'être was combating poverty. Insisted Blatchford, ACTION's director: "UYA is, above all, a program to assist Americans of low income and [in] disadvantaged circumstances."[53] VISTA and UYA fought the scourge of poverty though from far different ideological perspectives.

UYA volunteers were directed to act as achievement models for the poor, not to participate actively in organizing community groups for social change. Poverty would be fought by showing the poor how to risc from their despair. UYA volunteers were to assist "the community. If this goal is kept as the clear and primary focus . . . the secondary goals will be achieved. By producing a successful result in the poor community, you will provide university involvement and a genuine experiential gain for the volunteer."[54] UYA volunteers would by their very lives demonstrate that poverty can be conquered by those who wish to achieve.

How would UYA's programmatic approach be an improvement over VISTA? Both VISTA and UYA volunteers would serve a one-year term in antipoverty project activities, but whereas VISTA volunteers must be supervised by a community organization, UYA volunteers would be university students earning academic credit ("work-study") for their antipoverty-project activities. By the end of 1971, UYA projects at twenty-two universities had placed more than a thousand volunteers in low-income communities.[55] Such rapid placement of UYA volunteers was possible because ACTION contracted with several independent consulting firms to guide universities through the devices of UYA grant-writing and student recruitment and training.[56] Described as "VISTA in education," UYA funds came from VISTA's budgeting allocation for program development.[57] Legally, UYA volunteers were classified as associate VISTA volunteers.

The reaction to UYA from the National VISTA Alliance (NVA) was vehement: "The simple fact," said Representative Frank Thompson, Jr., "is that it (UYA) had been funded at the general expense of VISTA and has contributed to the weakening of the program."[58] Nonetheless, after its pilot years, UYA was judged a success and was transferred to full operational status within ACTION; by late 1974, UYA's budget and volunteer strength were almost half that of VISTA itself.

Now VISTA confronted a rival for already scarce resources in the ACTION budget. Without increasing overall appropriation requests, ACTION established an ideologically acceptable alternative to VISTA. UYA's own political survival, strengthened by strong clientele support from fifty-five universities with UYA contracts, appeared secure. The universities and the UYA volunteers were mobilized to appear repeatedly before congressional committees in an effort to resist NVA attempts to reduce UYA spending.

In the eyes of conservative policymakers and administrators at ACTION, UYA offered several important advantages over VISTA:

First, volunteer activism would be controlled. Only upper-division, full-time students would be selected as UYA volunteers, thereby avoiding college dropouts and nonserious students, two groups the conservatives viewed as inclined to gravitate toward VISTA.[59]

Second, UYA volunteers would serve in their own communities. Conservatives were convinced that sending VISTA volunteers into unfamiliar poverty communities was a mistake. "American communities which previously had accepted young volunteers recruited nationally now wanted locally recruited volunteers, who reflected the cultural profiles of their own population . . . local volunteers who conformed to local mores and lifestyles and avoided the culture clashes and social and political confrontation [that] characterized VISTA's early years."[60] Conservatives felt that community needs could better be served by local volunteers who possessed the virtue of increased access and credibility.

Third, UYA volunteer activities were guided and controlled through academic requirements and faculty demands on their time. With their studies, UYA volunteers would have little time or inclination for community organizing or radical action. Supposedly achievement-oriented volunteers would be in the final stages of completing their baccalaureate degrees.

Service by UYA's student volunteers would be limited to projects in such areas as the delivery of health services, economic development, education, consumer protection, the administration of justice, housing, and environmental protection.[61] Clearly, community organizing of the poor was not deemed an appropriate emphasis for UYA. As a demonstration project, it theoretically would exemplify the achievement ethic to poor people in America.

Fifth, VISTA's promise to lead the poverty crusade came under attack from more radical activists who doubted that VISTA actually attacked the root causes of poverty. The September 1968 issue of *VISTA Volunteers* carried an article that asked why so little progress had been made in fighting poverty. "It is because we have been dealing with effects and not with causes. And the primary causes of poverty in affluent twentieth-century America are simply these: racism and classism that inherently pervade almost every level and facet of white American society today. . . ."[62] The proposed solution to white racism and classism: two parallel movements of blacks working with blacks, whites working with whites. Accordingly, middle- and upper-class whites should stay out of the ghettos. Rather, "they must deal with their own racism and classism, whether individual or institutional."[63] Therefore, progressive or activist whites were advised to stay home and change their own race first.

Other radical critics echoed the view that VISTA was hamstrung by having to address what these critics perceived as the environmental causes of poverty. Marshall Windmiller gives the VISTA bail project in San Francisco as an example. Under the project, VISTA volunteers work with local officials in arranging for poor people who are arrested to be released on their own recognizance without bail. Even though this helps the poor who can't afford bail and relieves already overcrowded jails, Windmiller charged, "it does nothing to attack the poverty in which the criminality is bred; it merely strengthens the legal system" that controls the poor.[64] According to the radical view, rich elites must be forced by community-organizing efforts to relinquish power; otherwise, poverty merely is perpetuated by cosmetic VISTA projects.

Radical activists and conservatives alike agreed—from quite different premises—that VISTA should either be reorganized or be abolished. By the early 1970s, VISTA had managed to offend groups at both ends of the political spectrum and thus had lost its lustre.

New Directions Program for the Peace Corps

From the conservatives' perspective, the Peace Corps' independent organizational status contributed to its inability or unwillingness to control open discontent with the Vietnam War among volunteers. Vocal discontent expressed by Peace Corps volunteers and returned volunteers persisted, just as it had during the Johnson administration. Hundreds of volunteers and former volunteers participated in antiwar activities, including the mammoth Vietnam moratorium demonstration staged in Washington on October 15, 1969. (Ironically, Sam Brown, the moratorium's organizer, became ACTION director during the

Carter administration.) Peace Corps volunteers in the field protested host-country visits by Vice-President Agnew and Secretary of State Rogers.[65] At home, sixteen returned volunteers
occupied the Peace Corps' Southeast Asia office in 1970 and flew
the Viet Cong flag from Lafayette Park, in view of the Oval
Office.

The issue of how to deal with politically vocal volunteers was
especially troublesome to ACTION administrators. Director
Joseph Blatchford defended the volunteers' right to freedom of
expression:

> Many believe that a Peace Corps Volunteer must be prohibited
> from speaking out in disagreement with his own government's
> politics or views. I reject that viewpoint.
>
> The Peace Corps Volunteer is not an agent of the United States
> Government; he is an expression of the good will of the American
> people.
>
> To place restrictions on the thought or speech of our volunteers
> would undermine what they best represent: The ability and
> imagination which free society can mobilize for the common
> good.[66]

Yet, under pressure, Blatchford subsequently acted to terminate
twelve volunteers because of their antiwar protests.

To conservatives, the Peace Corps and its volunteers needed
both direction and better control. Thus Blatchford initiated a
"new directions program" intended to dismantle the activism of
the Corps by redirecting volunteer recruitment so that it would
be aimed at more acceptable volunteer applicants.

First, Peace Corps recruiters concentrated on attracting more
older volunteers. As a consequence, by 1976, the average age for
Peace Corps volunteers rose from 24.5 to 27.6 years. Over 5
percent were above 50 years of age. Director Blatchford would
later warn Carter administration officials against relying on
young college graduates who were often emotionally imma-
ture.[67] Blatchford also criticized the myth of the self-reliant
young: "The fact is, Americans aren't particularly self-reliant,
cutting the jungle on their own in a foreign land."[68] Clearly, the
conservatives' New Directions Program sought an older volun-

teer, one more compliant and less likely to protest American foreign policy.

Second, in order to accommodate older volunteers, the Peace Corps dropped its long-standing ban on family placements. By accepting volunteers with families, the Corps might improve recruitment of occupationally skilled volunteers and also might improve the image of the United States presented to host countries.

Third, the conservatives' New Directions shifted an emphasis away from the "B.A. generalist" volunteers, who had comprised almost 80 percent of all volunteers since 1961. These were recent liberal-arts graduates who served a Peace Corps stint before continuing on with graduate school or their chosen careers. Instead, ACTION proposed sending older, more skilled volunteers with established expertise in a particular area, such as mechanics, egg production, carpentry, etc.[69] Activists had argued that volunteers who were "highly trained but not necessarily highly certified" were more adaptable, and thus more effective, than less flexible specialists.

Furthermore, activists believed that generalists were more effective agents of development than technical specialists because of their broader, more interdisciplinary perspective on community problems. The ideal volunteer should function as "a political receptacle" by converting environmental resources, "as an engine converts fuel, into meaningful energy." A generalist volunteer, as an "engine of change," must "be sensitive to the entire problem cycle and be capable of dealing with several facets, as appropriate, more or less simultaneously. This volunteer must be able to work in the political, social, and economic sectors of the cycle."[70] Conservatives believed that generalists were so concerned with the problem cycle that they lacked specific and applied problem-solving skills.

Fourth, New Directions promoted an integration of host-country nationals with Peace Corps administrators. The Peace Corps in the 1960s had functioned almost entirely with U.S. administrators. By 1974, over 76 percent of the overseas staff were non-U.S. citizens.[71] Moreover, Peace Corps training that had formerly been conducted almost exclusively in the United States was shifted to host-country locations and administrative control. Even final selection of volunteers was carried out over-seas.

Fifth, New Directions hoped to better utilize the skills of Peace Corps volunteers upon their return. ACTION was portrayed as the volunteerism agency where domestic and international volunteerism could be coordinated. Director Blatchford believed that ACTION should facilitate an exchange of ideas among volunteers at home and abroad. He envisioned utilizing returned Peace Corps volunteers to raise volunteer levels to hundreds of thousands of volunteers, even millions.[72] To assist in helping returned Peace Corps volunteers overcome "reverse culture shock," ACTION set up Transitional Centers to help "put these people back in touch with America."[73] The agency designed a three-week course that it hoped would redirect volunteers "back to the urban scene." By understanding contemporary domestic issues, volunteers would also be given career counseling to help them best utilize their Peace Corps skills at home.

The conservatives' New Directions initiatives were firmly in place by the time of the election campaign of 1972. Conservatives hoped that New Directions would control the political excesses of volunteers and return the Peace Corps to its earlier status of a nonpolitical agency, an "altruistic expression of America's good will toward the world—our desire to help, our will to serve mankind."[74]

Increasingly, however, there were signs that the Peace Corps could never return to the activist vision of politically neutral volunteers. Perhaps most disturbing to conservatives was the radicalization of the Committee of Returned Volunteers. More and more, the CRV saw itself as a component of the growing antiwar movement. In the summer of 1969 it sent two delegates to Cuba to evaluate the Cuban revolution. In a report that would hardly make the best-seller list in conservative circles, Bonnie Parker summarized the feelings of the CRV:

> We learned to appreciate that radicals have a role in the United States to undermine the capitalist structure so that not only would imperialism be destroyed at home, but would also be destroyed in the Third World. In a certain sense, the peoples of the Third World look to the radicals in the U.S. to help them, not by

coming to fight in the mountains but to do our revolutionary thing here. We had a vision of imperialism being attacked on all sides.[75]

When the CRV general assembly met in September 1969, it passed a position paper criticizing the Peace Corps for supporting reactionary regimes in countries where volunteers are assigned. "We have come to the unavoidable conclusion that the Peace Corps should be abolished," it concluded.[76]

The Peace Corps, like VISTA, was under fire from conservatives and radical activists alike. Neither ideology agreed with the activist values that had guided both programs since their inception. Later, during the Carter and Reagan administrations conservatives and radical activists, in turn, would try their hands at formulating more acceptable organizational programs. For the time being, however, conservatives hoped that winding down the Vietnam war, plus reorganizing ACTION, would allow the Peace Corps and VISTA to be recast ideologically in a conservative image.

On the Eve of Watergate

As we have noted, neither antipoverty programs nor the Peace Corps suffered annihilation during Richard Nixon's first term. Rather, the period 1969–73 was marked by program reassessment followed by the agency reorganization that typified Nixon's first term. Though bruised and battered in some cases, no War on Poverty agency was terminated during those years. Agencies were reorganized and delegated, and budgets were cut; but none were eliminated. Still others, such as the new ACTION agency and its University Year for ACTION, were created. Even those antipoverty programs most heavily criticized by conservatives—VISTA, Legal Services, and the Job Corps— persist even into Ronald Reagan's second term.

In large part, the survival of these agencies is attributable to the truism that it's simply more difficult to terminate a government program than to initiate one. Once programs are in place, clientele groups with ties to particular government programs exert influence to prevent dismantlement. In the case of VISTA and the Peace Corps, former volunteer groups were particularly influential, as were career civil servants at both agencies.

A deeper and less explored reason, however, concerns the ideological perspectives of political appointees to government agencies. With a few notable exceptions, such as Howard Phillips at OEO and James Burnley at VISTA, presidential appointees generally do not seek to destroy agencies to which they are appointed. Frequently, though, they are at odds with either the organizational culture or the policies of their partisan predecessors. Conservative policymakers and appointees in the Nixon, Ford, and Reagan administrations usually did not seek to eliminate VISTA programs or the Peace Corps; nor did radical activists during the Carter presidency. They worked vigorously to change organizational values so that they would fit in an ideologically acceptable framework.

Richard Nixon's abbreviated second term and Gerald Ford's interlude as president brought new issues to ACTION, the Peace Corps, and VISTA. The early Nixon years of reassessment and reorganization were over. ACTION was a reality, as was the forced marriage of Peace Corps and VISTA. At issue now: How far can presidential appointees go, legally and ethically, in reformulating agency goals? Stated another way, what are the moral constraints on administrative decision-making, especially in agencies that rely on volunteers to implement their programs? To what extent could career employees be coerced to accept new organizational values?

The Peace Corps and VISTA offer fruitful, if perhaps unfortunate, case studies in exploring ideological struggles over administration. With its international mission, the Peace Corps raises ideological implications for foreign policy but not domestic policy, which is more center stage in the ideological struggle between activists and conservatives. VISTA, however, is caught in an ideological maelstrom. Attempts to control VISTA have persisted through every recent administration, while the Peace Corps is periodically demoralized when its volunteers and staff are offended by U.S. foreign policy.

Four

Political Education
at
ACTION

There is a well-worn maxim of politics that the purpose of elections is not to throw their rascals out, but to throw your rascals in. Each presidential election allows voters to choose not only a presidential candidate who is well known but thousands of unknown appointees as well. As John W. Macy, Jr., points out, these political appointees are not extensions of the chief executive. "Unelected, often unknown to the press and public, they bring to their work a personal history and leave an imprint, at least by interpreting regulations and forming a staff, that sets a pace and direction of its own."[1]

From where does the President select his "rascals"? Most influential jobs are set aside as political spoils for the victorious party. Yet, for incoming presidents, the spoils of victory seldom are sweet. Appointees to key administrative posts must be selected almost immediately and on the basis of political considerations that may have little to do with proven administrative competence. Rival party factions must be included, regional considerations recognized, campaign loyalty rewarded. Campaign workers often are even more ideologically committed to their values than either the voting public or the candidates themselves, who must learn the art of compromise during the course of the campaign.

Small wonder, then, that the appointment of campaign workers to an agency staffed by career civil servants frequently marks the onset of organizational conflict and tension. This conflict is heightened when top vacancies remain unfilled—often for more than a year—as the recruitment and selection process drags on and on at minor agencies such as VISTA and the Peace Corps. Even after selection, the new appointee arrives on the scene only to confront civil servants who resent the "new boss whose selection was not based on any expertise in subjects within the organization's jurisdiction and who was provided no careful preparation for the position he or she was to assume."[2] This unfavorable situation is exacerbated when political appointees feel that it is their mission to redirect agency programs and policies.

Despite the insistence of presidential candidates that government is guided by issues and policies, it is in fact run by men and women—candidates' appointees. Political campaigns seldom clarify or elucidate policy preferences; instead, policy and programmatic direction comes, if it comes at all, from the new appointees. All too frequently, deep conflict occurs in organizational values and direction. On one side are the partisans with their ideological beliefs, while on the other is an organizational culture adhered to by career employees. It is often much more than a mere difference of opinion; frequently there are profound differences between appointees and civil servants in their career patterns, decision-making styles, and experience. The list below contrasts these differences, as conceptualized by William Timmins:[3]

Political Appointees	Career Employees
Short-term appointment for specific time period	Lifetime or long-term, career-oriented commitment
Oriented philosophically toward policy pole of agency positions	Aligned with stable, long-term objectives and values of agency activities
Partisan (usually, politically appointed)	Responsible for policy implementation, not usually for formulation
Oriented toward short-term options and accomplishments	Seeking equilibrium, even when balance requires unnatural postures

Loyal to administration, an insider	Equanimitous, not easily perturbed or disturbed
Sensitive to political needs	Responsible more to profession than to party
Attuned to client groups and political publics	Inveterate, firmly established through long persistence
Ego and self-esteem needs can seem paramount	Aligned with "general public," not party or administration
Executive/management/ administration oriented	Management doctrines shared with other careerists
Sensitive to own career after public service	Sensitive to importance of merit system, career service, long-term values

As Timmins stresses, appointees and careerists often have little in common. And as VISTA and the Peace Corps demonstrated all too well, value conflict between the groups is often intense and unrelenting.

Value conflict, of course, is not felt equally in all governmental organizations; in some organizations or jurisdictions it may be virtually nonexistent, particularly when presidential appointees are already recognized experts in a policy field or where there is a strong commitment to the organization's mission. For example, it is clear that a hawkish appointee to the post of Secretary of Defense will not produce consternation among top agency administrators, military leaders, or defense clientele groups. Nor is it likely that presidential appointees to agencies with no strong commitment cultures—G.S.A., I.R.S., the U.S. Postal Service—will arouse concern among careerists whose primary concern is with their job security.

Conflict between careerists and appointees is inescapable in governmental organizations where two forces collide: an identifiable organizational culture widely shared among career (non-exempt) employees, and presidential appointees who hold opposing ideological values. Both sets of conditions existed and continue to exist in a number of governmental organizations but perhaps most vividly in such programs as the Peace Corps and VISTA, which began with intensity of purpose and high morale.

Redirecting Errant Activist Cultures

By the beginning of Richard Nixon's second term, conservatives were demonstrating a newfound political intensity. Far Right spokespersons had become distrustful of Richard Nixon. Once the ideological champion of staunch anticommunists, Nixon was now the cause of concern among many New Right faithful who had "adopted the view that Nixon's defense policies and his overtures to China were signs of a fatal weakness in the anticommunist ideology." For many, Richard Nixon had been supported in 1968 on the premise, "my enemy's enemy is my friend." He was now an uncertain ideologue.[4]

What better way to recoup lost political support from the Far Right than to nominate two outspoken conservatives as directors of OEO and ACTION? First, President Nixon appointed Michael P. Balzano, Jr., the "President's envoy to the world of ethnic blue-collar workers," as ACTION director.[5] Second, he nominated the founder of the Conservative Caucus as director of the Office of Economic Opportunity. As OEO director, Howard Phillips was charged with dismantling the agency. Balzano's mission was to destroy ACTION's activist values, particularly at the Peace Corps and VISTA.

It is difficult to stress too much the intensity of conservative opposition to activist-initiated programs. Ideologically committed conservatives and others were convinced that the poor actually had been *harmed* by the programs of the Great Society.[6] They allegedly were misled by welfare ethic values which included the activist premises: the socioeconomic system is unjustly controlled by a powerful elite; being poor in America constitutes a social injustice; the poor need government programs that exclusively address their problems. Policymakers and administrators, especially those on the Far Right, believed (and believe) that the activist welfare ethic encourages the poor to place the blame for their plight on external forces, thereby distorting a Rousseauistic instinct of people to improve their lot through their own efforts. With their contrived concepts of class consciousness and interclass warfare, programs designed by activists cheat the poor of any hope of escaping poverty.[7]

Many conservative thinkers assert that poverty in the contemporary United States is relative when compared with that of the Great Depression or with conditions in the Third World. Unlike the widespread poverty of the 1930s, today poor people constitute a minority of the U.S. population. Myriad examples of materialism appear daily on television, and from time to time the poor are told by activists that it is immoral to prevent the poor from attaining the good life. In effect, conservatives claim, poverty is no longer defined economically; that is misguided thinking, they say. The poor have been made unhappy by misdirected government programs that focus on the relative condition of the poor as compared with that of middle-class consumers. "By standards that have prevailed over much of history," Victor Fuchs wrote in 1967, "there are few poor people in the United States today. Nevertheless, there are millions of American families [which], both in their own eyes and in those of others, are poor. As our nation prospers, our judgment as to what constitutes poverty will invariably change."[8]

Basically, conservatives attribute the persistence of poverty to misplaced perceptions on the part of the poor, who feel cheated because, in their view, they are denied the affluence others seem to achieve almost effortlessly. Government programs must be restructured, conservatives say, so that a work ethic is instilled in the poor. If OEO or ACTION bureaucrats cannot accept such a work ethic, they should be fired or should work elsewhere.

Some conservative critics have gone so far as to link antipoverty values to Marxism or at least to claim that such values parrot a "Marxist idea" in assuming the inevitability of class conflict. These values, it is claimed, theoretically are based on the false premise that "it is wrong to governmentally treat the poor as a class apart, with interests and aspirations separate and distinct from those of society as a whole."[9] That only encourages an artificial class-consciousness among the poor and thus breeds dissatisfaction and rebellion such as that which surfaced in the urban riots of the 1960s.[10]

Conservative policymakers conceive of the poor as numerous heterogeneous subgroups, each with its own particular needs.[11] The poor are not unique, conservatives argue; they merely lack motivation. Consequently, government programs that attack the economic roots of poverty are unnecessary, even detrimental. Generally, the poor should be served by the same programs that serve everyone else. Their concerns, so the argument goes, are adequately addressed by existing programs in housing, employment, and education, among others.[12]

At the same time, "social change is not necessarily desirable per se . . . the kinds of changes that OEO has tended to work are in many cases undesirable."[13] Especially offensive is the social change, or "social programming," of activists in bureaucracies. Conservatives prefer a policy that instead encourages philanthropic efforts and voluntary action by private citizens.[14]

Thus the conservative ideologues Michael Balzano and Howard Phillips had little sympathy for existing organizational cultures. Conservatives viewed activist assumptions about poverty and the poor through quite different ideological lenses. As appointed "outsiders," these men were determined to redirect values of a recalcitrant bureaucracy committed to activist beliefs. Nor would conservatives be the only outsiders. Radical activist appointees during the Carter administration again confronted an unacceptable organizational culture and its bureaucratic defenders (see Chapter 6). During the Reagan administration, political appointees to the Peace Corps and ACTION experienced the same conflict between organizational culture and partisan ideology. In each case, presidential appointees came to the Peace Corps and VISTA from strikingly different ideological vantage points, hoping to make their mark by changing organizational cultures.

A Conservative Ideology at ACTION

Created by the Nixon administration in 1971, ACTION brought together under one organizational roof several activist programs, as well as new programs created by conservative appointees. Undoubtedly, VISTA and the Peace Corps brought with them to ACTION strong commitment organizational cultures. Following Nixon's landslide victory in 1972, conservative appointees to VISTA and the Peace Corps and to ACTION undertook aggressive campaigns to reshape organizational cultures by transforming them politically and ideologically.

In ideologically redirecting activist organizational values, two strategies were employed by conservatives: partisan politicization and reeducation institutes for career employees. Both strategies raise the issues of what is a proper balance between political responsiveness and the requirement of a politically neutral civil service. Stated another way, how far can a politically appointed administrator go in pressuring career employees to support the administrator's ideological values?

Politicizing the Bureaucrats

Soon after winning his overwhelming reelection in 1972, Nixon gave Frederick V. Malek, OMB's assistant director, a specific directive to develop a strategy to mute the perceived indifference and hostility of a predominantly "Democratic civil service."[15] Malek's subsequent proposal to neutralize the civil service became known as the Federal Political Personnel Manual, or, more commonly, the "Malek Manual."[16]

The manual's underlying thesis was stated succinctly for loyal department heads: "You cannot achieve management, policy, or program control unless you have established *political* control."[17] Presidential appointees within each agency or department were instructed to designate secretly a special assistant and support staff as a political personnel office, to provide "placement in all key positions of substantively qualified and politically reliable individuals."[18] Malek's secret manual goes on to outline such detailed strategies as "frontal assault," "traveling salesmen," "layering," and "isolation," designed to change the activist thinking of supposedly disloyal federal bureaucrats.[19]

Personnel offices were to identify and evaluate high-level decision-makers within each federal agency. If deemed disloyal to the administration, an administrator would be subjected to persuasion as outlined in the Malek Manual. The strategy was to pressure the recalcitrant administrator either to become more cooperative or to resign.[20] Political personnel staff also recruited politically reliable applicants for job openings from among Republican congressional and White House sources.

How effective was the Malek Manual during the brief span of its implementation? In such federal agencies as HEW, HUD, GSA, OEO, and ACTION, the manual was surprisingly effective. Briefly: At GSA, Civil Service Commission investigators formally charged eight top administrators with operating a political referral system; at HUD, a Senate committee investigation revealed that agency political watchdogs kept partisan files on more than 4,000 HUD employees and applicant referrals; meanwhile, HEW political personnel staffers conducted an "operational talent search" whereby White House and Congressional Republicans relayed job applications from loyal applicants.[21] Apparently, however, nowhere was the political personnel system espoused by the Malek Manual implemented more vigorously than at ACTION and OEO.

Abuse of merit-system protection and of the guidelines for public employee behavior undoubtedly was a fact of life in some public agencies. Surprisingly, throughout the history of the merit system, there has never been a criminal prosecution of a federal official for abusing merit regulations, which suggests that abuse stemming from partisan tactics is likely to continue.[22] Thus, ACTION and OEO, while hardly unique, apparently were unusual in the extent of their partisan abuse in personnel administration during the Watergate period.[23]

Consider only the partisan abuses reported at ACTION during Watergate. Early in 1975, ACTION employees filed a complaint with the Civil Service Commission, accusing the White House of systematically recruiting party loyalists while at the same time discriminating against classified employees who were active Democrats.[24] The complaint charged specifically that Alan May, former director of ACTION's Office of Staff Placement, had devised a screening system for rating the loyalties of potential ACTION employees in civil service jobs.[25]

Under May's rating system, job applicants for positions with ACTION were rated according to "P.Q.M.", officially an abbreviation standing for *p*ersonality, *q*ualifications, and *m*aturity. In actuality, applicants were rated in part on their demonstrated partisan loyalties, for, unofficially, May's staff used the abbreviation to rate an applicant's *p*olitics, *q*ualifications, and *m*inority status.[26] For instance, one applicant for ACTION's state director in Colorado possessed the following P.Q.M. "qualifications": "She has been active in politics in Denver for some years and has done such things as: Republican Committee Woman for Denver precinct 1410 since 1960; was co-chairman of U.S. Senate Campaign, co-chairman of Shoemaker for Mayor, and was in the state campaign committee for state legislators in 1964, 1966, 1968, and 1970. She has been active in the Colorado Federation of Republican Women."[27] As another example, a former staff member and campaign manager for Elliot Richardson was recommended as ACTION's Massachusetts/Rhode Island director. Though admitting that the nominee's qualifications were only "fair," it was noted that "he would be very reliable for our purposes."[28]

It would be unfair to suggest that political appointees automatically are unqualified to administer federal agencies. Clearly, party loyalty must be a factor by which qualified appointees are selected. However, the use of a political classification system for rating career civil servants is another matter. At ACTION, career employees who rated low by P.Q.M. criteria could expect repercussions along the lines suggested by the Malek Manual: job reclassification, reassignment, demotion, even the elimination of regional office functions.[29]

One must assume that the number of complaints filed against ACTION in the early 1970s indicates merely the tip of a partisan iceberg. ACTION's Region IX employees in San Francisco, for example, filed a complaint before the Civil Service Commission, complaining that they had been pressured and harassed by the local Committee to Reelect the President to support President Nixon's campaign.[30] The preponderance of the evidence suggests a wholesale attack on the political values of career employees in ACTION. Region IX employees who were politically undesirable were transferred from regional offices to headquarters in Washington, lest they "do irreparable damage to the election campaign" in California.[31] Another Region IX employee was targeted for transfer because of his opposition to Richard Nixon's gubernatorial bid in California in 1962. One critic accuses Alan May, while head of ACTION's personnel department, of "having fired the Peace Corps director and 33 of the country directors for partisan disloyalty."[32] Their positions remained unfilled during the Nixon and Ford administrations.

Further chronicles of examples of partisan abuse during and after the 1972 campaign probably are unnecessary; for most contemporary readers, the abuses of Watergate make for monotonous reading. Nor will we ever know the full extent of the partisan perversions of merit. Critics from the Democratic camp are quick to single out Republican violations. One of them has charged that 250 senior staff members of the Peace Corps were replaced by presidential appointees in the early 1970s; supposedly the Peace Corps became the "great dumping ground for Republicans."[33] Finally, given the Democrats' track record concerning VISTA and the Peace Corps, there is no empirical evidence supporting the virtues of one party over another when it comes to keeping partisan feelings out of personnel considerations.

At OEO headquarters, career employees were subjected to similar disregard by political appointees for the Hatch Act. At one point a local of the American Federation of Government Employees (AFGE) demanded that political-clearance procedures for OEO's classified employees be stopped. The grievance specifically identified a covert political evaluation unit housed in director Gallegos' office.[34] The AFGE complained that the OEO's partisan activities were an unlawful intrusion into the merit-selection process.

Again, it is not the concept or the practice of appointing political officeholders who are otherwise qualified that is troublesome; it is the planned politicization of career employees that deserves concern. Especially disturbing are those occasions when widespread ideological harassment permeates even such relatively small agencies as OEO, the Peace Corps, and ACTION. Whereas partisan activities along the lines of those recommended in the Malek Manual clearly are illegal, other forms of pressuring civil servants are not so clear-cut. For example, using one's influence to get a job for a "qualified" friend or relative is viewed by most people as neither unethical nor illegal, as long as it is not done with partisan considerations in mind.

Indoctrinating Career Employees

President Nixon, perhaps disappointed with the easygoing style of Joe Blatchford, ACTION director, decided that the agency needed a new leader and in early 1973 appointed Michael Balzano, Jr. The contrast between the leadership styles of the two directors was felt immediately. Whereas Blatchford was diplomatic, almost laid-back, Balzano prided himself on his direct, confrontational approach. Even Balzano's supporters observed that he "waded in and literally turned ACTION inside out and upside down."[35]

His critics portrayed Balzano less charitably, as ideologically to the right of Attila the Hun. No doubt Balzano's conservative values had been formed in large part by his own up-from-the-bootstraps career. Originally an "illiterate" high school dropout who became a sanitation worker, Balzano returned to school, completed college, and subsequently worked in Nixon's 1972 reelection campaign under Charles Colson. He evidently believed that he had a special mission in the campaign by being "the President's envoy to the world of ethnic blue-collar workers; the resident hardhat in the White House; and Nixon's favorite garbage collector. Because of my overt commitment to America, its government, its flag, and its traditional values, I have been called 'a middle American cheerleader.'"[36] Unlike his boss, Charles Colson, who later spent time in federal prison, Michael Balzano kept out of trouble.

Others, even within CREP, viewed Balzano's campaign activities as "shady." He was known as a political hatchet man and dirty-tricks specialist who was remembered in a less complimentary light by John Ehrlichman:

> Unknown to me [Ehrlichman], one of Charles Colson's people was sent to make inflammatory anti-busing speeches in Michigan, to the great distress of local officials. I called Bob Haldeman to find out why one of his staff members, Mike Balzano, was up in Michigan stirring up trouble. He made clear what I had already guessed: that Balzano was working for Colson. When I called Colson, he said he was operating in Michigan on the President's

instructions. If I didn't like it, then I didn't understand what was good for Richard Nixon.[37]

Clearly, Balzano proved an effective yet controversial member of the campaign.

Balzano's selection in 1973 as director of ACTION, however, was not based solely on his ability to make inflammatory anti-busing speeches or his appeal to ethnic groups. Shortly before the start of the campaign, while working for OEO, Balzano completed a Ph.D. dissertation critical of the design and training of VISTA's program.[38] He was particularly upset with a training program at the University of Maryland, where, he felt, VISTA volunteers were being indoctrinated with community-organizing values.

Even when Dr. Balzano took over as director of ACTION in 1973, he was hardly pleased with what he found: "a confrontation, anti-establishment effort, manned by nationally recruited young people, mostly college-educated, mostly middle-class, who, by their dress, code of behavior and style were viewed by strangers as outsiders. Their behavior, as far as the traditional U.S. community was concerned, was extremely poor."[39] ACTION's activist administrators and volunteers were not seen by Balzano as the type of achievement-oriented individuals who could help the poor work their way out of poverty, and he was determined to change ACTION's organizational culture and activist programs.

If conservative changes were to occur, certain assumptions had to be incorporated into the programming and design of ACTION. Conservative values must replace activist ideology. A restructured, conservative organizational culture would be based on the tenets listed below.

Volunteerism must replace antipoverty as an ACTION goal.[40] During the Democratic era of activist values, reduction of poverty in the United States was the major policy focus in VISTA and Peace Corps projects. Led by President Nixon, Republican conservatives proclaimed a new reliance on voluntary efforts and the provision of volunteers with a new level of public recognition. In addition, the President created the National Program of Voluntary Action while promising that volunteerism would be a major goal of his administration.[41] He also placed several voluntary action programs—that is, Senior Core of Retired Employees (SCORE), Retired Senior Volunteers Program (RSVP), and Foster Grandparents—in the ACTION agency, along with VISTA and the Peace Corps. This centralized consolidation in ACTION of voluntary-action programs that appealed to predominantly middle-class volunteers and retirees, together with several traditional antipoverty programs, marked a decided policy preference in favor of volunteerism.

ACTION projects should be expanded beyond the poverty community.[42] Local voluntary-action projects, if supported by ACTION, must follow local priorities as set by "those organizations which have the financial means to support volunteer work," namely, local government and civic groups.[43] Dr. Balzano felt that activist-designed programs in ACTION unnecessarily antagonized local leaders "by focusing on the poor and minorities and considering everyone else the problem."[44]

Conservative policymakers continually reaffirmed their belief that the problem of poverty and the aspirations of poor people were neither unique nor distinguishable from those of other Americans. The poor had simply lost sight of the American success ladder. Their vision was clouded by activists and community organizers. The poor must once again be invited to join the "achieving society." No longer would Balzano permit ACTION projects to assume, as they had done previously, that local elites were adversaries of the poor.[45]

When describing his vision of a conservative ACTION, Balzano evoked patriotism and theology. He proclaimed the achievement ethic as "consistent with the American tradition, i.e., God helps those who help themselves."[46] ACTION projects would be based on the American ideal that "in this country it is indeed possible to improve oneself"; voluntary-action programs would be designed so that the poor could be "trained and encouraged to participate in the American dream."[47]

All the community, not just the poor, should be served by ACTION. Conservatives believed that antipoverty programs had been too narrowly focused on traditional poverty and minority clienteles, with the result that other groups had been alienated from ACTION. Accordingly, white ethnic minorities would now be included in ACTION goals and objectives; ACTION would no longer focus exclusively on Appalachian whites, blacks, Chicanos, and Indians. New target clienteles might include such groups as Poles, Ukrainians, and Italians.[48]

Income levels or economic dimensions of poverty would no longer be used by ACTION agencies in defining appropriate clientele for voluntary-action projects. Any local community organization that requested ACTION's assistance, regardless of the income levels of its members, would be eligible for agency assistance.[49] The poor had been superseded by the larger community as ACTION's clientele.

In passing, it should be mentioned that conservatives were not alone in their criticism of antipoverty programs for their exclusive focus on the poor—on, for example, those many individuals whose annual income fell below an arbitrarily determined level. Community organizers who used the Saul Alinsky model had long preached building "as broad a coalition as possible within the community."[50] As "radical activists," organizers from the Alinsky mold would be given their day in court during the Carter administration.

Achievement-oriented volunteers must be recruited from among those who could motivate the poor and mobilize the community's voluntary-action efforts. Conservative administrators at ACTION worked to redirect agency recruiting and training in order to select achievement-oriented volunteers.[51] Conservatives believed that the achievement ethic was passé among most college-age students; thus ACTION's traditional recruitment of recent university graduates was, in their eyes, misdirected.

ACTION administrators redirected agency recruitment toward those individuals who supposedly had already embraced the achievement ethic, the blue-collar working class: "There would be no need to tell these people about the achievement ethic. . . . These people are trying to work their way into the middle class. [If] the children of the middle class, who constitute the bulk of VISTA's volunteers, do not believe it, how can they be expected to motivate anyone?"[52]

Since their inception, the Peace Corps and VISTA have recruited "A.B. generalists" or liberal-arts graduates to serve in their far-flung community-development projects. Volunteers were selected from the best universities, but they were not flag-wavers or overt patriots; to conservatives, they were outside the true American mainstream, still adhering to the liberal values epitomized in the films of their generation, *The Graduate* and *Easy Rider.* In the eyes of conservatives, activist volunteers in community-organizing projects constituted a doubly unpalatable situation: the wrong type of volunteer was being placed in poorly conceived projects.

Instead, ACTION during the Balzano era devoted considerable effort to attracting a new type of volunteer: the older, achievement-oriented individual—from a different vocational background, possibly with a family—who was expected to carry the message of the American dream. For VISTA, in order to maximize their credibility, volunteers were recruited locally. At the Peace Corps and VISTA, their mission was to mobilize local volunteers and community groups. Achievement-oriented volunteers were reminiscent of early American volunteerism. Conservatives envisioned a renewed volunteerism that would "be restored to its traditional American scope: the full-time volunteers of OEO formulation are to be diluted as much as possible by part-time volunteers."[53]

Properly trained, mature volunteers theoretically motivate low-income persons by demonstrating and exemplifying the validity of the achievement ethic. Part-time community volunteers helping their neighbors represented an ideal model for conservatives, thus spreading the achievement ethic among the poor.

Recruiting achievement-oriented volunteers alone, however, would not change the activist mentality at ACTION. The ACTION staff, particularly at the Peace Corps and VISTA, clung to activist values born of the Great Society. Former volunteers and volunteer groups worked diligently to preserve these values.

Organizational cultures would change only if employee values changed, that is, if they were converted to a different ideology.

Dr. Balzano had long believed that the key to organizational culture lay in changing employee attitudes. Conservative policymaking was futile if career bureaucrats operated from assumptions based on activist decision-making. Convinced that ACTION employees must understand and accept a new policymaking consensus, and intent on implementing a comprehensive approach to policymaking, Balzano set conservative goals and objectives.[54]

Changing a widely held organizational culture among ACTION's 1,800 career employees would not be easy, however. These employees were dispersed among seven ACTION programs located overseas, in ten U.S. regional offices, and at headquarters in Washington. Most staffers, including many former volunteers, came on board during the 1960s and, despite the Malek Manual, were protected by their civil-service status from overt political harassment. Furthermore, active groups of former volunteers and sympathetic congressmen were ready to defend the Peace Corps and VISTA against the perceived political sacrilege proposed by conservative appointees.

As a strategy for bringing about organizational change, a series of "programming institutes" attempting to break down the existing activist culture and replace it with a conservative ideology were put together by Balzano and his staff. These institutes would bring about employees' attitudinal changes that "must occur from regional staff all the way through headquarters personnel." As publicly explained, Balzano's purposes in organizing the programming institutes were presented in a somewhat benign light. He thought that they would "provide ACTION employees with a clear picture of the direction in which I intended to lead the agency."[55]

ACTION's programming institutes allegedly were intended to improve the agency's sagging morale. Dr. Balzano was persuaded that low employee morale was caused in large part by the mistaken belief that President Nixon intended to dismantle agency programs. Balzano insisted that nothing could be further from the truth and that his programming institutes would

get across that message.[56] The agencies and programs of AC-
TION would be continued by conservatives, though not under
the aegis of an activist organizational culture.

Specifically, ACTION's programming institutes were designed to convince employees that community organizing, or
confrontational politics, no longer was workable. Accordingly,
ACTION would shift its activist emphasis from "a program of
confrontation with the establishment to one of working harmo-
niously with the establishment in a low-key fashion. The AC-
TION institutes sought to encourage the agency's staff to favor
less volatile means for achieving social change."[57] The outmoded activist values of employees supposedly would be transformed into a more conservative viewpoint.

Attendance at the programming institutes was mandatory for
everyone, including the ACTION director (and his wife). Finally,
Dr. Balzano assured employees, "though we never promised that
employees would not be transferred, demoted, or dismissed, we
did promise that all those who worked hard would be rewarded
by career advancement and promotions."[58] Whether "semi-
nars," "institutes," or "indoctrination sessions," the institutes
clearly were intended by conservatives to be the first step in
changing the agency's organizational culture.

To carry out his reeducational goals, Balzano contracted with
an outside consulting group to conduct and evaluate five regional institutes. In virtually nonstop sessions, participants in
the institutes were saturated with conservative policymaking
assumptions and ideology. Various pedagogical techniques (lectures, small group discussions, project teams, films, and ques-
tion-and-answer periods) were used to reiterate selected
conservative themes.[59] Each was intended to help change employee value positions from those of activists to those of conservatives.

The extent to which Balzano's programming institutes redirected activist values can be measured by several assessments
given participants. First, each person who attended was
provided with pre- and post-institute attitudinal surveys. Second, participants were required to keep program-assignment
forms in which the response to each presentation was recorded.
Third, ACTION employees turned in daily logs, with their com-

ments on program activities. Collectively, the pre- and post-institute surveys, and the program assessment surveys, furnish insights into what happens when political appointees undertake to change organizational cultures. Three generalizations are derived from the participant data.[60]

1. *Participants generally gained a greater understanding of conservative ideology.* Analysis of employee responses indicates that a significant statistical change occurred in 31 percent of 51 responses *(N* = 16). At first glance, this result might appear impressive, suggesting that considerable attitudinal change took place during a five-day institute. Attitudinal change centered on two narrow propositions, however, that ACTION should expand its clientele in order to serve European ethnic groups and that more administrative efficiency was a worthwhile goal at ACTION.

By comparison, there was seemingly no significant attitudinal change by institute participants toward *acceptance* of conservative values. Participants showed only slightly more positive responses to the achievement ethic (or "Horatio Alger") items. There was no shift at all toward the political values of the Nixon administration or toward conservative ideology.

In effect, institute respondents gained a greater understanding of and perhaps sympathy for certain conservative values. On only two issues related to agency expansion was there a major transformation. First, the issue of increased organizational efficiency is arguably neither an activist nor a conservative position. Second, ACTION employees apparently became more receptive to the idea of expanding agency clientele to include new ethnic groups. They did not, however, reject the poor as a target population for ACTION programs.

2. *Participants learned that activist value orientations toward antipoverty programs were unacceptable to conservative appointees.* Institutes served to communicate both acceptable and unacceptable viewpoints. Employees who deny or criticize prevailing conservative assumptions risk criticism, harassment, demotion, transfer, or dismissal. Ethically, the role of advocating unacceptable views in any organization is admirable but seldom rewarding. Perhaps the most telling obstacles to

"honest" participant feedback were the pre- and post-test surveys that required identification numbers for employees.

3. *ACTION institutes generally were unsuccessful in changing the orientation of participants toward poverty.* Statistically significant evidence suggests that activist participants did not change their own values, but rather that participants redirected their behavior and went home wiser because of their participation. Numerous responses to open-ended questions asking for an assessment of the institutes as an instrument corroborate the institutes' negligible effects in changing employee attitudes toward the poor as ACTION's primary clientele. Nor do survey responses suggest that most participants changed their activist assumptions that poverty is an economic problem perpetuated by an unjust political system.

No doubt, many institute participants rejected the conservative message because of the way it was presented. Intensive education sessions hardly constitute an ideal learning environment regardless of the subject. Ideology can be transmitted through indoctrination or brainwashing, but long-term change is unlikely. ACTION employees learned through negative reinforcement about Dr. Balzano's values and plans for ACTION, but few changed their own activist values. At the same time, they learned from the institutes to keep their opinions to themselves.

The Changing Organizational Culture at ACTION

An organizational culture is not easily changed, especially in cases where strong organizational values are widely held by nonexempt, or civil service, employees. Michael Balzano's programming (or "informational") institutes provide a case study in the difficulty of changing an organizational culture. Refusal to change among ACTION's career employees was vividly demonstrated the morning after Jimmy Carter's narrow electoral victory in 1976. Balzano remembers a sign (placed in the lobby at ACTION headquarters where he would see it) that read: "We Won!"[61] The activist organizational culture at ACTION emerged largely intact from the Republican administrations of Richard Nixon and Gerald Ford; neither the activist culture at the Peace Corps nor that at VISTA was seriously eroded by the conservative ideological assault.

Several inescapable lessons emerged from the conservatives' efforts to change the organizational culture at ACTION. First, Dr. Balzano's programming institutes ran counter to usual strategies for organizational change and development. And second, as long as political appointees and career employees assume adversarial roles, cultural conflict in government organizations such as ACTION will continue. (In Chapter 7 we explore managerial options in minimizing conflict between political appointees and career employees in government.)

Once Again, Changing Organizational Cultures

Much has been written about organizational culture and change, in both public and private organizations. Much less is known, however, about governmental cultures or about strategies for encouraging strong organizational cultures. A major obstacle occurs because many presidential appointees are appointed to agencies with values antithetical to the appointees' own ideological beliefs. Coercive tactics, ideological indoctrination, or other pressure measures are seldom if ever effective. What options, then, are available to those who would change organizational cultures in governmental agencies? Is there a viable alternative to intimidation or to machinations à la the Malek Manual? Finally, once created, can a commitment culture be nourished despite ideological attack? Each of these questions will be addressed as we continue the Peace Corps and VISTA odyssey during the 1970s and the 1980s.

We conclude this chapter with a simple assessment of one of the more thoughtful efforts to change a corporation's culture. In the early 1970s, the Honeywell Corporation undertook a strategy designed to change its corporate culture. Honeywell's approach to changing corporate culture places the ACTION indoctrination fiasco in its proper perspective.

Honeywell's managers began with a basic premise that "change occurs gradually and may entail many false starts and slip-ups along the road."[62] Unlike political appointees who frantically attempt to reshape agency values during the first hundred days, Honeywell managers knew that changing to a participatory management style takes years, not months. Nine principles were enunciated and followed:

1. A charter statement of organization values must be articulated and practiced.
2. Managerial competencies must be developed through a well-conceived employee development plan.
3. Management must be of the "top-down" variety, and it must be participatory.
4. "Bottom-up" support must be encouraged by such techniques as annual employee-opinion surveys.
5. Corporate heroes and symbols must be created. "Together We Can Find Answers" became the ubiquitous motto at Honeywell.
6. Psychological ownership must be obtained by Honeywell employees through participatory groups such as quality circles and problem-solving task forces.
7. Reward and incentive systems must reinforce efforts at cultural change. Personnel subsystems must appraise and reward people who are effective.
8. An iterative learning model must be used to teach new corporate values.
9. Patience is required. Cultural change takes at least three to five years and occurs as employees see it actually practiced by top management.[63]

Managers were viewed as cultural carriers, or role models, within the organization.

The Honeywell goal essentially was to convert the organization's culture from one based too frequently on command and control to a participative one that emphasized employee involvement.[64] Unlike political appointees at ACTION, VISTA, and the Peace Corps, who ignored prevailing organizational cultures, Honeywell executives knew that cultural changes could not be attained with a quick fix or even with programming institutes.

Furthermore, it was understood that organizational leadership is a mutual-influence process among employees and managers, that employee motivation centers on the needs, perceptions, and expectations of the individual employee. As one Honeywell vice-president put it:

> We should worry a little less about the Work Ethic in America and think a little more about our company's employment ethics. The challenge is to pick up the ethics of democracy, dust them off, breathe new life into them, and install them in the workplace. Think of it as an ethical undertaking. That will ensure that programs like Quality Circles, participative management, and quality of work life help our people achieve their objectives, and do not degenerate [into] more manipulation.[65]

Intensive staff re-education institutes and Malek-type political harassment such as that imposed on ACTION employees during the Nixon and Ford administrations hardly are recognized strategies for changing organizational values or increasing productivity among schools of public administration and management. Even so, Balzano's supporters argue that Balzano was tremendously effective in cutting costs while increasing services to clients.[66]

Again, Honeywell's approach to cultural development is not intended as an example for governmental organizations; there obviously are many differences between a corporate organization and agencies such as the Peace Corps and VISTA. Nonetheless, a commitment culture can be created and preserved in any organization, be it public or private. Strategies for organizational development and cultural enhancement certainly will vary, but in both environments, a commitment culture is possible. Political ideologies need not be a dominant, disruptive organizational force.

Efforts to modify ACTION's organizational culture did not cease with Jimmy Carter's election. Indoctrination efforts by Carter appointees were, if anything, intensified, this time from a radically different ideological perspective. Both Carter and Reagan continued with the time-honored practice of appointing loyal campaign workers to top positions at ACTION. From both the New Left and the New Right, these presidentially appointed ideologues brought new ideologies into direct conflict with existing organizational cultures at the Peace Corps and VISTA. Again, the result was a lessening of employee commitment and a heightening of organizational conflict.

Ironically, Michael Balzano's programming institutes and the infamous Malek Manual did not mark the height of conflict at ACTION—only the opening salvo.

Five

A New Left Ideology

Sam Brown, President Carter's appointee as director of AC-TION, was viewed by members of his own party as an ideologue, just as Balzano had been regarded by Republicans when he was director of the agency. Brown had played a key role in Carter's campaign and in his self-proclaimed crusade to free the administration of Washington insiders.

Ideologically, Brown and Balzano came from opposite ends of the political spectrum. Perhaps the most frequent speaker on behalf of the New Left, Brown could not be ignored within Democratic party circles. Spiro Agnew went so far as to call him a hard-core, professional dissident, a charge that endeared Brown to the Democratic party's left wing. Others, some of them within the party, viewed Brown as politically unreliable.[1] John Ehrlichman dismissed him as "power lustful," and the historian Theodore White described Brown in 1968 as devoted to a single cause—the antiwar movement.[2] Robert Howard, writing in 1979 about the debate on amnesty for Vietnam draft evaders and deserters within the 1976 Democratic Platform Committee, said: "The Carter forces were in total control except on the amnesty vote. Sam stood up after the vote, made a little speech about compromise, and just gave away the victory . . . *after* we won! I went along with it, but to this day, I hate myself for not screaming." Although Brown later reflected that he had made a lot of mistakes, his ideological vision apparently was unclouded by self-doubt in the 1970s.[3]

From the time when he was student body president at Redlands College, Sam Brown had loved to organize people. An early staff member in Senator Eugene McCarthy's presidential primary campaign, he later became national coordinator of Mc-

91

Carthy's grass-roots political organization, "Clean for Gene," often called the Children's Crusade. After McCarthy's defeat in 1968, Brown "conceived of, and then directed, the largest peaceful petition of the U.S. government in U.S. history, the Vietnam Moratorium."[4] Even Brown's hawkish critics conceded that the moratorium had proved an unparalleled success in demonstrating the strength of the antiwar movement.

Brown's activism was not, as some charged, limited to the antiwar issue. His long-standing belief in community organizing as a strategy of change included broader issues. Brown articulated his philosophy in *Storefront Organizing,* a book published in 1972.[5] After election as Colorado state treasurer, Brown worked to mobilize opposition to the Winter Olympics for Colorado in 1976.

For Sam Brown, the New Left ideology was neither a theoretical nor an ivory tower exercise. It was meant to be *practiced.* Brown summarized his pragmatism as wanting "to figure out how you make life better for people who really don't have much of a shot."[6] To accomplish this objective, Brown proposed organizing the grass roots for social action. He advised college students to eschew university studies, as "irrelevant," and turn to direct social action as a way to bring about change: "The rhetoric of government is outmoded—the problem is how to affect your government."[7]

It is interesting to note that both Sam Brown and Michael Balzano are party infighters. Both mix ideological fervor with hardball politics. Both became adept at gaining their president's attention, particularly during a presidential campaign: Balzano served as Nixon's envoy to ethnic Europeans, Brown as Carter's liaison with former antiwar activists.

Ironically, after Senator Fred Harris dropped out of the Democratic primary race, Sam Brown, a key campaign coordinator of Senator McCarthy's presidential bid in 1968, was approached by Carter's campaign strategists, who asked him to play a key role in derailing Senator McCarthy's presidential hopes. Brown agreed; under his guidance, former McCarthy campaign staffers from the 1968 race placed advertisements in national publications and such newspapers as the *New York Times.* The ads criticized McCarthy's campaign as divisive to the Democratic party and harmful to Jimmy Carter's effort to unseat Gerald Ford. Not everyone appreciated Brown's treatment of his former boss, however. Unidentified McCarthy supporters sent Brown what they considered an appropriate present—thirty dimes, or "pieces of silver."[8]

After the election, Jimmy Carter made Sam Brown his new director of ACTION. Carter's selection of Brown seemed a natural match. The former community organizer and antiwar activist supposedly would revitalize the Peace Corps and VISTA after a hiatus under the Republicans. Most agency employees and volunteers, when they heard about Brown's appointment, were described by one observer as "euphoric [and] overjoyed . . . we thought that he was going to be our savior." Despite Brown's earlier reservations about the Peace Corps and his alleged view of its "cultural imperialism," many believed that Sam Brown "would put the Peace Corps back together."[9] After the partisan vendettas of the Balzano era and the excesses of the Malek zealots, ACTION had been delivered to a kindred soul—or so thought activist employees and former volunteers in the Peace Corps and VISTA.

A far different scenario unfolded during Sam Brown's administration of ACTION, however. By the end of the Carter administration, the agency was mired in political infighting, bitterness, and congressional charges of mismanagement on Brown's part. Both VISTA and the Peace Corps had been severely damaged by ideological conflict and by purges of the "unfaithful." As Michael Balzano had attempted before him, Brown was determined to reshape the organizational culture at ACTION to reflect his own ideology. The ideological difference between Balzano and Brown was no less than the chasm that existed between the Far Right and the Far Left; yet both extremes believed in the truth of their convictions, and both were intent on changing organizational cultures. Indeed, to many former volunteers and employees who came to VISTA and the Peace Corps during the Great Society era of activist values, Brown seemed a welcome change. That career employees, especially in the Peace Corps, would be more outraged by Brown's ideology than by Balzano's, came as a shock. The deep conflict that emerged between political appointees and civil servants in both voluntary-action agencies had entered a more troubling phase.

The Not So Peaceful Corps

As with many "perfect" marriages, some of which end in divorce, it is easier in hindsight to see irreconcilable differences than when vows were exchanged. In the euphoria following Jimmy Carter's victory, it seemed logical to activists that the Peace Corps would prosper under Brown's leadership of AC-TION. Brown's appointment of Dr. Carolyn Payton, a former Peace Corps staffer, augured better days ahead. In addition, Brown's determination once again to stress recruitment of Peace Corps volunteers from among recent liberal-arts graduates indicated a return to an activist-oriented Peace Corps, one reminiscent of the Great Society. Encouraging as these moves were to former Peace Corps staffers and volunteers, Brown had a far different vision of the mission of the Peace Corps, one that was to plunge the agency into deep organizational conflict.

The Return of the Liberal Arts Volunteer

Brown began by redirecting the Corps' recruitment strategy. As we saw in Chapter 4, conservative appointees to ACTION moved away from the traditional "B.A. generalist" volunteer in the Peace Corps, who was viewed as suspect, too liberal, and unprepared to be effective in helping Third World countries. Instead, during the Nixon and Ford administrations, under "New Directions," conservatives pushed for the recruitment of older, more skilled Peace Corps volunteers. In the activist resurgence under Brown, B.A. generalists as well as younger applicants would again be recruited from college campuses.[10]

Brown attacked the Corps' recent technical emphasis as wrong.

> It has excluded those who have moderate skills, which are the most useful abroad, and people who can be trained in basic skills.

Rather than sending a water engineer, maybe we need to send people who can build a catchment basin or dig an artesian well. It's that kind of skilled person, not the type who knows how to run a giant drilling rig, that is needed now.[11]

In other words, the B.A. generalist volunteer might not be as technically skilled, but he or she supposedly would be more adaptable and persevering than the technician when confronted with a difficult mission overseas. Supposedly, too, the generalist volunteer tended to be more "altruistic, and could be placed in remote locations where trained personnel or even host-country nationals won't go."[12] Dr. Carolyn Payton, Brown's Peace Corps director, pledged to rejuvenate a corps of generalist volunteers. "I believe very strongly that the ability to provide technical assistance should be secondary to a volunteer's motivation. ACTION is the only federal agency designed to transmit human qualities and understanding. I would like the Peace Corps to get back to this level."[13] Applicants who were older, those more technically skilled, and those with families still would be accepted into the Peace Corps; but, once again, the emphasis would be on recruiting recent liberal-arts graduates.

Conservative administrators at ACTION during the Republican administrations of Nixon and Ford disputed the supposed advantages of generalist volunteers. As ACTION director Blatchford warned, "I'm in favor of using people with social commitment, but if we're going to do this in great numbers we should first experiment with it in our own land. . . . We can't afford to let young people work out a period of their lives at the expense of these very poor countries."[14]

Others disagreed with the notion that volunteers with a liberal-arts background were survivors. "The fact is, Americans aren't particularly self-reliant cutting the jungle on their own in a foreign land. These are a percentage of real pioneers, and there should be room for them in Peace Corps. But these people are rare." In congressional testimony, critics charged that, in the early years, Peace Corps domination by white middle-class volunteers "failed to accomplish much of any enduring consequence to its hosts."[15]

Despite opposition from conservatives, the Peace Corps once again returned to college campuses as its primary source of volunteers. Dr. Payton hoped, in addition, that new recruitment efforts would shatter the "white, middle-class stereotype of the Peace Corps" by attracting more minorities as volunteers.[16] In retrospect, it can be seen that the percentage of minorities in the Peace Corps has not increased significantly since the agency's inception. Despite the efforts of conservatives to recruit blue-collar people, and despite activists' campaigns to attract minorities, Peace Corps volunteers have been overwhelmingly white and college graduates. Not only did young, liberal-arts graduates traditionally form the core of Peace Corps volunteers, they were the heart of Sam Brown's political and community-organizing efforts. These were true believers. They had long since responded to Kennedy's call, "Ask not what your country can do for you." Later they had been in the vanguard of civil rights marches in the South, in the women's liberation movement, and in protests against the Vietnam War. In effect, they were Sam Brown's shock troops.

Despite Brown's call for a return to generalists, and to less technically specialized volunteers, the call did not signal his desire to bring back the Peace Corps of the 1960s; volunteers would be recruited, as they had been earlier, from among recent college graduates. But if Brown prevailed, the role of these volunteers would in the future be far more sensitive politically. Peace Corps volunteers would work to achieve political change; they would become radical activists abroad.

The Peace Corps and Third World Realignment

In order to redirect the Peace Corps, Brown nominated Dr. Carolyn Payton, the black director of counseling at Howard University and a Peace Corps director in the Caribbean during the 1960s. Her appointment was proclaimed by ACTION's deputy director as a "powerful statement," proof of the Carter administration's commitment to "put the Peace Corps back together."[17] Within a year, however, because of irreconcilable ideological differences with Brown, Dr. Payton was forced to resign. An article in the *Wall Street Journal* described the differences as a conflict between a "young white male committed to change, and an older black woman seeking to preserve the traditional Peace Corps."[18]

At issue was much more than a difference of opinion about the appropriate types of projects for the Peace Corps. It was a major ideological divergence, a conflict of values, of different strategies of social change long practiced separately by the Peace Corps and VISTA. Although both Payton and Brown supported a return to reliance on generalist volunteers instead of technical specialists, they differed significantly when it came down to what these volunteers should do in the field.

Carolyn Payton represented the traditional Peace Corps culture, one that emphasized strict political neutrality and the volunteer as a teaching role-model for host-country nationals. To Sam Brown and other political appointees with community-organizing backgrounds in the United States, the Peace Corps' traditional approach erred in two respects. First, projects were designed from the one-way perspective of cultural imperialism by the United States. Volunteers were assumed to be teachers rather than learners. Second, Peace Corps administrators, when deciding where to send Peace Corps volunteers, did not consider stages of economic development or human-rights practices by host-country governments. The self-proclaimed political neutrality of these countries no longer was acceptable to Sam Brown and the radical activists.

Liberation from Cultural Imperialism

Soon after his appointment as director of ACTION, Brown was quoted as saying that the Peace Corps had been in the "vanguard of American cultural imperialism" and that the Corps should recognize "we are not a missionary band out to save the world, that we don't have the answers."[19] In Brown's view, the Peace Corps' mission was confused by nostalgia for a Pax Americana when Americans had a monopoly on technology. As such, the agency was "one of the few remaining symbols of our innocence."[20]

The misplaced missionary zeal of the Peace Corps supposedly was reflective of Kipling's "white man's burden": by definition, *our* way is superior. As an example of this zeal, Brown cited the Corps' approach to housing-assistance projects: "We will take our way of building houses and teach you how to do it. Well, that's bullshit. What we've learned in the past ten years in the Peace Corps is how to build houses that don't require sand and concrete shipped in from 1,000 miles away; we've learned to use local materials to build permanent structures for people who've never had permanent structures."[21] Essentially, Brown thought that the Peace Corps spent too much time *teaching* other cultures when it should be *learning* from them. Because of this one-sided approach, Brown regarded the Peace Corps as "the sheep's clothing on American adventurism abroad." Cultural imperialism, Brown believed at the time, starts with the assumption that Americans "know everything," that the world is "ours to shape in our own beautiful image."[22] Brown's cultural pluralism, on the other hand, supposedly begins with recognition that other cultures can make contributions to us.[23] By 1979, Brown was persuaded that the reorganization of the Peace Corps into ACTION in 1971, along with domestic volunteer programs, had measurably demonstrated to Third World governments that the United States does not have paternalistic motives abroad: "Third World people should see that the Peace Corps acknowledges that development is not so much what we can do for them, as what we as global citizens can do together to abolish the worst aspects of global poverty."[24] In Brown's view, cultural imperialism occurs any time one culture is imposed upon another, and it begins when the assumption is made that one culture is superior to another.

Traditional activists in the Peace Corps acknowledge that a certain amount of paternalism may be present any time someone volunteers to help someone else in need. As a former volunteer observed, "I suppose we had an exaggerated idea of our own importance and usefulness. There was an element of the white man's burden in it. But it was more a case of paternalism than imperialism. We saw ourselves coming to the rescue of people neglected by their own community. We never expected to change the community itself."[25] For Sam Brown, however, it was essential that community change be an outcome; otherwise, the Peace

Corps was wasting time and money. Even worse, cultural imperialism would be perpetuated in the Third World.

Symbolic of the Peace Corps' supposedly misplaced emphasis, Teaching English as a Foreign Language (TEFL) projects proliferated overseas. Frequently volunteers taught English to students as a *second* foreign language, that is, in former French and Spanish colonies of Africa and Latin America. In most countries where illiteracy rates were high, English was taught to a small elite. Brown charged that teaching English was "not a fundamental task of development."[26] Accordingly, Brown ordered that planned TEFL programs be scrapped and that volunteers be shifted from cities to rural areas.[27] Similarly, Peace Corps projects that focused on recreational development and university teaching were discarded in favor of projects that stressed what Brown called "basic human needs."

In addition to the redirection of overseas Peace Corps projects, cultural imperialism should, Brown believed, be alleviated if volunteers from developing nations ultimately could serve as VISTA volunteers in the United States. As a prototype of the program that would break down American paternalism in the Third World, Brown proposed creating a "Jamaican Brigade," a proposal that Director Payton later categorized as a "crackpot idea."[28] About 200 poor American black youths from inner cities such as Oakland and Detroit would be selected and sent to Jamaica to work with Jamaican youth, learning such skills as land-clearing, soil conservation, and terrace farming.[29] Later, they would return and apply their new skills in the United States.

Payton recounted the proposal's reception in Jamaica: "Some of Mr. Brown's aides [went] to Jamaica to talk to Prime Minister Michael Manley. They showed up in safari jackets and boots. The prime minister jokingly told the Americans to see his brother. The brother is to the prime minister what Billy Carter is to the President."[30] To put it mildly, the Jamaican government was unimpressed. "It already has great difficulty with youth unemployment and is experiencing increasingly violent political unrest. What would it do with two hundred inner-city youths?"[31]

Apparently, it was controversy over the proposed Jamaican Brigade and other radical approaches that culminated in the forced resignation of Dr. Payton after only thirteen months on the job. Among other "deep differences" cited was ideological divergence over where the Peace Corps should be sent and what constituted appropriate projects for volunteers.[32]

A Neutral Corps of Peace

Carolyn Payton represented as well the traditional activist approach to projects overseas, whereby the Peace Corps entertained requests from nations throughout the Third World regardless of their economic stage of development or human-rights policies, so long as they maintained official relations with the United States. Peace Corps projects of all types could be requested and often funded, irrespective of the political practices of host governments. To Sam Brown, however, Peace Corps neutrality and passivity were intolerable. He later said of Dr. Payton: "She was all for going into any countries that asked and doing whatever they asked us to do. If Chile wanted a baseball coach, Carolyn would send them a baseball coach."[33] Payton, as had administrators of the Peace Corps before her, accepted the host country's request at face value, without reference to the political regime in power or the regime's human-rights policies.

Fundamentally, Peace Corps volunteers since the agency's inception in the years of Camelot had been trained to work with community leaders and local officials regardless of their politics. Volunteers were warned against advocating social or political causes that might result in their dismissal from the community. Projects such as TEFL or recreation were primary vehicles to be used in influencing or gaining the trust of local elites and "key influentials." Once that trust was gained, community changes could be implemented. The quickest way to go home would be to openly organize people in host countries against those in power. Peace Corps training in the United States and in the host country stressed circumspection and a diplomatic approach. Peace Corps volunteers were forbidden to get involved in local politics. They were reminded that in all their activities they represented the United States, twenty-four hours a day.[34]

In sharp contrast, Brown and the community-organizing approach he represented took a direct-action solution. Volunteers, whether in VISTA or the Peace Corps, would serve as a catalyst in organizing the community for change. By *community* it was generally meant those who are powerless, who are not listened to by elites. It is their basic human needs, Brown believed, that should concern the Peace Corps volunteer abroad and the VISTA volunteer at home. Social or recreational programs supposedly diverted attention from the key mission of organizing a community for change—that mission being essentially an exchange of power between haves and have-nots, or at least a change in the relationship of power held by the two groups. Mary King, Brown's top deputy, described the Peace Corps' redirected mission as one intended "to address basic human needs and direct our assistance to the poorest of the poor. This has meant shifting some long-held notions, and it hasn't always been pleasant."[35]

Specifically, Brown rejected the elitist approach, one he felt had for some time been practiced by the Peace Corps. In his view, the Corps had wrongly stressed aid at the highest levels of a society in hopes that it would trickle down to the truly poor. "This is precisely what the Peace Corps should not stand for," he said.[36] Brown proclaimed a new era for the Peace Corps, one in which "basic human needs" at the village level, rather than government ministries or urban elites of Third World countries, would receive emphasis. In Brown's view, Peace Corps volunteers should be trained as "development workers" in order to address the most urgent needs of poor countries.

In an effort to radically reorder the priorities of the Peace Corps, and much to Dr. Payton's dismay, Brown decided to remove volunteers from those Third World economies that were relatively well developed. Radical-activist administrators at ACTION adopted a "physical quality of life index" (PQLI), designed to assess which nations the Peace Corps should work in and which it should leave. Dr. Payton opposed this assessment on the grounds that if a country's PQLI "was above the magic figure of 40, we were supposed to get out."[37]

According to the PQLI measure, the Peace Corps would have pulled out of some sixteen countries, including Brazil, South Korea, Chile, Malaysia, and Costa Rica. "Korea had undergone heavy development," Brown said in rationalizing the process. "We are no longer needed there so much. We were in some of the wealthiest nations in the Third World, but we weren't in Bangladesh. Humanity demands [that] we make more reasonable decisions."[38] Put another way, does South Korea, the host country of the 1988 Summer Olympic Games, need Peace Corps volunteers?

Under Brown's proposal, as the Peace Corps departed more affluent Third World countries, it would enter new ones. In addition to Bangladesh, Brown was eager to send volunteers to Tanzania, Jamaica, and Cuba, or, as an observer noted, "countries with progressive leaders who had captured the imagination of American radicals."[39] Brown frequently cited "workplace democracy" as an example of what Americans could learn from developing nations. "We know that workplace democracy is a concept ill-developed in American society. It is another of the [areas] where we stand to learn from Jamaica, from Tanzania, from Cuba, from Yugoslavia." Brown's critics, however, labeled workplace democracy a totally phony, vague thing.[40]

Undaunted by the criticism, Brown asserted his belief that authoritarian regimes whose policies violated citizens' human rights should be excluded as possible locations for Peace Corps volunteers. He viewed the human-rights policy of President Carter as a guide to selecting the appropriate host countries for Corps volunteers. As indicated by PQLI indices, however, human rights was only one measure, along with "quality of life."

Perhaps Brown's greatest miscalculation lay in assuming that countries that scored lowest by PQLI measures would not be in violation of Carter's human-rights policies or that authoritarianism existed only among those regimes controlled by right-wing dictators. Brown made little or no effort to reconcile the fact that a country such as Cuba, with which the United States had no diplomatic relations, scored low in its treatment of political dissidents, or that Cuba already had one of the highest overall standards of living in Latin America. Nor did he seem reluctant to consider organizing a Jamaican Brigade in a country such as Jamaica, whose poverty and recent high unemployment had been exacerbated by Michael Manley's socialist government. Brown's New Left ideology was not always consistent, especially when an attempt was made to transpose a domestic philosophy onto foreign affairs. Although radical activism was still a force within the Democratic party, it was unwelcome in U.S. international relations.

According to the traditional organizational culture of the Peace Corps, volunteer assistance bore little relation to host-country politics. It was assumed that the large Peace Corps contingents in the Shah's Iran, Somoza's Nicaragua, and Marcos' Philippines were unrelated to official U.S. support of these regimes. From a comparative perspective, the entry of Cuban or other Soviet bloc advisers (or "volunteers") into Latin American or African nations was viewed by many U.S. national security advisers as the first stage of communist infiltration. At the same time, traditional Corps activists did not subscribe to the view that American Peace Corps volunteers were not a similar extension of U.S. foreign policy.

The United States had never actually withdrawn Peace Corps volunteers from a country for overtly political reasons, though Sargent Shriver originally had declined to send volunteers to Paraguay and Nicaragua because, he said, "those are governments totally opposed to every principle the Peace Corps stands for."[41] Later, Jack Vaughn, the Corps' second director, sent volunteers to both countries. In light of the impending deterioration of U.S.-Nicaraguan relations following the *Sandinista* revolution in Nicaragua, perhaps President Somoza's support for Corps projects highlights the precarious status of political neutrality in such situations: "General Somoza has embraced the Peace Corps as a . . . pet project. He greets each arriving contingent personally, often inviting them to his Pacific coast ranch for the day and frequently has pictures of the gathering published in the papers. Clearly, he has done everything he can to co-opt whatever good will the volunteers engender with the hope that some will rub off."[42]

Sam Brown was determined to rid the Peace Corps of its neutrality in foreign policy; but Payton opposed turning the Peace Corps into an arm of U.S. foreign policy, as had traditional Peace Corps supporters from the beginning. "To make the Peace Corps an instrument of foreign policy," Secretary of State Rusk noted in 1961, "is to deprive it of its contribution to foreign policy."[43] To activists, the Peace Corps was politically neutral; to Brown, it was politically naïve.

Brown was afraid that Third World countries would interpret as a statement of foreign policy the fact that Corps volunteers were in countries governed by authoritarian regimes, such as Korea and Chile, "which historically have been close to American policy interests." Rather, Brown believed that the Peace Corps should make it clear that "we are open to a relationship with a broader range of countries."[44] Brown expressed a special interest in countries with which the United States had no relations or severely strained ones.

A broad spectrum of critics charged that Brown, by attempting to dictate their needs to developing countries, was implementing his own ideological elitism. By cutting back on TEFL projects, Brown stood open to accusations by Payton and others of denying Third World nations access to Western technology. Michael Balzano accused Brown of promoting his own cultural imperialism by ignoring the efforts of developing nations to promote their own domestic volunteer programs rather than imposing "exported volunteers" from the United States.[45]

Several years later, Brown, pursuing a career as a real estate developer in Colorado, mused on the turmoil at ACTION while he was director. "I screwed up—approached things in a way that was confrontational."[46] Viewed from another vantage point, Sam Brown, as Balzano had, suffered from ideological myopia, or the "curse of the true believer." In truth, purging oneself of "cultural imperialism" is probably best approached as an individual-level life-long quest. Peace Corps trainers trying to make trainees "aware of their cultural baggage" undoubtedly were engaged in a lost cause. Countless interviews with former volunteers bear out a common theme: most volunteers who completed the two-year assignment were changed significantly by their experiences in the Peace Corps.[47] Whatever cultural pater-

nalism volunteers brought to their service overseas usually van-
ished after two years of extensive acculturation. Many
volunteers, upon returning to the United States, even experienced reverse culture shock. Most returning volunteers did not
impose on their unsuspecting hosts American cultural values,
but rather acquired new, or broadened, cultural perspectives
themselves.

Even those volunteers deemed unlikely to change succumbed
to the culture and language of their host countries. The jacket
blurb of a book subtitled *The Tale of Another Peace Corps Grandmother in India* (an allusion to President Jimmy Carter's
mother) summed up the author's experiences: "For two years the
indefatigable Mrs. Visel lived as villagers lived, sharing their
concerns, hopes, and misfortunes." In large part, the most significant cultural change occurred not in the Indian village of
Vellore but in Adele Visel, who returned "sari bedecked and full
of stories."[48]

It was a truism among Corps volunteers during the 1960s that
a two-year stint overseas produced one of the following personality changes: from Asia and the Middle East, volunteers returned more philosophical; from Africa, they returned more
cynical; from Latin America, they returned more angry. Many
volunteers believed that they were able to change little but that
they themselves were greatly changed. Paternalism was a frequent casualty. Most Corps volunteers experienced a stage of
"culture fatigue" in which, after nine months to a year in a
country, reality set in and world-changers began to come to
terms with the limits of their own idealism.[49]

Sam Brown, too, believed that the Corps' choice of host-country requests for volunteers must be determined in light of U.S.
foreign-policy goals and by taking economic development into
consideration. (Ironically, Reagan appointees later took a similar stance.) Even though the organizational culture of the Peace
Corps was based on belief in the value of political neutrality,
Brown moved vigorously to reshape the Corps' firmly entrenched values, but without lasting success. In part, Ronald
Reagan's election in 1980 cut short his radical activist efforts.
Brown's failure stemmed as well from his appreciation and acceptance of a drastically different organizational culture, one

true of VISTA and other community-organizing groups where direct political action on the part of volunteers was a valued behavior.

In the final analysis, the debate over whether Peace Corps volunteers are a dimension of U.S. foreign policy may be more abstract than real. Unlike their VISTA volunteer counterparts, to most peasants and slum-dwellers overseas, Peace Corps volunteers *are* the United States. Although, in reality, a dichotomy between official U.S. foreign policy and the Corps' presence in the field is unlikely, the distinction remains an article of faith in the Corps' organizational culture. Certainly this distinction was not made concerning the more than twenty-one countries that terminated Peace Corps projects.

Whether they like it or not, volunteers are trapped by actions taken in implementing U.S. foreign policy. During the Johnson administration volunteers were forced to "explain" the presence of U.S. Marines in Santo Domingo and, later, Vietnam; during the Carter administration, the U.S. human rights policy; during the Reagan administration, the "invasion and rescue mission" of Grenada, the meaning of U.S. Marines in Lebanon, and support for anti-Sandinista guerillas in Nicaragua.

Finally, Brown perhaps was technically correct in his perception that the Peace Corps is an extension of U.S. foreign policy. He wished to demythologize the Peace Corps, to mold it into an instrument for accomplishing foreign-policy objectives which he believed were more humane. Still, Brown, as had Balzano before him, failed to appreciate the role a strong organizational culture could play in providing positive meaning for agency volunteers and staff.[50]

Volunteers were not attracted to the Peace Corps in order to carry out State Department priorities or to serve as junior Foreign Service officers; they were attracted to the Corps' reputation for political neutrality. The Peace Corps culture held that volunteers are not employees of the U.S. government; they are private citizens who have volunteered their services on a person-to-person basis. Volunteers did not accept the role of pawns in international diplomacy or a foreign policy promoted by the White House. The volunteers' organizational culture stressed political neutrality and a teaching tradition on their part. The result, in the 1960s and early 1970s, was a clearly defined organizational mission and a commitment by volunteers and an activist staff.

The Peace Corps: Out from under ACTION's Umbrella?

Activists in the early 1970s charged that President Nixon's reorganization and creation of ACTION were motivated by a desire to "play down, even hide the Peace Corps because of its close identification with John F. Kennedy."[51] Not surprisingly, many Peace Corps observers hoped that a new Democratic president would once again liberate the Peace Corps from a Republican-created ACTION. Ironically, independence for the Peace Corps came under Reagan, not Carter.

During the ACTION years, the Peace Corps suffered from confusion as to its true identity, from a kind of organizational schizophrenia. Was it the autonomous agency for international volunteerism begun under the New Frontier or a group of volunteer programs under the aegis of ACTION? Officially, the Peace Corps was referred to as the International Operations division of ACTION. The term *Peace Corps* disappeared from official stationery, and recruiting brochures stressed voluntary opportunities offered by all ACTION programs. Congressman Don Bonker deplored the Corps' loss of purpose and its low morale: "Peace Corps people, once the most vibrant bunch of go get'm Americans, now have all the spark of the losing team's locker room after the big game."[52]

Harlan Cleveland, a respected scholar at the Aspen Institute, thought a cure for the malaise at the Peace Corps was obvious. After conducting a comprehensive assessment of the Corps' performance in ACTION, Cleveland concluded that ACTION "has made Peace Corps a more routine, less exciting adjunct to the foreign-aid function, rather than a uniquely valid and vibrant expression of the best that is in us."[53] He urged the removal of the Corps from ACTION and its reconstitution as an independent foundation or public corporation.

Sam Brown remained unconvinced, however. It was his view that the idea of an independent Peace Corps was little more than nostalgia on the part of former volunteers. Brown, after all, viewed the Peace Corps' traditional neutrality as a barrier to New Left foreign-policy objectives in the Third World. In his view, the Corps needed redirection to help the truly needy and to rid itself of its "cultural imperialism." Brown could accomplish this mission only if the Peace Corps remained within ACTION. Brown's willingness to force Carolyn Payton to resign merely underlined his resolve to reform the agency's activist culture. Thus, Brown, who had bitterly opposed Richard Nixon on the Vietnam War, came to believe that the Republican reorganization of ACTION begun in 1971 merited continuation. After three years as director of ACTION, Brown voiced his approval of the Corps remaining in ACTION.

Joint administration of the Peace Corps and ACTION domestic volunteer programs was defended as helpful in demonstrating to the Third World that the United States harbored no "paternalistic motives" in sending volunteers overseas.[54] Also, Brown's deputy director Mary King argued, despite their obvious self-interest, an independent Peace Corps could collapse if it were pulled out of ACTION. An independent Peace Corps was "not strong enough to stand up against the OMB and Congress without the ACTION umbrella. Besides, who would do a better job of rebuilding it than Sam and I?"[55] It should be noted in passing that during its ten years of autonomy (1961–71), Peace Corps administrators regularly gained attention in the Washington press by voluntarily returning unspent appropriations to the national treasury.

Brown, less than a year on the job, increasingly found himself under intense attack from several ideologically diverse groups. Numerous former Peace Corps volunteers and staffers were upset with his attempt to change the traditional values of the Peace Corps, while Congressional conservatives were incensed by his politicization of VISTA. Criticism of Brown, however, centered on his decision-making style as much as it did on the substance of his decisions. By allowing an acrimonious public vendetta against a Peace Corps director with strong links to its early years, Brown signaled liberals that he intended to attack the agency's traditional culture. Not only had Payton opposed Brown's "Jamaica Brigade" and his PQLI approach to the placement of volunteers, she had also been forced to compete with ACTION officials for control over budgetary allocations. Former Corps volunteers in Congress were especially vociferous in their attacks on Brown, charging that while the Peace Corps received only 40 percent of the total ACTION budget, it was saddled with 60 percent of ACTION's "shared administrative costs."[56] Representative Michael Harrington expressed profound disappointment at Brown's lack of originality and "pedestrian approach to Peace Corps problems."[57]

Nor were Brown's problems diminished by Dr. Payton's departure in December 1978. A few months later, the General Accounting Office released a report highly critical of Corps administrative practices. The report pinpointed three problems: (1) questionable program design; (2) poor host-country relations; and (3) slipshod volunteer recruitment, placement, and retention.[58] In the third problem area, the GAO found that ACTION recruiters had failed to screen applicants adequately, with some candidates being interviewed by telephone and others not at all.

In addition, ACTION staffers were criticized for failing to give adequate information to volunteers about poor living conditions in host countries. As a costly result in both human and financial terms, "many volunteers are terminating service before scheduled completion—frequently within the first months of service."[59] The GAO report, unrelenting in its assessment of Peace Corps volunteer recruitment, concluded:

> Recruitment is . . . slipshod [in] almost every instance. . . . Certainly no other organization but that of the government could afford to operate in such a manner.
> The first time accepted applicants are able to discuss in detail work they will be doing or the quality of life they will have to endure is a two-day medical and administrative orientation immediately before being sent overseas.
> Unless there are serious problems, it is usually too late for applicants to change their decisions, because at this point they have already prepared to leave the country.[60]

Without assigning total blame to Brown, Balzano, or other political appointees, the Peace Corps by the late 1970s had reached a new low in both management and morale. Indeed, it no longer had a coherent organizational culture.

Throughout 1978, bipartisan momentum built to remove the Peace Corps from the control of ACTION. Representative Bonker introduced legislation that would establish the Peace Corps as an independent foundation funded by the federal government and answerable to an independent board of directors appointed by the President.[61] Another bill, introduced in 1978 by Senator Hubert Humphrey, proposed placing the Peace Corps in a new department, together with the Agency for International Development. In April, Bonker's bill passed the House (276 to 116). Its backers called it the first step in removing the Peace Corps from "the tentacles of ACTION."[62]

The Senate, however, later defeated a move to remove Peace Corps from ACTION and establish it as an independent agency.[63] Nevertheless, Brown's efforts to radicalize the Peace Corps were dashed. After the House vote, President Carter interceded through an executive order that stripped ACTION's director of any real control over the Peace Corps. Although, organizationally, the Peace Corps was left within ACTION, its director, Richard Celeste, was given complete autonomy over his own budget, administrative and policy decisions, and personnel operations. Under pressure from Congress, Carter restored the Peace Corps to semi-independent status.

Interestingly, several of the congressmen and White House aides who pushed for autonomy for the Peace Corps within ACTION have something in common: former service as Peace Corps volunteers. A likely decision-making catalyst for them was Brown's unseemly removal of Payton. Perhaps socialization to an organizational culture is a process Sam Brown had underestimated.

Once Bonker's bill passed the House, former Corps volunteers now within the White House and Congress moved to gather support for an independent Peace Corps. First Congressman Christopher Dodd, who had been a volunteer in the Dominican Republic in the late 1960s, urged that the proposed merger with AID not be approved, arguing that to do so would erode the Peace

Corps' people-to-people role and "cloak it in an agency concerned only with our short-term policy goals."[64] Second, Senator Paul Tsongas, a former volunteer in Ethiopia, worked
behind the scenes to effect a compromise with House conferees
that would insulate the Peace Corps adequately from "potential
political involvement."[65] Third, Tim Kraft, a former volunteer
in Guatemala and a key White House adviser, coordinated communication with the House and Senate, helping draft the President's executive order guaranteeing Peace Corps autonomy
within ACTION. To these former volunteers, ACTION's stran-
glehold on the Peace Corps had become intolerable.

Equally intolerable was Representative Bonker's bill to force
the marriage of AID and the Peace Corps. If successful, the bill
would forge a linkage of the agency with U.S. foreign aid programs worldwide, a move that was unacceptable to former Peace
Corps volunteers. It was apparent that the Senate would not
approve an autonomous Peace Corps; therefore, the only viable
option seemed to be to keep the Corps organizationally within
ACTION while guaranteeing its programmatic integrity, which
was accomplished by executive order.

The Peace Corps' semi-autonomy within ACTION occurred at
a time when Richard Celeste, who had narrowly lost his gubernatorial bid in Ohio after serving as lieutenant governor, was
selected as the new director of the Peace Corps. Celeste, possessing an uncontested power base within the Democratic party,
won out over Brown's choice of his former director of recruitment
for the job. (Celeste ran successfully for governor of Ohio in 1982.)

Sam Brown, whose political fortunes had seemed so bright in
1976, now found himself in the position of having lost President
Carter's confidence. Because of his overt efforts to politicize ACTION
in general and the Peace Corps in particular, Brown had forfeited the
privilege of naming a key program head within ACTION.

Radical Activists at the Peace Corps

By the last months of the Carter administration, Sam Brown
had alienated many Peace Corps volunteers, former volunteers,

and staffers. Offended by his heavyhanded efforts to politicize the agency and change its organizational culture, most of those alienated agreed with Georgie Anne Geyer, who protested that ACTION was *not* Brown's personal "Fund for the Spreading of My Own Ideology."[66] An editorial in the *New York Times* lamented that Brown had turned ACTION into a "virtual playpen of the New Left."[67]

Others attacked Brown for departing from the "original purpose and philosophy of the Peace Corps."[68] To this charge, Brown pleaded guilty. He worked to alter organizational goals and culture, which, he felt, were mired in nostalgia and bound by paternalistic assumptions. In doing so, however, he apparently never understood the nature of his opposition or the intensity of the reactions from its members. Unlike the predictable responses from conservatives when he had redirected VISTA funds to more radical projects, Brown's initiatives for the Peace Corps were opposed by activists, by former Peace Corps volunteers, and by staff. These people might have been expected to oppose Balzano—but why Brown?

In large part, Sam Brown never truly appreciated the Peace Corps experience, nor the organizational culture that was instilled during Peace Corps training. That is not to say one can generalize about a single Corps experience for almost 100,000 former volunteers. Yet, if one listens to numerous interviews and reads what former volunteers wrote for publications as diverse as *Seventeen* and the *New York Times,* some common themes emerge. "I learned far more than I contributed," Tim Kraft said.[69] A former volunteer in Tonga expanded on this theme: "But in the last analysis, what seemed to leave the [greatest] impact on my hosts was my willingness to speak Tongan, to live and eat and celebrate among Tongans, to share birth and death and sickness and success."[70] To Brown and the community organizers at home, however, these statements merely underscored the irrelevance and innocence of the Peace Corps.

In fairness to Brown and other political appointees, the three goals of the Peace Corps as stated in its original legislation have never been ranked by priority. The agency is required to provide aid to host countries, to give Americans an opportunity to learn about host countries, and to offer host countries a chance to learn about Americans. Which of these laudable goals is most important? which least important? Perhaps Brown and the radical activists were guilty of emphasizing only one goal: the need to learn about host countries. Ironically, activists at the Peace Corps and in Congress stressed volunteers' contributions to the economies and welfare of the host countries; yet most volunteers, upon returning, believed they had received much more than they had given.

Thus it is likely that Brown and those who argued for restructuring the Peace Corps' priorities failed to appreciate the cross-cultural values imbibed by most Corps volunteers. These values, or organization cultures, had little to do with political change or economic reform, however. Again, even though the Peace Corps' mission was to provide aid to communities abroad while at the same time improving communications among people, even the most cynical returned volunteer measured his or her Peace Corps experience by the degree to which the volunteer's life had been changed.[71]

It is difficult to imagine readily a VISTA volunteer making a similar assessment. The prevailing view among VISTA volunteers was that a volunteer should be a catalyst in bringing about changed relationships of economic and political power. Results were to be measured by the extent of change effected. In the Peace Corps, though such would not be argued before a congressional committee, the Corps' primary contribution lay in changing the volunteers themselves.

In the final analysis, Sam Brown wanted to reshape the Peace Corps as an *overseas* VISTA committed to community organizing in "progressive," nonauthoritarian nations. However, activists who viewed the Peace Corps as a politically neutral organization, as a medium for enhancing their personal values and expanding their cultural horizons, carried the day.

VISTA: Returning to Grass-roots Organizing

Unlike the Peace Corps, ideologically, VISTA was close to Sam Brown. Its volunteers were charged with working under community-action agencies to give the poor greater control over their lives. In Brown's view, though, VISTA had not gone far enough; it had not been allowed to organize for political and social action. Even in the heyday of the Great Society, VISTA had been hamstrung by local politicians and elites. Brown believed that VISTA volunteers were constrained by antipoverty programs, programs that became massive, anonymous nightmares and whose primary beneficiaries more often than not were bureaucrats and social planners.[72]

Government programs, Brown believed, caused a malignant, social dependency among the poor:

> Despite our best intention, the government programs we have supported have unwittingly made the poor dependent and created a new bureaucratic and expert elite that too often denies poor people the opportunities to help themselves.
> We have allowed those who wish to scorn the poor the opportunity to foster the myth that poor people will not pull their own weight.
> We have, in short, created a system of helping that encourages the poor to be passive rather than active, dependent rather than self-reliant, recipients rather than producers, clients instead of people proud of their own work.

Sam Brown was fond of parables. One of his favorites was, "It is good to give a hungry man a fish; it is better to prepare him to do his own fishing."[73]

To correct the dependency created by liberal welfare programs, Brown thought that VISTA and other ACTION programs should move away from directly serving the needs of the poor to a more aggressive community-action model. He envisioned a community-development approach in which everyone affected by economic injustices, including those living below the poverty line, banded together to achieve concerted action. VISTA would once again accept the premise of the War on Poverty, that effective community organizing would lead eventually to the elimination of poverty.[74]

Brown moved to redirect VISTA projects away from conservative priorities. VISTA efforts in education, social services, and other areas, which had been emphasized by Republican conservatives under Balzano, were soon terminated. To the activists, community organizing was the cornerstone of VISTA as well as its building blocks.[75]

VISTA, as had other antipoverty programs initiated under the Great Society, again worked directly with self-described grass-roots organizations and community groups with the aim of bypassing government bureaucracies and local politicians (though Brown subsequently was compelled to give mayors veto power over VISTA projects in their cities). Basically, Brown's controversial community-action process worked according to a simple theoretical model (shown in Figure 1). Proudly, VISTA proclaimed itself a "partner in a community project run by community people."[76]

VISTA volunteers, the key to community organizing, were catalysts. They would organize community residents and teach them to raise funds and fight for their own interests. Under Brown's leadership, VISTA volunteers would help tenant groups organize, assist consumer food co-ops, and work for better sewers and streets, in poor neighborhoods.[77] Further, VISTA's official recruiting literature served notice that volunteers would be expected to help address the problems of maldistribution of city and rural services, lack of health-care facilities, utility rate reform, substandard housing, women's rights, and ethnic and cultural identity.[78] The activist agenda under the Great Society was expanded; now VISTA volunteers would attack a much broader range of issues confronting the poor. Radical activism had arrived.

Brown's self-help, grass-roots approach was, in some respects, reminiscent of earlier VISTA efforts conducted during the War on Poverty. It attempted, however, to distinguish itself from the activist programs of the past, in several important respects. First, Brown's radical activism rejected the view that VISTA volunteers could be recruited from outside the poor communities where they served. Marge Tabakian, VISTA director and protégé of longtime community organizer Saul Alinsky, warned VISTA not to recruit middle-class youths and bring them into poor communities to teach the poor.[79] Instead, volunteers would be selected by local community groups, "*genuine* community groups, not those who claim to speak for the poor."[80]

VISTA's Model of Community Organizing

Citizens
aware of
problems,
want
improvement.

Sponsoring Organization
local, nonprofit group brings people
together, defines problems,
sets goals,
calls on VISTA for help
(and often other
resources as well),
supervises volunteers.

**The
Community**
continues with
its own skills,
resources, and
know-how when
the volunteer
leaves.

VISTA
recruits,
assigns, and
trains volunteers,
who work under
local project
supervisors and
directors.

Volunteers
live in
communities they serve,
provide skills, work with the
community to develop local resources toward achievement of
goals outlined by sponsor.
Phase out their involvement
as community gains self-
reliance, skills, resources.

Source: ACTION, January 1978, p. 3.

Second, Brown ordered an approach to the design of community-organizing projects that was much more decentralized. Whereas in the 1960s, VISTA's state directors had played a major role in formulating and implementing projects, Brown's staff now went directly to local community groups. Toward this end, Brown initiated the National Grant Program (NGP), in which VISTA headquarters made grants directly to community groups. There were few strings attached; all that recipients had to do was mobilize and train VISTA volunteers for their projects.

VISTA's National Grant Program

Supposedly, the NGP facilitated efficient redirection of VISTA from the conservative-designed service projects of the Nixon and Ford administrations. Instead, to achieve economic redistribution and social change, VISTA volunteers theoretically returned to activist coalition-building in poor communities.[81]

Budgetarily, ACTION's ability to support VISTA's National Grant Program was secured in fiscal 1980, when ACTION's overall appropriation increased from $25.6 million to $40 million. Concurrently, VISTA dropped the conservative-initiated University Year for ACTION (UYA) and reallocated an additional $3 million to the NGP.

Predictably, this action quickly brought howls of protest from such conservatives as Robert Michel, who believed the NGP was ample demonstration that Brown was converting VISTA into a "cell for the training and practice of confrontation politics." Michel, who was also House minority whip, accused Brown of using the NGP to "siphon grants to radical friends."[82] Conservative representatives Michel and Ashbrook were irked by the militant reputation of many NGP grant recipients, such as the National Association of Neighborhoods, the National Council of La Raza, the Federation of Southern Cooperatives, and the Ohio Public Interest Campaign.[83] Brown countered that these genuinely authentic community groups—as well as others such as ACORN, Fair Share, and Mass Advocacy—were trusted advocates of the poor whom he had known over a period of years.

Nonetheless, conservatives attacked NGP as an ideological scam of the New Left, a front for political organizing. They believed it was immoral for government-supported VISTA volunteers to "tell people what's wrong with their lives and prod them into changes they don't really want."[84] Conservatives charged that in addition NGP had assumed that local officials and government bureaucrats frequently were willing, even unwitting, enemies of the poor. As VISTA volunteers in Indiana's welfare advocate program complained, "too often local officials were used to an unquestioned power position."[85] In effect, the direct approach of NGP was similar to OEO's premise in the War on Poverty—state and local officials generally oppose true redistribution of political power. Therefore, VISTA and NGP supposedly had no choice but to bypass local officials and go directly to community organizations representing the poor.

Nor were NGP grants given to social or civic groups that represented broader community interests; only community organizations controlled by the poor qualified for grants. At a retreat for senior staff in rural Virginia, Brown debunked the validity of such voluntary organizations as United Way, Junior League, and Red Cross, proclaiming: "I think we ought to bust them."[86] Charitable and civic organizations merely enabled the poor to feel better while doing nothing about the root causes of poverty. Radical activists have accused conservatives of defining the proper role of a VISTA volunteer as driving "welfare recipients down to get their checks."[87] NGP grants to truly community-based organizations allowed VISTA volunteers to reassume their activist role as shock troops fighting poverty. This time, however, they would be employed directly by community organizations rather than by a federal agency.

John Brown and Sam Brown

Although only indirectly, some parallels may be made between John Brown of Harper's Ferry and Sam Brown of the Vietnam Moratorium. Each man saw himself as a man of action (or ACTION), as a visionary of social change. Both men believed that a catalyst was needed to liberate those enslaved, whether by race or economic poverty. Both misjudged the willingness of their fellow Americans to accept the need for confrontational politics.

At the Peace Corps, Sam Brown assumed that volunteers and staffers would accept his plan to make the agency a more active political agent. He completely misgauged the depth of feeling about political neutrality as practiced since the Corps' founding under the New Frontier. At VISTA, Brown's philosophy of community organization was acclaimed within the agency but vociferously attacked outside it. His radical values did not square with those of society or Congress. His aggressive (or confrontational) approach to community organization was opposed by those who thought that he had lost the ability to compromise, that he had "been unable to communicate a concrete program for fighting poverty in the late 1970s [or to communicate] ACTION's role in the fight."[88]

By 1981 and the end of President Carter's term, VISTA found its organizational culture clearly out of touch with mainstream America. Both the Peace Corps and VISTA were now perceived as arcane relics of the 1960s. Conflicts among organizational values in the Peace Corps had taken a devastating toll of staff and volunteers. After a decade of infighting among political appointees, staffers, and volunteers, the Corps had lost sight of its purpose and its volunteer commitment. It languished in confusion and disarray. Critics charged that budgets soared while accomplishments dwindled.[89]

VISTA, by contrast, had regained a strong organizational culture based on radical activist values; but VISTA's clarity and commitment were not to last. Once again, under a new president with conservative policymaking values, VISTA entered a period of organizational conflict, this time between political appointees, civil servants, and volunteers. The seemingly inevitable cycle was coming around again.

Six

Reagan's
Peace Corps
and
VISTA

Ronald Reagan's victory in 1980, though a landslide, carried with it no clear mandate from the voters on the future course of the Peace Corps and VISTA. Once again, a new crop of political appointees would direct these agencies and determine their future; once again, partisan appointees, career employees, and former volunteers would engage in intense, internecine conflict over ideology and organizational culture. As we saw in Chapter 5, VISTA emerged from the Carter years with a radical activist culture, while the Peace Corps floundered in confusion and a state of malaise. Neither organizational environment was tolerable to the Reagan policymakers with their strongly conservative ideology.

A Frontal Assault on VISTA

Beginning, perhaps, on Inauguration Day, 1981, Reagan staffers in the White House marked VISTA for elimination. They intended to succeed where Richard Nixon had failed. President Reagan, however, like his Republican predecessors, could not simply abolish VISTA by a stroke of the presidential pen. True, VISTA had made enemies during its sixteen years of existence, but at the same time it had gained strong supporters in Congress. It also had the Friends of VISTA, former VISTA volunteers. Both groups were determined to prevent VISTA's demise during the Reagan administration.

The conservatives, in particular, planned sweeping changes under Reagan. Outraged by the extent to which VISTA had been radicalized by Sam Brown during the Carter administration, they saw Brown as the "New Left in government" and felt that unpatriotic Vietnam War protesters had taken over VISTA policymaking.[1] Conservatives were correct in believing that Brown had radically changed VISTA while failing to redirect ideologically the Peace Corps' strongly activist culture.

Under Brown's controversial National Grant Program (NGP), VISTA's operation had become much more decentralized. Most VISTA volunteers were recruited locally and worked directly for local community organizations. By 1980, some 4,800 volunteers worked in approximately 900 community-action projects around the country. Over two-thirds of the volunteers who were paid subsistence stipends each month were residents of communities in which they worked.[2] VISTA, more than ever before in its fifteen-year history, responded directly to neighborhood activism. Despite assertions by *The Wall Street Journal* that VISTA "provided an offensive, large subsidy to middle-class kids," such was not the case.[3] Most VISTA volunteers were now low-income or neighborhood residents; nearly 15 percent were over fifty-five years of age.[4] The role model of the VISTA volunteer had changed from that of the 1960s.

During the period when Brown was encouraging radical activism, VISTA became a vehicle for community organization. He is quoted as having "rejoiced . . . that eighty percent of the neighborhood groups have started in the last seven years," because these groups afforded a "burgeoning chance to change long-term politics."[5] One might add: but not if Reagan's conservative appointees had their way.

To what extent Ronald Reagan encouraged the elimination of VISTA (or whether he himself decided to eliminate it) is difficult to know—any more than one can know the extent to which presidents Nixon and Carter participated in similar decisions regarding VISTA and the Peace Corps. Though housed in the executive office, presidents rarely concern themselves with the fate of relatively minor agencies; that is the task of presidential aides and appointees. Nixon's and Carter's official memoirs contain no mention of either agency. What is clear is that Reagan followed the path taken by his presidential predecessors, both Democratic and Republican, in appointing campaign loyalists to top positions in ACTION, the Peace Corps, and VISTA. Once again, these and other agencies were spoils for devoted party workers, most of whom believed the campaign rhetoric and ideology.

Accordingly, President Reagan appointed Thomas Pauken, a former White House aide and army intelligence officer in Vietnam, director of ACTION. Loret Ruppe, a coordinator for George Bush in Michigan, became director of the Peace Corps. Reagan selected a top official in his North Carolina campaign, James Burnley, as director of VISTA. As Howard Phillips had said of OEO during the Nixon administration, Burnley now proclaimed: "I'm working as hard as I can to be the last director of VISTA."[6] Believing that nothing succeeds in eliminating a government program faster than lack of operating funds, VISTA's conservative administrators dramatically reduced their appropriations request. Although the reauthorization bill for fiscal 1982 specified a funding floor intended to thwart attempts to eliminate VISTA, its appropriation was only $16 million for 1982 (down from $30 million in fiscal 1981). In fiscal 1983, ACTION itself requested only $700,000 over the congressional funding floor of $8 million for operational programs. In fiscal 1984, the agency requested a mere $231,000, an amount that would administratively dismantle VISTA by September 30, 1983.[7]

Operationally, VISTA's conservative administrators initiated plans for the phase-out process. Burnley justified his mandate to support VISTA's phase-out on the grounds that the program supposedly had failed when measured against three questions:

1. *Is the program fulfilling goals set by legislation authorizing it?* Instead of focusing on self-help for the poor, Burnley charged that VISTA "funded and supplied volunteers to numerous left-wing groups."[8]

2. *Is the program cost-effective?* Even though Burnley admitted that VISTA did not cost much, it "had failed to make a serious dent in the problem of poverty."[9] Thus the $400 million spent on VISTA since 1965 had been wasted.
3. *Is the program a proper function of the federal government?* Burnley believed that VISTA was unmanageable, and that even local communities could not control objectionable community-organizing activities.

To Burnley, Pauken, and other conservative appointees, VISTA should be separated from ACTION and eliminated because of its alleged failures and its left-wing leanings.

ACTION appointees began their dismantling of VISTA with a group of individuals determined to resist them: career civil servants. In early 1982, ACTION announced its intention to close down more than a dozen state offices of the agency and lay off nearly 90 other employees. During 1981, the first year, 188 VISTA employees lost their jobs because of a federal reduction-in-force, reducing its staff to about 500.[10] VISTA's own administrators proclaimed their intention to halt VISTA activities by the end of fiscal 1983, ostensibly because its "limited successes do not justify the continued outlay of federal funds."[11]

As had Howard Phillips' heralded goal of dismantling OEO during the early 1970s, the conservative announcement of VISTA's demise proved premature. The conservatives' attack served to alert Friends of VISTA, while also offending congressmen who considered it another manifestation of a budding imperial Reagan presidency. One wonders whether VISTA might not have been more easily terminated by presidential appointees not as ideologically minded, who possessed greater diplomatic skills and who were less impetuous about issuing press releases.

Alarmed by the oncoming conservative juggernaut, the Friends of VISTA began campaigning among VISTA supporters on Capitol Hill to reinstate VISTA appropriations. They were particularly effective with two House committees that claimed oversight of VISTA—the Subcommittee on Manpower and Housing, headed by Representative Cardiss Collins, and the Subcommittee on Select Education, chaired by Representative

Austin Murphy. Each subcommittee conducted extensive hearings on alleged improprieties by VISTA's new administrators.

These subcommittees used a technique that a *Wall Street Journal* editorial called "torture by questionnaire." Simply put, VISTA administrators were asked to answer hundreds of questions, such as:

> Provide an updated list of all Schedule B employees, Schedule C employees, consultants, experts, part-time, full-time, and temporary since April 1, 1981. Please indicate grade, rate of pay, date of service, and job description. List all VISTA projects approved, renewed and denied since Dec. 31, 1981. Indicate reason for denial. Why were FY'81 monies not used to recruit, train and place VISTA's from May 1 through September 1, 1981, since that is the purpose of the funds, and no VISTA's were placed during that period? How many new initiative projects had clear anti-poverty missions?[12]

Evidently, the torture-by-questionnaire tactic proved successful; VISTA administrators were so beleaguered the agency could not be terminated immediately. Congress subsequently passed a VISTA appropriation of $11.8 million for fiscal 1983. Thus Pauken capitulated to congressional pressure to train and place 1,800 additional VISTA volunteers. Congress, however, could not as readily dictate where these volunteers would be placed or what manner of training they would receive. Thwarted in their attempt to terminate the agency, conservative appointees fell back to a strategy of reconstitution. If VISTA had to remain, let it be as a conservatives' VISTA.

Changing VISTA's Radical Activism

Despite setbacks in Congress, ACTION and VISTA administrators remained undeterred in their conviction that VISTA must be purged of radical activism. If VISTA could not soon be eliminated, at least its organizational culture and community-organizing projects would be remolded in the conservative image. In an implementation strategy similar to Balzano's efforts, conservative appointees pursued three interrelated objectives:

—eliminate unacceptable VISTA projects, thus community organizing

—create alternative VISTA projects that reflected conservative volunteerism

—increase the number of conservative appointees at VISTA.

The Heritage Foundation, known for its conservatism, summed up the underlying premise of the strategy: "VISTA is an established program with much support in Congress and the media . . . it would be far easier to change the character of VISTA than to eliminate it."[13] Changing VISTA's organizational culture thus became a consuming passion for conservative appointees.

Disbanding VISTA's Community Organizing

Conservatives wasted no time letting the other shoe fall. On June 19, 1981, ACTION director Thomas Pauken addressed a policymaking retreat hosted by four right-wing organizations: Conservative Caucus, headed by Howard Phillips (formerly of OEO); the Committee for the Survival of a Free Congress; the American Legislative Exchange Council; and the Washington Legal Foundation. Known collectively as the "Kingston Coalition," representatives from the four groups planned to redirect agency policymaking and programming toward a conservative ideology. At the retreat, Pauken distributed what his critics later called a "hit list" containing thirty-nine pro-left organizations with which VISTA was to have no further relations.[14] Organizations on Pauken's hit list would no longer receive government funds, which had allowed "social engineers" to "push society further to the left."[15] (It must be noted that Pauken later denied the hit-list allegation, claiming instead that the list was merely a "random selection of typical projects funded by the previous administration."[16] Whether selected randomly or intentionally, the organizations named were conducting community-organizing activities that were unpalatable to conservatives.

A year after publication of Pauken's list, only three of thirty-nine community organizations still had VISTA volunteers.[17] Though supposedly not on a hit list, these community organizations clearly were "hit" by VISTA's new conservative administrators. They, along with other community groups perceived by the Kingston Coalition as "engaged in activities [that] place them in a confrontational mode with state and local officials and community leaders," no longer received VISTA support.[18] Even James Burnley, considered a tough director of VISTA, admitted that "not all VISTA projects are confrontational in nature and based on leftist community organizing theory." He argued that "quite a few are objectionable."[19]

The hit-list controversy, however, was not limited to debate over how organizations came to be placed on the list. If we assume that the list included only the most objectionable organizations or projects, there apparently is no common denominator among the groups listed. The group of thirty-nine runs the gamut from true community-based organizations to traditional United Way members. Several of the groups appear to resemble the middle-class civic groups Brown wanted to destroy because of their supposed conservatism.

Certain community groups were especially puzzled and offended by inclusion on Pauken's list:

> "Activism to improve your community doesn't strike me as a left-wing activity," protested Rich Freisen, executive director of the Whitmore Neighborhood Corporation in Kansas City, one group on the list. Whitmore has worked to preserve its neighborhood and to prevent traffic into the community from being blocked by train crossings. The group's president, Mary Rose, a sixty-nine-year-old retired special education instructor, described herself as "a middle of the road conservative, and this is essentially a working class neighborhood." She expressed her feelings: "The people here are good, law-abiding citizens and they are not involved in anything fanatical."[20]

Other community groups on the list of those that would no longer receive VISTA volunteers reacted similarly:

> Walter Cross, vice-president of the 20,000-member Massachusetts Association of Older Americans, which was on the list,

pointed out that the organization had always prided itself on avoiding politics. The 51 locally-recruited senior-citizen volunteers had been involved in a long series of community-betterment efforts: construction of 135 units of housing for the elderly; the transfer of 50 seniors from dangerous housing projects to safe homes; the creation of an eye clinic; a training program in self-help weatherization.[21]

These groups certainly were not in the same class as the Underground or the Black Panthers; they probably weren't even as militant as the Gray Panthers. Still, they apparently were too radical for President Reagan's first-term appointees to ACTION and VISTA.

How, then, did groups with no radical ties end up on ACTION's list of prohibited VISTA recipients? Mimi Mager, the director of Friends of VISTA, offers one explanation. She believes that Pauken's list was compiled in the Washington headquarters after a cursory review of descriptions of VISTA projects in the field. Mager speculates that any community groups whose project descriptions used the following "suspicious" words were placed on the list: *community organizing, consumer rights, advocacy,* or *citizen participation.*[22] Evidently, conservatives at ACTION viewed the world in simplistic terms, as a struggle between good and evil. Any organization that espoused community organizing was by definition the enemy. Ironically, these conservatives assumed an ideological mind-set, just as had Sam Brown, who regarded "the rich, the corporations, Republicans in general as the forces of evil."[23]

It would be mere speculation to wonder whether Pauken's thirty-nine community groups were more confrontational than others that received VISTA volunteers. At least a few were respected, if not established, organizations. Apparently, it was inevitable that *any* community organization allocated VISTA volunteers during the Carter administration would have its political loyalties challenged by the political appointees of the Reagan administration.

Strong pressure was applied by conservatives to restrict VISTA's "powerful leftist political tendency."[24] Spokespersons for the Far Right considered Sam Brown, Marge Tabakian, Mary Brown, and other Carter appointees to ACTION and

VISTA little more than unwitting fellow travelers of the Communist party. Although New Right conservatives did not assume that Brown and other ACTION appointees "were necessarily pro-Communist," they claimed that the behavior of these appointees "speaks for itself"—that it was leftist-oriented.[25] The issue was clear and simple: appointees viewed such government organizations as VISTA as ideological battlegrounds where old ideologies were to be purged and new ones instilled.

There were abundant examples of VISTA radicalism that offended conservative appointees at ACTION. For instance, the Toledo Metropolitan Mission in Toledo, Ohio, had ten VISTA volunteers, who were "organizing around school desegregation [and] senior citizens' welfare rights, [as well as] organizing a citywide coalition of people and organizations to bring about social change." Another example was the Susquehanna Legal Services organization, in Philadelphia, which had three VISTA people who were to "organize, train and develop self-sustaining community welfare advocacy groups in seven counties." Still another example was New Orleans, where VISTA activity involved statewide community organizing of low-income people in neighborhood affiliates along with such issues as state tax reform, health-care issues, property tax reform, and tenants' rights.[26]

The *Conservative Digest* cited other "leftist causes" sponsored by organizations receiving VISTA volunteers during Brown's tenure at ACTION:

Tom Hayden's and Jane Fonda's Laurel Springs Institute, in Los Angeles—a training school for Hayden's political arm, the Campaign for Economic Democracy—received $189,000 from VISTA in August 1978. Numerous CED staffers were serving on the institute's board.

In 1981, the American Civil Liberties Union, in Atlanta, had six VISTA volunteers who, according to VISTA, were organizing a local lobby on "decisions relating to public assistance and the criminal justice system."

The New York PIRG Citizens' Alliance, in Albany, received funding for nine VISTA volunteers in 1981. PIRGs (public interest research groups) are affiliated with Ralph Nader's national network.

In 1981, the Dane County Welfare Rights Organization, in Madison, Wisconsin, received funding for five volunteers in order to lobby for more welfare, training leaders, and "acting as change agents at the local level."

With the help of eleven VISTA volunteers, a study called "The Reagan Cruelty Index"—and another, called "The Greed Index—A Guide to Reagan Tax Reductions"—were produced in March 1981 by the Institute for the Study of Human Values, in Philadelphia.

In 1980–81, the Iowa Gray Panthers, in Iowa City, received assistance for organizing a Gray Panther network from five tax-funded VISTA volunteers.

In September 1977, ACORN (the Association of Community Organizations for Reform Now) received $470,475 to train 100 volunteers. According to a congressional report issued in 1979, ACORN's tax-funded volunteers were openly active in political campaigns in Arkansas and Missouri, and five volunteers helped with union organizing in New Orleans.

The Midwest Academy, an ultra-left training school in Chicago, received $432,235 in September 1977 and prepared VISTA volunteers for their duties throughout the Carter administration. A congressional study found that two volunteers were made full-time union organizers in Rhode Island and that others were sent to bolster leftist organizations in the Midwest.[27]

As can be gathered from their vitriolic attacks, Reagan appointees to ACTION did not accept these community groups as representative of community interests. Nor did they intend to underwrite what they considered leftist community-organizing projects with either federal funding or VISTA volunteers.

VISTA's organizational culture would be restructured by presidential appointees so that it reflected conservative ideology.

A Conservative Vision of VISTA

Throughout this book we have seen an intense struggle between opposing value systems, as expressed in organizational cultures at the Peace Corps and VISTA in opposition to partisan ideologies held by political appointees to both agencies. These contrasting value systems posit quite different views of poverty, its causes and cures, as well as the role and mission of full-time volunteers in both programs. Included among antagonists in this project were career employees, volunteers and former volunteers, political appointees, and politicians. As is true of the seemingly unending sequels to the *Star Wars* movie saga, the struggle continues without apparent victory by either side. Even on the simplest level, that of good and evil, good forces and evil forces vary, depending on one's values and ideological assumptions.

Reiterating a theme first proclaimed at ACTION during the Nixon administration, conservatives argued that VISTA should be service-oriented and achievement-directed so that the poor could be motivated to work themselves out of their poverty.[28] Accordingly, VISTA volunteers should be role models of achievement from the community. Only *legitimate* community organizations or civic groups were qualified to receive VISTA volunteers, and then only for nonconfrontational activities. Conservatives "commonly envision volunteerism as a *cultural* undertaking, affiliated with local churches and other established civic groups. VISTA volunteers supposedly need to change attitudes of despair, not empower the poor to revolt; they should help tutor kids rather than organize tenant associations."[29] Apparently, neither conservatives nor activists nor radical activists would grant the validity of the other's ideological premises.

Thomas Pauken's hit list of thirty-nine community organizations that would no longer receive VISTA volunteers, though widely publicized, was merely the conservatives' opening salvo during the Reagan administration. As VISTA allocations dropped dramatically in the early 1980's, so did the number of volunteers available to community organizations. Across the country, the VISTA volunteer became an endangered species. Community organizations that depended on VISTA volunteers and CETA workers were the hardest hit. No doubt, conservatives viewed their dependence on federally funded support as proof that they were not truly community-supported organizations.

For many organizations, the effects of VISTA's pullback during the Reagan administration were devastating. A study by the respected Catholic Campaign for Human Development (CHD) underscored these effects. Under the Carter administration, almost half of the 143 community-organizing projects supported by CHD used VISTA volunteers.[30] Under Reagan, nearly 60 percent of the CHD projects experienced significant reductions in operations because of cutbacks in the number of VISTA volunteers.

Two Illinois projects typify the impact of VISTA curtailments during the Reagan administration:

> In Decatur, Ill., a unique program called DOVE, which has provided financial counseling and a credit union for some 500 low-income families, lost 11 of its VISTA staff in 1982 and has been forced to curtail its service drastically. Also lost was a CETA-paid van driver who chauffeured 100 senior citizens to the market weekly. "I guess they needed the money in Washington to finance more missiles," says one frustrated, elderly DOVE customer. "So now we can walk to the store—if we can."
>
> The Greater Illinois Peoples Cooperative is struggling on even after losing all eight of its VISTA staff and seeing four of its member food co-ops fold. The description of this cooperative (which provided low-cost food to fixed-income households) is especially disturbing because the project would have required only one more year of full-scale operation to become self-sufficient.[31]

From the conservatives' perspective, too many VISTA projects were being used (or "misused") for engineering purposes by volunteers who supposedly were "white middle-class youth attempting to impose their beliefs and standards on poor black communities."[32] In fact, Sam Brown's National Grant Program had changed the image and reality of VISTA to one of predominantly white, middle-class volunteers.

In the early 1980s, VISTA volunteers were rapidly pulled out of existing community-action and related projects. Newly trained volunteers were placed in projects more acceptable to conservatives, projects activist critics categorized as at best "paternalistic."[33] Conservatives, however, simply ignored activists who caricatured them as "racist, uncaring and devoid of compassion."[34] Only community organizations with projects in such areas as literacy education, drug treatment, Head Start, refugee resettlement, or remedial tutoring were given VISTA assistance. These projects reflected the conservative values of self-reliance, hard work, and individual motivation.

Community organizing and advocacy on behalf of the poor had ceased to exist. Father Mottet, director of the Campaign for Human Development, deplored VISTA's conservative direction. "There's no advocacy going on anymore at all," he said. "Organizers are now involved in setting up soup kitchens and shelters for the homeless. It's the worst situation in forty or fifty years."[35]

Nevertheless, conservatives were convinced that community organizing and advocacy were false activist approaches that only made the poverty problem worse by pitting the poor against the affluent. They were especially opposed to such Carter-era activities as "union organizing and lobbying state and local governments and legislatures." Conservatives believed that VISTA was advocating programs and developing intervention strategies that "were basically antithetical to American political and economic usage."[36]

Once again, VISTA's organizational culture was caught in a raging attack on its political underpinnings and organizational values. As had occurred in the late 1960s, conservative appointees moved to rid the agency culture of community-organizing concepts which, in their view, were "designed to elicit a confrontation between poor people as a group and government and non-government institutions in their communities."[37] From the conservative perspective, confrontations were harmful because "such confrontations are usually designed to encourage expansion of programs, entitlements, rights which serve to enhance dependency, not self-reliance."[38] Conservatives claimed that VISTA had become the "outside agitator," unnecessarily provoking the poor to revolution.

Conservatives in the Reagan administration envisioned and supported a different approach to community organizing, one "that arises as a very natural response by members of a certain community group to address a specific problem through self-help, through sharing information."[39] Conservative appointees promoted, as had their predecessors in the Nixon administration, a national, voluntary-action effort whose success would spell the end of activist community-organizing projects. Conservatives considered voluntary action contagious, a part of the American spirit since the frontier era. Once voluntary action programs caught on, supposedly they would be taken over by private sponsors or charities.[40] Mark Blitz, of ACTION's policy-planning staff, described the agency's mission as reinforcing "those activities by which people in a community deal with their own problems and learn once again not to be dependent on government."[41]

To encourage the poor to solve their own problems rather than expect economic redistribution, new VISTA programs would have to be designed and old activist concepts discarded. As had occurred under Nixon and Ford, conservatives created alternatives to VISTA that were more ideologically acceptable, alternatives designed to replace VISTA's misguided community activism with VISTA's local volunteerism. In previous Republican administrations, conservatives had launched the University Year for Action as an alternative model for VISTA (see Chapter 2). Similarly, ACTION's Office of Policy and Program Development (OPPD) once again formulated pilot programs intended to prove the viability of voluntary community action. As demonstration projects, OPPD had virtually free rein to design and implement voluntary-action projects. If successful, Congress would be asked to approve them as authorized ACTION programs.

Several volunteer projects reflecting conservative ideology were quickly approved and implemented: the Vietnam Veterans

Leadership Program, Young Volunteers in ACTION, the Drug Abuse Prevention Programs, Literacy and Food Banks. Each project embodied the conservatives' values of and perceptions on community self-help. Each was funded largely with ACTION discretionary funds, which historically had been used for VISTA organizing operations.[42] Once operational, conservative experiments in volunteerism were expected to survive because of their demonstrated successes. More cynically, they would last until the next Democratic president appointed an activist or a radical activist administrator as director of VISTA. At that point, the cyclical conflict between organizational culture and partisan ideology would begin anew.

Vietnam Veterans Leadership Program

The Vietnam Veterans Leadership Program (VVLP), formally dedicated to boosting the self-image of Vietnam veterans, was designed to attract "veterans who are in good shape and can give other vets advice on how to be likewise."[43] ACTION director Pauken, himself a Vietnam veteran, believed that the VVLP also would destroy "the false stereotype of Vietnam veterans as everything from drug-crazed psychos to guilt-ridden victims."[44] The hope was that Vietnam-era veterans would gain, as volunteers, "a sense of pride and integrity . . . a strong sense of self-worth."[45] Who better could help Vietnam veterans than Vietnam veterans themselves? Who better could serve as role models? These objectives were set forth:

> Increase the receptivity of the employers to hiring Vietnam veterans through contacts with Vietnam veterans occupying key positions in business and industry.

> Persuade local institutions to make more resources available for solving Vietnam veterans' problems.

> Encourage and help Vietnam veterans to make full use of all federal, state, and community government activities that support them.

> Aid and support, where appropriate, the Veterans Administration's Vietnam veterans counseling centers.

Encourage membership in veterans volunteer programs.[46]

To many Conservatives, the Vietnam War had been, in the words of Ronald Reagan, a "noble crusade." Far too little had been done to improve the self-image of those who participated in that crusade. To the conservatives' dismay, the Carter administration appointed a leading antiwar activist as head of ACTION. Now the VVLP supposedly would help Vietnam veterans regain their self-respect and dignity.

Conservative appointees at ACTION immediately pronounced VVLP a success. ACTION's fiscal 1984 budget allocated approximately $2 million for VVLP programs in fifty communities. Coordinated by the program's national director, each local VVLP project selected its own director and community advisory board. Congress was assured that by fiscal 1985, local VVLP programs would be self-sufficient. Few, however, ever attained complete financial independence.[47]

Assessing the cost benefits of VVLP is perhaps misleading. On paper, the program was relatively inexpensive; thousands of hours were volunteered and hundreds of jobs committed to veterans. To what extent the VVLP contributed to changing the public's attitude in the 1980s is impossible to say. Whereas Vietnam veterans were largely ignored immediately after the war, by the mid-1980s there seemed to be a greater public understanding, if not acceptance, of America's role in the war. Or, possibly, most Americans now thought that it was time to put the war behind them.

Young Volunteers in ACTION

Conservatives at ACTION and elsewhere wished to demonstrate the vitality of voluntary action in all age groups of American society. They were convinced that most Americans, if given a chance, would voluntarily contribute their time and skills. This conviction had been the basis of ACTION's creation by executive order in 1971.

Under the Nixon and Ford administrations, however, ACTION appeared to display an anti-youth, or pro-retiree, position on volunteerism. The Peace Corps' New Directions project openly solicited older, more skilled applicants, and its recruiters avoided college campuses. ACTION's Older American Program was a centerpiece of Nixon-Ford volunteerism. The Foster Grandparents Program, designed for low-income and older citizens, recruited volunteers to work with handicapped children confined to institutions. The Retired Senior Volunteers Program (RSVP) coordinated older volunteers on a part-time basis in not-for-profit organizations. In the early 1970s, ACTION initiated its Senior Companions Program (SCP), whereby low-income elderly were recruited to assist the home-bound elderly. Though not explicitly stated, ACTION's early years reflected widespread conservative doubt about the reliability of youthful volunteers. (Conversely, activists and radical activists were distrustful of older volunteers.)

The University Year for ACTION, intended as an ACTION alternative to VISTA in 1971, was an exception to the agency's graying image. Although the UYA was disbanded during the Carter presidency, its brief success demonstrated to conservatives that voluntary action by youth was possible if properly administered. Thus Reagan appointees to ACTION focused on demonstration projects for younger volunteers in areas of literacy, drug prevention, and community service.

Young Volunteers in ACTION (YVA) was designed to give fourteen- to twenty-two-year-olds at least eight hours' work each month in approved projects. Acceptable YVA activities are indeed a far cry from the activist-designed community-organizing projects only a few years earlier. Two YVA programs were typical of the conservatives' approach to local voluntary action: YVA volunteers in El Monte, California, worked as visiting public guardians, parks and recreations staff, and volunteers in county hospitals; and in Everett, Washington, YVA volunteers served as program aides in gymnastics, swimming, and basketball, as clerical workers, canvassing, repairing toys, and boxing gifts for retirement homes.[48]

Young Volunteers in ACTION got teenagers involved in the types of social service activities conservatives considered both safe and constructive for society. In fact, conservative appointees at ACTION and VISTA were convinced that YVA could bring about long-term changes in attitudes of American youth toward voluntary action. "We have to look at the long haul here, and we have to look at the spirit of volunteerism in this country. Over the long haul, a volunteer who learns at the age of 14 or 16 or 17 that it is his or her civic obligation and right and pleasure and joy to serve the needy in his or her own community will contribute, we believe very firmly, as has been the case in this country, an immense amount of volunteer resources over time."[49] YVA would emphasize community service and individual achievement as conservative values for young volunteers.

YVA's volunteer strength in the field was projected to equal that of VISTA within a few years; it has grown only slightly during Reagan's second term, however. To conservatives, YVA was the capstone of a full array of programs designed to encourage part-time voluntary action among Americans of all ages. If conservatives had their way, voluntary service would no longer be left to full-time volunteers in projects aimed at community-organizing goals.

VISTA's Drug Abuse Prevention Project

VISTA's effort to develop programmatic alternatives to traditional VISTA community organizing focused on the prevention of drug abuse as well. In a prototype of what the agency hoped would be cooperation with the private sector, ACTION turned to pharmaceutical companies for assistance in designing a drug abuse prevention project. The joint venture turned out to be excellent public relations for both the companies and ACTION.

For its part, ACTION agreed to disseminate "up-to-date scientific information on the dangers of drug abuse."[50] Participating pharmaceutical companies, in turn, promised to produce a descriptive brochure on the topic. ACTION offered cooperating pharmacists a training program in advising parents and children on the dangers of drug abuse. ACTION's funding, which totaled approximately $100,000, also supported a toll-free number that interested parents and others could call for assistance. And the actor Michael Landon of the television series *Little House on the Prairie* agreed to do a public-service announcement on the dangers of drug abuse.

How exactly did ACTION go about sponsoring such a program? It seems that the program actually was an "outgrowth of the White House briefing that ACTION co-sponsored with Mrs. Reagan for corporate, labor, not-for-profit and other organizations on the dangers of drug abuse. Many of them are adopting a drug prevention program as a result of that conference, and this is one of [the programs]."[51] The number of children who ultimately were rescued by the efforts of Mrs. Reagan, ACTION, and the pharmaceutical companies is not known. As an alternative model of voluntary action, VISTA's Drug Abuse Prevention Project demonstrated that VISTA's potential clientele extended far beyond the activists' poverty community.

Of Literacy and Food Banks

By 1983, VISTA had nearly 330 volunteers working in literacy projects around the country, most of them as reading tutors. VISTA's director of policy and planning advocated using volunteers as tutors because they had "the skills—the right kind of training—to do something about the problem." As literacy tutors, VISTA volunteers had an advantage in that they "often perform their services in environments which are much more conducive than are school settings to the learning of people that they are training."[52]

In another project, one that reflected the conservative values of self-help and the delivery of service, 140 VISTA volunteers were assigned to forty food banks nationwide. VISTA volunteers became so critical to the functioning of the food banks that one congressman expressed concern that the banks would stop functioning if VISTA volunteers should ever be withdrawn.[53]

Thus, by the end of President Ronald Reagan's first term, VISTA's organizational culture had changed dramatically, from a culture of radical activism to one of conservatism. VISTA's projects for community organizing were dropped, and local organizations, which traditionally had relied on VISTA volunteers, were now denied VISTA assistance. As had occurred during the Nixon and Ford administrations, ACTION's political appointees moved to reshape organizational values ideologically and to redirect projects already in place. Conservative initiatives in voluntary action involved Vietnam veterans, the illiterate, youth, and the elderly. No longer were the poor considered VISTA's target clientele. No longer would local community groups be the sole recipients of VISTA grants. Conservatives envisioned a voluntary action agency that would serve a wide variety of citizens, that would spread a network of volunteerism among all types of civic, social, and community groups. VISTA's mandate from the conservatives was to mobilize volunteers, not the poor.

Whatever Happened to the Peace Corps?

Ronald Reagan became the sixth president to preside over the Peace Corps or, more accurately, what remained of a once proud program. As the Peace Corps began its third decade it clearly was in trouble. "After so many ideological spasms," one observer noted, "the agency was confused." Organizational malaise pervaded the Peace Corps, and its organizational culture was nonexistent. The Peace Corps needed, "more than anything else, to be guided around those riding ideological hobby horses and passing out glib phrases."[54] The Corps' experience demonstrates the truism that it often is easier to tear something down than to build it up.

Quite simply, the strong organizational culture of the Peace Corps in the early 1960s disintegrated under successive attacks by politically appointed administrators and by radical activists of the Carter administration and conservatives of the Nixon-Ford period. Further, the Peace Corps' ten-year alliance with ACTION had been like "putting apples and oranges together," since the Peace Corps often played a role subordinate to ACTION's domestic programs.[55] As a result, Peace Corps staff and volunteers suffered, morale was low, and organizational values were confused.

Symptoms of organizational anomie were abundant. Numerous complaints from the field regarding poor planning and staff support suggest something substantially less than a strong organizational commitment to achieving excellence. As one journalist commented, "When 4,452 volunteers—about 75 percent of those in service—were polled in 1979 about their positions, 25 percent did not believe that the staff had visited their sites to plan assignments before their arrival and almost 50 percent felt that the staff had never discussed details of their jobs with local supervisors."[56]

Following the intra-agency turmoil of the Nixon, Ford, and Carter administrations, the Peace Corps clearly was at its lowest ebb. Its purpose was confused and the commitment of its staff and volunteers diffused. Senator Charles Percy lamented that the Peace Corps had been losing its identity for some time and that it lacked esprit de corps.[57] Sargent Shriver compared the Corps' once proud organizational ethos with that of another corps: "The Peace Corps is the kind of entity which requires a prophetic, almost spiritual leadership—more so than any other agency in government. . . . It's like the Marine Corps. It is a service which depends for its quality and motivation on this spirit."[58] It almost goes without saying that by the early 1980s, the Marine Corps ran decidedly ahead of the Peace Corps in esprit de corps.

During Reagan's first term, the Peace Corps, in most respects, followed a now familiar pattern: political appointees enforced partisan agendas; career civil servants, volunteers, and former volunteers protested the agendas. Again, the Peace Corps' role in and relationship to the foreign policy goals of the United States were debated. Accompanying the Reagan administration were several important policymaking shifts. The Peace Corps, freed of the albatross of ACTION, regained its independence, only to be racked again by intraparty partisan conflict. In short, conservatives used the Peace Corps as a whipping boy to test partisan loyalties to President Reagan and Vice-President Bush.

Independence from ACTION and the CIA

In 1981, the Peace Corps marked its twentieth anniversary with the passage by the Senate of a bill calling for separation of the Peace Corps from ACTION. After ten years under the ACTION umbrella, the Peace Corps lacked only House approval to gain its independence. Senate action on the Peace Corps, however, would not have occurred had partisan politics not again confused the agency's mission. The Peace Corps, already given virtual autonomy by President Carter's executive order following Sam Brown's efforts to politicize agency policymaking and programming, faced a new threat to its organizational integrity. Because of Carter's decision, the Peace Corps, practically speaking, operated autonomously within ACTION, with its director reporting directly to the President. Thus, on the surface, there seemed no compelling reason for complete independence or separation from ACTION.

Partisan infighting, though, sometimes supplies just such a compelling reason. This time, ACTION's director, Thomas W. Pauken, did *not* produce a hit list of Peace Corps projects, as he had done in the case of VISTA. Now it was Pauken's past that was the problem. Pauken had served as a U.S. Army intelligence officer in Vietnam; that fact would not disqualify the director of most governmental agencies, but the Peace Corps was different. Since its beginning, Corps regulations explicitly barred from employment anyone who had served in the intelligence branches of the armed forces during the past ten years. And this was one regulation that was strictly enforced.

Perhaps no other issue so threatened the Peace Corps' neutral image. One cannot overemphasize the extent to which the agency had over the years avoided any appearance of involvement in intelligence work. The mere rumor of CIA involvement cost the Peace Corps its India program (terminated by New Delhi in 1976). Sargent Shriver remembers that the CIA was quick to cast covetous eyes on the Peace Corps during the early years of its existence but that President Kennedy had ordered a strict hands-off policy.[59] Soviet propaganda often portrayed Peace Corps volunteers as CIA "covers" overseas, and the agency could ill afford any appearance of espionage involvement that lent credence to anti-American propaganda.

Exactly what intelligence could be gathered by Corps volunteers living in rural villages or urban slums is difficult to discern, especially in the developing nations of the Third World. Nonetheless, many educated, middle-class citizens in these countries took the view that a few volunteers might actually be undercover agents.

I remember with shock and dismay the final English class I held for a group of young high school students in Brazil. The elite of local society, most went on to the university. For two years their studies were conducted in English; I spent many hours visiting their parents' homes. Following a touching good-bye party at the end of my two years' service, the students gathered around to say farewell. Some even promised to visit me in the United States someday. One young woman, considered a leader by the others, clearly waited to say something on behalf of the group. After some hesitation, she asked in Portuguese: "Now tell us the truth. We won't tell anyone. Are you really a CIA spy?" Only the Peace Corps volunteer laughed.

Pauken dismissed the notion that his army intelligence background implied the intelligence-gathering use of Peace Corps volunteers. "I don't believe, first of all, in getting the Peace Corps involved in intelligence. And I don't have sway over the policy of the Peace Corps."[60] Despite Pauken's objections and mild opposition from the Reagan administration, an amendment to the foreign aid bill establishing the Peace Corps' autonomy passed the House and the Senate in late 1981. No longer could critics try to link the Corps to the CIA because of Pauken's past. No longer could ACTION submerge the Peace Corps in its domestic voluntary-action programs. Once again, the Peace Corps was on its own. Organizational autonomy, however, did not insulate the Corps from intense ideological rivalry among its political appointees.

Conservative Rivalry at the Peace Corps

The Peace Corps' victory in Congress proved to be troublesome for Loret Ruppe, the Corps' highly vocal director. Ruppe expressed her support for autonomy, thus provoking what some observers called "one of the most angry behind-the-scene conflicts, with a heavy ideological overlay." On the surface, certain hard-line conservative groups and ACTION officials were upset with Ruppe for supporting Peace Corps autonomy against the wishes of the White House, feeling that Ruppe's actions demonstrated disloyalty to the President.[61]

Under the charges of disloyalty lay a deeper ideological struggle. Ruppe became the focus of a fight between party liberals who had supported George Bush, and conservatives who had backed the President in the presidential primaries. As a "preconvention supporter and a social friend of the Bushes in Washington," Ruppe exhibited a lack of commitment to the President that supposedly was obvious to Reagan supporters.[62] Conservative ideologues believed as well that Ruppe was protecting an agency that should have been purged ideologically some time ago. Not only was Ruppe disloyal to the President, they said, she was ideologically suspect, too.

Despite support from Barry Goldwater and other conservatives, the Peace Corps developed no substantial support among archconservatives. When Ruppe's "deviationism" proved insupportable, therefore, these conservatives launched a vicious counterattack. One conservative journal referred to the Peace Corps' twentieth-anniversary celebration as a forum for "virtually every anti-Reagan freak around."[63] Others described the Peace Corps as representing a "repository and a dangerous anti-Reagan instrument, within the U.S. government, of Third World animosity."[64] Why would someone loyal to the President defend or lessen control of the Peace Corps? David Broder, after interviewing Ruppe, charged that her conservative critics were sexists who thought that she was "an uppity woman, making trouble, instead of staying home in Michigan and helping her husband" run for the Senate.[65]

Nor were Ruppe's fortunes among conservatives helped by the actions of William G. Sykes, a deputy director of the Peace Corps in the Carter administration. Despite strong criticism from conservatives, Ruppe kept Sykes aboard as acting director of the African division. After ten months, Sykes departed, leaving behind a letter mailed on Peace Corps stationery to his colleagues and aides. In the letter, Sykes announced that he and others were donating $100 to the gubernatorial campaign of Richard Celeste, a former Peace Corps director and a Democrat. Sykes denounced "right-wing ideologues inside and outside the agency."[66] His encouragement to agency professionals to resist the agency's political ideologues is particularly revealing:

As life at the agency becomes more and more confusing and as the
mission of the Peace Corps becomes more and more submerged in
political rhetoric, I know the professionals among you who know
and love the Peace Corps can be counted on to try and help the
organization regain a sense of its priorities.

I am confident that the Peace Corps can survive this dark period of attack . . . and [that] *it will survive the personnel that are
being imposed on the agency without regard for ability, sensitivity
and present or potential competence.*[67]

Sykes undoubtedly expressed pent-up frustrations among numerous career employees who accepted a strong organizational
culture and were offended by political appointees with conflicting ideologies.

Ruppe's political problems with conservatives did not end
with Sykes' departure, however. Three years later, her running
feud with archconservatives erupted again in an incident reminiscent of Watergate. According to press accounts, Director
Ruppe secretly tape-recorded a supposedly private conversation
with deputy Edward Curran during a meeting six months earlier, in which Ruppe reportedly grilled Curran regarding his
opposition to her politics. Supposedly, Ruppe intended to trick
Curran into making disloyal statements to be used to convince
her White House supporters that Curran should be fired. It
seems the taping incident occurred after Ruppe had stripped
Curran of his major responsibilities, including serving as acting
director in her absence. Curran protested, took his case to the
White House, and received vindication.[68]

The confrontation of Ruppe and Curran was more than a personality clash between two inflated egos; ideologically, it pitted
archconservatives against liberal conservatives, Reagan versus
Bush wings of the Republican party. Loret Ruppe, wife of former
Representative Philip Ruppe and co-chairperson of the Bush
campaign in Michigan, found herself appointed Peace Corps
director even though she "had no previous professional experience when she took over."[69] Curran, a staunch conservative and
former headmaster of Washington's National Cathedral School,
gained support for the agency's deputy director position even
though Ruppe opposed his appointment. The resulting organi-

zational climate produced what one agency official characterized as "like the old Nixon days around here."[70]

The Ruppe-Curran quarrel had deeper implications for the Peace Corps. Tensions between political appointees and career employees are at best manageable; but in this case, appointees with opposing, intensely held ideologies were appointed Peace Corps director and deputy director, respectively. Both had strong friends among the White House staff; both maintained cliques of loyalists among agency employees. The director fired, or tried to fire, several employees viewed as loyal to Curran. The result was the triumph of internecine warfare over organizational development. For instance, Ruppe ordered her Inter-American director not to give Curran information on the Peace Corps' policy toward Grenada "or to notify him of meetings about whether the agency should send volunteers back to Grenada."[71] Agency decisions were made not on the basis of policy analysis and information-gathering but on the basis of personal positions taken by key actors.

Assigning the ultraconservative Curran as Ruppe's deputy is reminiscent of the commissar-commander practice prevalent in the Soviet Union, where both party commissar and military commander were co-leaders of the organizational unit, one to ensure partisan purity, the other tactical direction. Typically, the result was continuous conflict and confusion. As co-leaders, Curran and Ruppe became locked in a stalemate.

Partisan activities at the Peace Corps, however, were not limited to the Curran-Ruppe brouhaha. Director Ruppe put off her critics by taking more than a disinterested role in her husband's 1982 campaign for the Senate. Critics were particularly irked when Ruppe took along her executive assistant on campaign trips in Michigan despite Hatch Act prohibitions forbidding government employees from taking an active part in political campaigns. Peace Corps spokespersons defended Ruppe's actions as essential. Ostensibly, her executive assistant went along with Ruppe "as a central reference point" to "maintain liaison" with the Peace Corps director and headquarters. "Have you ever tried to reach a campaigning person?" a testy spokesman for the agency asked.[72] Although Ruppe took accrued leave for campaigning on her husband's behalf, her aide went along on agency time. (Despite Ruppe's efforts and the diligent support of her staff, her husband lost.)

Undismayed, Ruppe continued to use her "central reference point" on travel plans of questionable political neutrality. Following her husband's losing Senate campaign, Loret Ruppe accompanied Barbara Bush, the vice-president's wife, on an extensive tour of Africa, and again, her executive assistant went along, albeit in a separate executive jet. As irreverent pundits noted, one wondered "whether someone needing to get in touch with the Peace Corps director wouldn't just forward a request through the Secret Service."[73] Viewed from a financial perspective, at a cost of only $4,700 to taxpayers, the American public kept in touch with its Peace Corps director as she toured the continent of Africa.

"Americans Abroad"

Numerous public opinion polls indicate, and commentators of varying political persuasion have observed, that an increase of patriotic feeling among Americans was noted in the early 1980s. No doubt, the Reagan administration considered the rise in patriotism as one of its proudest accomplishments. After the long despair over American hostages held in Iran, and the feeling of helplessness during the Arab oil embargo, Americans eagerly awaited better times. Ronald Reagan, a master at political symbolism, quickly capitalized on this longing. Such events as the invasion (or liberation) of Grenada by U.S. forces, the success of American athletes in the 1984 Olympic Games boycotted by most communist bloc nations, and the suicide bombing of U.S. Marines in Lebanon were easily turned into patriotic benchmarks by the President.

The Peace Corps did not escape the nation's renewed patriotic fervor. Several policy options were pursued by conservative appointees at the Corps during the early Reagan years. First, Peace Corps volunteers traditionally kept apart from their government's foreign policy, were redefined by conservatives as "Americans Abroad"—cultural and political emissaries of their country. Second, overseas projects that stressed up-by-the-bootstraps themes were favored over social-intervention approaches.

In short, Director Ruppe pushed the "pull-them-up-by-their-bootstraps type of program" because it was "the kind of foreign aid that appeals to conservatives" in Congress.[74]

Conservatives intended to make sure that Peace Corps volunteers, as "Americans Abroad," understood the "philosophy, strategy, tactics, and menace of communism."[75] Therefore, conservative appointees to the agency redesigned the training of volunteers to teach them to defend themselves intellectually against communist propaganda. Beginning in the activist days of the New Frontier, volunteer trainees had attended classes with assigned readings in Marxism and U.S. foreign policy. By the late 1970s, however, such readings and topics had disappeared from training sessions because, as the agency's deputy director said, "It was absolutely total bullshit."[76]

Beginning early in the Reagan administration, however, "Patriotism 101" found its way back into the Peace Corps training curriculum. Owing to pressure from several conservative members of Congress and to such Far Right groups as the Committee of One Hundred to Defund the Left and the Christian Anti-Communist Crusade, the Peace Corps paid $50,000 to a consulting firm to produce an audiovisual presentation of high patriotic content for volunteer training. The result, "Americans Abroad," offered the following observations:

> *On Vietnam:* We were moved to solve problems which were not of our making, and we inherited both the problems and the blame for causing them.

> *On U.S.-Soviet relations:* Soviet strategy continues to view the United States as the adversary in the world struggle. . . . Make no mistake; we are engaged in a world-wide struggle for control— an ideological confrontation.

> *On open societies:* A secret police force cannot exist, because the system does not tolerate secrets.[77]

Ironically, both ultraconservatives and activists were upset by "Americans Abroad," the former group because the film allegedly did not go far enough, and the latter because it went too far.

Liberal critics charged that "Americans Abroad" simply fit into Corps plans to create for volunteers a readily identifiable enemy: the Godless Glaring Communist. "To smite that dragon, it wants to send forth a phalanx of young Americans who will explain with flashcard simplicity what's good and what's evil."[78] Shriver, among others, decried the Peace Corps' efforts to convert trainees into "philosophical Green Berets."[79] He might have added that section 8(c) of the legislation establishing the Peace Corps requires extensive indoctrination of trainees.

Conservatives under Reagan believed that properly educated volunteers should support the legitimate aims of U.S. foreign policy. Activists and returned volunteers alike charged Reagan appointees with declaring the Peace Corps "an instrument of United States foreign policy and a tool of the Reagan administration."[80] Debate over the Peace Corps' relationship to U.S. foreign policy erupted as Reagan appointees proposed to expand rapidly the number of volunteers in Central America and the Caribbean. No less a group than the Bipartisan Commission on Central America (known as the Kissinger Commission) proposed adding 3,000 volunteers, in addition to the 600 already there.[81]

Activist reaction to the "Kissinger Report" was typified by a former volunteer, now a sociologist at Cornell University: "I'm very much against expanding our Peace Corps volunteers operations and expanding our military operations simultaneously. It's just a tragedy to give this mixed message and to make volunteers feel like they're a part of a mopping-up operation."[82] Activists despaired that a rapid build-up of the number of Peace Corps volunteers in Central America, while volunteer levels in other parts of the world remained constant, "would be perceived as a tool of the hawk wing of the United States foreign-policy Establishment and its Central American clients."[83]

Throughout Central America and the Caribbean, Peace Corps volunteers took on greater importance among conservatives who wished to build the region's resistance to what they viewed as Soviet-Cuban-Nicaraguan aggression. However, a spokesperson for the Returned Peace Corps Volunteers Committee on Central America asserted, "Honduras already is running over with volunteers, and with the introduction of American troops, the place is swarming with Americans."[84] Still other volunteers and returned volunteers sharply disagreed, perhaps agreeing instead with the old adage, "Don't look a gift horse in the mouth." After all, for the first time since the 1960s, proposals were being made to *increase,* not decrease, Corps volunteer levels. As former volunteer Thomas J. McGrew argued, "I would take 3,000 more volunteers serving rural Central America as long as they can be free, as Peace Corps volunteers always have been, of any involvement with U.S. security and espionage organizations. If I could raise the total to 10,000 volunteers, I'd be for that, too."[85] Senator Paul Tsongas, himself a former volunteer in Ethiopia during the early 1960s, agreed. "It's important to demonstrate to the countries that we can do more than just send arms," he said.[86]

Honduras, viewed by Reagan administration policymakers as the key bastion against Sandinista expansionist aims in Nicaragua, became a widely proclaimed success story of the Peace Corps. According to U.S. embassy polls, 86 percent of rural and urban Hondurans view the United States favorably. Why? According to the embassy's public affairs counselor, this favorable impression was attributable in large part to the Peace Corps volunteers, especially in the rural areas. "They saw real aid. They were grateful to the volunteers for living with them in their dire poverty and giving them a sense of human dignity."[87] Corps volunteers were a key ingredient in the Reagan administration strategy for Central America.

Perhaps nowhere did the Peace Corps face a greater dilemma than on the Caribbean island of Grenada. In late 1983, the United States, in concert with Grenada's sister islands, launched a successful "liberation" (or, to Reagan's critics, "invasion") of the island. According to the administration, the military action occurred just in time to prevent a Marxist takeover. Regardless of whether such a takeover would indeed have occurred, and regardless of the President's motivation, to many liberals and opponents of the President, Grenada was merely the most recent example of American imperialism. Thus, when Grenada asked the United States to send Peace Corps volunteers to rebuild agricultural, health, and educational services as soon as possible, many believed the volunteers would be little more than political agents.[88]

The activist-conservative, as well as the conservative-ultra-conservative, conflicts continue over the degree of involvement of volunteers as extensions of United States foreign policy. Even during the early years Peace Corps volunteers often had tried to explain their country's involvement in Vietnam and the Dominican Republic while maintaining their own political neutrality as volunteers. Insistence on the absolute separation of the Peace Corps from U.S. foreign policy priorities was, at best, only abstractly possible. In reality, to poor villagers and slumdwellers around the world, volunteers *are* the United States.

At issue was whether Peace Corps volunteers and Peace Corps projects, as had happened during the Carter and Reagan administrations, should be selected primarily on the basis of foreign policy goals. It was the difference between individuals volunteering to serve and volunteers being trained as "Americans Abroad." Both radical activists during the Carter administration and ultraconservatives under Reagan have argued that the Peace Corps should function as an extension of U.S. foreign policy, whereas traditional activists and conservative appointees opposed such a role.

Self-Help and Private-Sector Initiatives

With two main goals in view, the Reagan administration's revitalization of the Peace Corps moved ahead. The first goal was to infuse the Corps with private sector support; the second was to return to basics in the field through such projects as agriculture, fisheries, and teaching. The practical result was a Peace Corps salable to Congress and to staunch conservatives.

John Williams, a former volunteer on loan from Chase Manhattan Bank, was named to head the "Peace Corps Income Generation Initiative." Williams envisioned a three-pronged program involving private and non-for-profit organizations, to increase the number of returned volunteers entering private-sector jobs, to coax corporate or not-for-profit personnel to join the agency by taking leaves of absence, and to design cooperative projects overseas with private-sector organizations.[89] In part, the Peace Corps emphasized private-sector initiatives because of sizable budgetary cutbacks before Grenada and the Kissinger Report proposals.

In theory, multiple benefits would be derived from greater Peace Corps cooperation with private voluntary organizations. The Peace Corps could lend these organizations trained volunteers for work in countries where the Corps had no current operations. Budgetary cuts had already forced the agency to terminate operations in Colombia, South Korea, and the Ivory Coast; joint projects with private organizations might be a way to avoid further cutbacks. For example, Peace Corps volunteers serving in a project operated by CARE would provide mutual benefits for both organizations. CARE would receive trained volunteers without support costs, and the Peace Corps would maintain its presence in the field. John Williams believed that the Reagan administration's "emphasis on voluntarism, on self-help" was particularly attractive to private-sector organizations; they were themes which "traditionally the Peace Corps has proven it can do, and do well."[90]

In returning to the basic programs of technical assistance and education, the Peace Corps stressed development of programs in agriculture, alternative sources of energy, and fisheries in order to bring "protein into areas where it is almost impossible to get meat." In a departure from the early years, when volunteers were asked in exit interviews to assess their accomplishments, "in its training program volunteers are taught not to expect to see changes in their two-year period of service." For example, according to the agency's regional director for North Africa, the Near East, Asia, and the Pacific, "it may be easier to raise rabbits than build fisheries," and, whereas locals readily eat fish, introducing rabbit stew into the local cuisine may take somewhat longer (up to six to eight years, by one estimate).[91]

A Conservative's Peace Corps and VISTA

Some believe that conservatives, activists, and radical activists were merely using different terms to describe the same concept or similar ones. Accordingly, conservatives speak of "volunteerism" while activists push for "community control." Conservative "self-reliance" supposedly is synonymous with radical activist "self-determination." "Capacity-building," a popular concept during the Carter administration, possibly is indistinguishable from "economic independence." In the 1980s, theorists talk of "empowerment" (a concept that has yet to become popular, much as "antipoverty" and "Appalachia" were unfamiliar terms before Kennedy's New Frontier).

To some extent, there undoubtedly is overlap of the ideological jargon of the Far Left and the Far Right. How much overlap is as yet a matter of speculation.

More important, ideological values are significant variables in organizational decision-making. The values held by political appointees help shape policies and agency projects, as do organizational values expressed by career employees and volunteers. Although at times the ideological rhetoric used by conservatives and activists may seem confusing, the values expressed by such rhetoric make a profound difference in agency policymaking and the setting of priorities. Strong organizational cultures reflect clarity and commitment to clearly articulated values, whether activist or conservative.

Ronald Reagan's presidency has followed patterns set by Democratic and Republican presidents since John Kennedy. As before, party loyalists were appointed to top positions at the Peace Corps and VISTA. None happened to be former volunteers or professional administrators (with the possible exception of Joe Blatchford, whose *ACCIÓN* resembled a private Peace Corps). Reagan—like Carter, Ford, Nixon, and Johnson—delivered VISTA and the Peace Corps to campaign workers as the spoils of victory. What followed in each case proved remarkably similar: open warfare between political appointees and their subordinate careerists, volunteers, and organized groups of former volunteers. In each instance, conflict between political ideology and organizational culture occurred.

Though not unique in policymaking style or substance for the Peace Corps and VISTA, the Reagan administration nevertheless demonstrates several trends worth noting. First, *intra*party infighting, with the Peace Corps and ACTION as pawns in that conflict, arose again. During the Nixon and Ford administrations, Republican appointees brought a conservative ideology to an activist organizational culture. Agency decisions during the Reagan years were points of conflict between conservatives and ultraconservatives. Few if any career employees found themselves drawn into this internecine struggle. Agency policymaking reached a stalemate as rival factions attempted to block each other's political agendas. Such ideological strife was typified by the Heritage Foundation's attack on Loret Ruppe and the Peace Corps for being out of step with Reagan.[92]

Second, the Reagan administration portends another unique feature for the Peace Corps and VISTA, as well as for all other government agencies. Ronald Reagan has been presented with the opportunity to become the first president since Dwight Eisenhower to complete two full terms. His appointees—or, if he is unable to complete his second term, those of his vice-president—could effect profound changes at the Peace Corps and VISTA. Assuming eight years of conservative and ultraconservative domination of both agencies, truly conservative organizational cultures could become a reality. Conservative appointees during a Reagan (or a Reagan-Bush) administration can, if they plan carefully, mold the Peace Corps into "Americans Abroad" in support of national-security objectives. VISTA appointees, so reliant on community-organizing projects in the late 1970s, might be enabled to remove the concept from the conservative lexicon. Instead, conservatives may turn VISTA into a catalyst for civic and social volunteerism or simply ask local governments to pick up the tab.[93] If established, conservative cultures at the Peace Corps and VISTA might be attacked by political appointees with activist ideologies in a future Democratic administration.

At present, however, conservative ideology has carried the day; activist cultures in either agency are virtually nonexistent. Traditional activists and community organizers alike are enduring this period of conservative bondage, hoping to regain power in the not-too-foreseeable future. Less ideologically committed people may ask whether the seemingly endless cycle of ideology-versus-culture is truly inevitable. *Could* there be a less disruptive way, one that actually would encourage rather than discourage commitment cultures at the Peace Corps and VISTA?

Seven

Epilogue:
A
Government
of Enemies

Throughout the presidencies of six men, from Kennedy to Reagan, presidentially appointed administrators to the Peace Corps and VISTA worked to change and redirect governmental programs in accord with their own ideological views. Program goals and organizational cultures supported in one administration were attacked by political appointees in the next. Nowhere was the resulting conflict between organizational culture and political ideology more intense than at VISTA and the Peace Corps. Both organizations began with strong commitment cultures whose message was spread by legions of young volunteers. For more than twenty-five years at the Peace Corps and some twenty years at VISTA, intense conflict has reigned. Throughout this period political appointees have been pitted against career employees, volunteers, and former volunteers in a struggle over organizational culture and its relationship to partisan ideology.

Ideological Swings at the Peace Corps and VISTA

Perhaps the greatest flowering of strong organizational cultures, at least in the federal government, occurred during

John Kennedy's New Frontier and Lyndon Johnson's Great Society. Together, these programs produced a plethora of strong organizational cultures in such programs as the Peace Corps, VISTA, the Job Corps, Legal Services, and Head Start. Each program, equipped at launch with a strong organizational culture, resulted in a high commitment and clarity of purpose among employees and volunteers. Although all the programs have survived, their once-strong organizational cultures have over the years suffered successive culture shocks. Each program has experienced progressive deterioration and/or cultural confusion as presidential appointees with differing ideologies used their administrative discretion to erode organizational cultures.

The Peace Corps and VISTA, begun with strong organizational cultures and values, share a common emphasis on voluntary action. Their cultures have been enhanced by the charisma of a martyred president and by extensive media coverage of young Americans helping poor villagers abroad and the once "invisible poor" in the United States. The Peace Corps and VISTA were designed and staffed by individuals who can be characterized as activists who believe in taking direct political action in solving community problems, especially poverty. At VISTA, these policy activists viewed the federal government as a key instrument in fighting poverty, which state and local governments seemingly ignored or addressed only reluctantly. Activists saw (and see) themselves as going forth to fight the dual enemies of ignorance and poverty at home and abroad.

Activist values have centered on the belief that poverty is caused by structural economic problems and political injustice. Accordingly, the poor are powerless to escape unless organized to break the vicious cycle of poverty that seems to be passed from one generation to the next. The Peace Corps and VISTA projects designed by policymakers have pursued a redistribution of power so that the poor could control their own destinies. Volunteers were and are intended to serve as catalysts in springing the poverty trap, although VISTA volunteers were much freer to organize the poor politically than were Peace Corps volunteers.

Similar to VISTA in its organizational values, the Peace Corps, as intended by activist policymakers in 1960, would promote peace and "combat the virus of Communist totalitarianism" by training volunteers to eliminate "the root causes of war, poverty, ignorance, hunger and despair."[1]

Activists believe, however, that the Peace Corps should be politically neutral, neither an arm of official U.S. foreign policy nor involved in partisan politics overseas. Ironically, both conservative appointees to the Peace Corps during the Reagan administration, as well as radical activists during the Carter administration, have sought to change the Peace Corps' tradition of strict political neutrality. Conservatives and radicals feel that the host countries and projects selected by the Peace Corps, and which it designed, should reflect administration priorities in U.S. foreign policy.

VISTA, in comparison with the Peace Corps' original organizational culture, accepted a political activism that differs considerably. VISTA volunteers learned during training that political and social intervention must occur before the poor can break the poverty cycle. VISTA, mislabeled the "domestic Peace Corps," has operated according to direct activist strategies and has been more controversial ideologically than the Peace Corps. The agency prepared full-time volunteers to work in poverty communities in the United States, usually in community-organizing roles. Frequently working with community-action agencies or other community-based organizations, VISTA volunteers helped organize the poor against the economic and political elites who, activists believed, kept the poor in poverty. Peace Corps and VISTA volunteers were socialized by activists' values in the 1960s, but VISTA volunteers were more likely to consider themselves part of the poverty communities; Peace Corps volunteers knew all along that they were guests in foreign lands.

Several factors contributed to the development of strong activist cultures at the Peace Corps and VISTA during the 1960s. Both programs drew strength from the Kennedy mystique, initially through the leadership of Sargent Shriver; in their first stage of growth, both agencies attracted large numbers of organizational advocates (or "zealots") common to many governmental programs. These advocates commonly put the agency's social mission above their own self-interests, and this phenomenon was especially true of such programs as VISTA and the Peace

Corps, which utilize humanistically committed short-term volunteers.

Thus, during the initial phases of each agency's existence, VISTA and Peace Corps volunteers, as well as career employees, experienced a formative sense of identity. The activist ideology—expressed as a secular missionary faith—proclaimed the goal of rescuing the poor from their misery. In short, it was an exceedingly powerful culture in both organizations; but during the Nixon presidency it came under intense attack by agency appointees holding strong ideological values.

With the election of Richard Nixon, a cycle of conflict between organizational culture and appointee ideology began. Nixon was presented with the opportunity to appoint agency administrators who held conservative ideological values. As ideological conservatives, his appointees made different assumptions concerning the causes of poverty, its cure, and the role of volunteers in government programs. Conservatives, while agreeing with the goal of alleviating (or eliminating) poverty, were less impressed with the severity of poverty than with what they viewed as the dangerous side effects of activist policies. They distrusted big government in Washington, which, they believed, omnipotently tried to solve local problems. Conservatives preferred local initiatives, private-sector partnerships, and self-help projects as the means of helping the poor.

Conservative ideology emphasized the role of individual motivation in defeating poverty. To conservatives, human liberation occurred internally, not externally. Conservatives advocate a work- or achievement-ethic role model as a means of fighting poverty. As a result, conservative appointees to the Peace Corps and VISTA have launched a variety of efforts designed to change organizational cultures from activist to conservative ones. In doing so, these appointees have employed the full range of administrative discretion, only to discover in the process that organizational cultures are not so easily destroyed, especially during a four-year presidential term.

Conservatives began by attempting to break down the strong agency cultures in the Peace Corps and VISTA. They made their first move as the agencies were brought together with several other volunteer action programs in a new agency—ACTION.

Designed as a supervolunteer agency, ACTION had a new raison d'être that stressed voluntary action rather than an anti-poverty focus. The Peace Corps became the international operations arm of ACTION. Second, ACTION appointees moved to suppress the opposition of Peace Corps volunteers to the war in Vietnam. Third, the Peace Corps administrators promoted a "New Directions" program intended to redirect volunteer recruitment toward recruits whose values are more compatible with the conservative redirection. Fourth, ACTION director Balzano required that all ACTION employees, from clerical workers through top management, attend "agency staff programming institutes." Convinced that both the agency's activist culture and its programmatic goals must change, he was intent on turning ACTION inside out and upside down, and he would start with these institutes. Balzano, who assumed that the key to agency productivity and effectiveness lay in coalescing employee values, moved to rid VISTA and the Peace Corps of their activist cultures.

Despite intensive efforts by conservative appointees to ACTION, the Peace Corps, and VISTA, career employees and volunteers continued to express their profound commitment to activist values. Dr. Balzano's institutes shook the organization's activist culture but did not alter it substantially. Jimmy Carter's election in 1976 cut short Balzano's efforts to modify the activist cultures at the Peace Corps and VISTA.

Carter ushered in a period during which the ideological pendulum swung to the opposite extreme. Many Peace Corps and VISTA careerists, volunteers, and former volunteers had anticipated a revival of activist values in which, once again, activists would fight the twin evils of poverty and ignorance, both at home and in the Third World. Their hopes soared when Carter appointed as ACTION director Sam Brown, former community organizer and an antiwar protest organizer. Following a succession of conservative appointees to VISTA and the Peace Corps during the Nixon and Ford administrations, agency careerists and former volunteers looked forward to a kindred soul as ACTION director.

A far different scenario unfolded. By the end of Jimmy Carter's term, the Peace Corps was mired in political infighting, bitterness, and congressional charges of mismanagement. Both VISTA and the Peace Corps were rocked by conflict and by purges of career employees who refused to accept an alternative ideology in lieu of an organizational culture. Brown, as Balzano had before him, attempted to reshape the organizational culture by imposing a strongly held ideology. With successive directors, the agency's ideological pendulum swung from a conservative position to one of radical activism. Once again, political appointees, career employees, volunteers, and former volunteers struggled over organizational culture and political ideology.

The conflict occurred because Brown, unlike the traditional Peace Corps activists of the 1960s, argued that volunteers should function as political organizers rather than as neutral observers. They should help organize oppressed peoples in developing countries rather than support petty right-wing dictators. Supposedly peripheral Peace Corps projects such as recreation or teaching English as a second language were scrapped in favor of projects that addressed basic human needs in underdeveloped societies.

VISTA did not undergo similar organizational stress during the Carter administration. Its organizational culture, set firmly on a radical-activist course, created inevitable conflict with Reagan appointees. Under Sam Brown's guidance, radical activists emphasized recruiting local community residents as VISTA volunteers. No longer would activist-oriented, middle-class youth be placed in poor communities to serve twelve months as VISTA volunteers. Instead, volunteers were selected and paid by community organizations rather than directly by VISTA in Washington. It was hoped that they would thus be freer to help community groups combat the forces that kept them in poverty.

Finally, the scope of acceptable VISTA projects was expanded to include greater emphasis on political organizing, consumer protection, food cooperatives, and self-help projects. VISTA, particularly through its National Grant Program to community organizations, later was labeled by its conservative critics as the "New Left in Government." When assessed at the conclusion of President Carter's administration, VISTA's organizational culture was shown to have demonstrated a strong radical activism. Many traditional activists apparently had been rejuvenated by Brown's enthusiastic support for community-organizing projects in VISTA; their enthusiasm, however, lasted only until Reagan's election in 1980.

Unlike previous administrations, which had attempted to redirect VISTA's organizational culture, Reagan appointees to VISTA announced their intention to eliminate it entirely. The efforts of conservative appointees were blocked, though, by organized groups of former VISTA volunteers and congressional sympathizers, which persuaded key congressmen to continue funding of VISTA.

Thus defeated in their attempt to abolish VISTA, Reagan conservatives adopted a strategy aimed at reconstituting the organizational culture and agency goals. Conservative appointees reasoned that if VISTA could not be abolished, at least its organizational culture of radical activism could be purged and replaced by conservative ideology. Appointees formulated three interrelated strategies for introducing conservative ideological values at VISTA: (1) purge unacceptable community projects; (2) create alternative VISTA projects that reflect conservative achievement values; and (3) recruit agency employees with conservative values. To varying degrees, all three efforts succeeded.

By 1984 and the end of Reagan's first term, VISTA's organizational culture of radical activism existed only among *former* volunteers. No longer were VISTA volunteers allocated to ideologically suspect community organizations. Many volunteers were assigned to noncontroversial projects reflecting the conservative values of self-help, achievement, and entrepreneurship. Finally, VISTA's top posts continued to be filled with loyal party workers. Radical activism was no longer alive at VISTA.

The Reagan-era Peace Corps experienced conflict of a different nature from that of VISTA. After the ideological turmoil of the Nixon, Ford, and Carter years, however, the agency's once strong organizational culture had disintegrated. The Corps' ten-year exile within ACTION had produced confusion of commitment and purpose among staff and former volunteers. The Peace Corps' distinctive organizational culture had succumbed to ideological warfare between political appointees, on the one hand, and activist volunteers and staffers on the other. Could its organizational culture be resurrected? Could a new conservative ideology perhaps be imposed?

Finally, in 1981, Congress voted to make the Peace Corps once again independent of ACTION. Activists at the agency soon learned that a return to activist values would not be tolerated by conservatives appointed by the Reagan administration, who had adopted an "up by the bootstraps" philosophy for the Peace Corps. Volunteers, trained as "Americans Abroad," would continue to be viewed as emissaries of U.S. foreign policy. Peace Corps projects, once formulated with no special regard for host-country relations with the United States, were again subject to foreign policy considerations. Conservatives were intent on an *American* Peace Corps making its presence felt overseas, though not in the same way that radical activists under Carter had intended.

Although conservative ideology was in sharp contrast with the activist culture of the Peace Corps and in even sharper contrast with the radical activism of the Carter years, conservative appointees were criticized for ideological impurity by conservative ideologues. Peace Corps director Ruppe was at times stridently attacked by her Far Right critics for such ideological sins as

—proposing to send volunteers, despite State Department objections, to Zimbabwe, "a war-torn Marxist nation."[2]

—not sending a large number of volunteers to Grenada following the U.S. "liberation."

—allowing the agency to support the U.N. Volunteer Programs and the U.N. High Commission for Refugees.

—failing to take seriously a Peace Corps legislative requirement to teach volunteers "in the tactics and menace of communism."

—not adequately supporting President Reagan's Caribbean Basin initiative.

—not implementing President Reagan's Income Generation initiative, in which the President "championed free enterprise as the surest way to combat poverty and unemployment around the globe."[3]

On these and other issues, the conservatives of the Far Right disdained the Peace Corps director's above-the-battle attitude, as well as her seeming reluctance to support U.S. foreign policy priorities.

Organizational Culture and Ideology: A Never-Ending Story?

During the 1960s, neither the Peace Corps nor VISTA were confronted by ideologies opposing their organizational cultures. Both imposed unitary, activist values on volunteers; no one doubted the truth of activist assumptions regarding poverty and the poor. By the mid-1980s, that situation had changed; cultures, ideology, and counterideologies waged incessant warfare in both organizations. Political appointees, career administrators, and former volunteers approached policymaking priorities from activist, conservative and ultraconservative, and radical-activist perspectives. A dominant organizational culture during one administration was ideologically suspect during the next. Because no president since 1961 had completed two terms in office, no single organizational culture at the Peace Corps or VISTA could survive long enough to achieve either permanent acceptance or temporary reprieve from ideological attack. Conflict and constantly changing values characterized the environment at both agencies.

On Inauguration Day, 1985, the Peace Corps and VISTA continued to function under conservative administrators. Activists or radical activists are expected to have to wait at least until 1989, if not later, before regaining control of either agency. Barring another scandal of Watergate proportions, conservatives possess the opportunity to destroy activist organizational cultures in the Peace Corps and VISTA. Staffers at the agencies who still cling to activist or radical-activist values can and may be purged, and organized groups of former volunteers can be nullified. Unfortunately, if adopted by conservative appointees, this strategy will merely increase organizational conflict; it will not achieve consensus or introduce a conservative organizational culture. With an eventual Democratic victory, the process of organizational conflict would begin anew.

We have noted that a key difference between corporate and governmental cultures consists in their staying power. Organizational cultures in the public sector that initially are strong, as in VISTA and the Peace Corps, have difficulty surviving when competing with opposing ideologies introduced by political appointees to those agencies. To be sure, some critics might argue that government organizations, unlike their corporate counterparts, should *not* be encouraged to develop strong corporate cultures. After all, in a democratic society, governmental programs need to be responsive to changing political currents, whereas corporate cultures are imposed "undemocratically" from top management down. Although corporate employees subsequently may accept corporate culture as their own, it is still initiated by those with authority.

In a democracy, it is said, government organizations should not be guided by an elitist outlook such as organizational culture. Perhaps. It would seem, though, that certain governmental programs transcend ideology and are more reflective of common, long-term goals. This applies especially to regulatory and symbolic policies where a substantial national consensus exists; the National Endowment for the Humanities and the Public Broadcasting Corporation are two examples.

Although the Peace Corps and VISTA are relatively minor efforts when compared with some government programs, nonetheless they are indicative of a national consensus on voluntary-action service. Few disagree that the Peace Corps and VISTA offer a much-needed outlet for individuals who wish to volunteer their services at home and abroad. The issue becomes one of how to guarantee opportunities for voluntary action in the Peace Corps and VISTA in an organizational environment free of conflict and partisan infighting, one guided by a strong organizational culture that emphasizes commitment and clear purpose. Voluntary-action opportunities can be realized by reducing, if not eradicating, the influence of partisan ideology in the programs of both the Peace Corps and VISTA.

Voluntary Action Is Nonideological

Ideologues from both political parties have long dominated the Peace Corps and VISTA. Their narrow world-views have perpetuated conflict over types of projects, volunteer selection, and agency culture. Perhaps we need to be reminded that radical ideologies, whether activist or conservative, are not very popular among most Americans. Nor do most career civil servants or the young (those aged eighteen to twenty-five) hold radical opinions despite conservatives' traditional mistrust of this age group. Sam Brown, too, misjudged the organizational values held by most Peace Corps volunteers and staffers. Actually, most federal employees are relatively middle-of-the-road in their values. A survey conducted in 1984 by Stanley Rothman and Robert Lichter suggests that top federal managers are more supportive of traditional values than are leading journalists, public-interest activists, or Hollywood TV producers, writers, and directors. They describe themselves in distinctly conservative terms "as desiring to improve the system rather than change it in fundamental ways."[4]

Radical values do not predominate even among the age group most likely to join the Peace Corps or VISTA, eighteen-to-thirty-year-olds. A *Los Angeles Times* poll of the baby-boom generation, conducted in 1984, indicated a decided preference for President Reagan's policies over those of all Democratic primary candidates, including senators Gary Hart and George McGovern.[5] A *Washington Post*-ABC News poll indicated that President Reagan's conservative *policies* are even less influential on voters than his perceived "warm personality."[6] Most Americans who are politically active, whether common people or federal bureaucrats, show little fondness for radical values.

Sam Brown's radicalism of the 1970s appeared outmoded less than four years after Reagan's election when Democrats became uncharacteristically conservative in their political pronouncements. Representative Geraldine Ferraro, the first woman nominated for vice-president by a major party, was introduced to the national Democratic convention in achievement-oriented terms: "Like most Americans, she's worked hard for everything she's achieved. She has a strong family life, deep religious convictions, and working Americans of average income will find in her a vice-president who knows them and who will fight for them." In accepting the nomination, Ferraro responded by invoking her Italian-immigrant background, speaking in words Michael Balzano would applaud, "In America, anything is possible if you work for it. . . . American history is about doors being opened."[7] Although Balzano might shout "Bravo," Sam Brown would despair at such rampant conservatism from the Democratic nominee.

Political theorists and observers, as well as others, have long marveled at the "irony of democracy," in which the common person in the United States generally is less committed to democratic values than are opinion leaders and elites.[8] Most Americans are not overly concerned with the burning policy issues of the day; few even discern policy differences between political candidates. Consequently, the plight of the poor or the status of social injustice finds little sympathy among Americans more concerned with variable mortgage interest rates or inflation.

Most Americans have not considered whether poverty is caused by forces beyond the control of the poor or whether it is a psychological phenomenon to be alleviated by instilling an achievement ethic. Many may attribute poverty's persistence to both causes. Again, Americans are not noted for their strong ideological views on these or other issues. At the same time, they do want to volunteer in large numbers, to give something of themselves.

In one month alone, the Peace Corps received 12,380 inquiries for 600 volunteer slots in Africa—no doubt reflecting a massive outpouring of sympathy for the African victims of famine. There are strong indications that, if the ideologues do not prevail, a Peace Corps renaissance is possible as the Corps completes its third decade.[9]

The Problem of Political Appointees

According to a facetious work by Howard K. Smith, "The Three Biggest Lies of a Politician Who Has Just Won" are:

1. Without my wonderful wife and terrific kids, I couldn't have done it.

2. I see my win [as] a clear mandate to change the way our government has been run.

3. Just because my first appointee is my campaign manager doesn't mean he's not qualified for the job.[10]

One might paraphrase Smith's last "lie" to read: Just because a campaign worker is appointed to run a governmental agency doesn't mean he or she is qualified—or does it?

Smith's barbs reflect a serious, deep-seated problem in American democracy in general and the functioning of government specifically: the large number of political appointees distributed over a wide range of high administrative offices, with overlapping lines between them and career civil servants.[11] When compared with Western Europe, the ratio of political appointees to top civil servants is 1:3.2 for the United States, approximately 1:9 for France, and only 1:40 for Great Britain.[12] Moreover, in France, most appointees are former civil servants instead of campaign workers.

Thus the question can be stated: Do political appointees, especially in smaller government agencies such as the Peace Corps and VISTA, cause these agencies inevitably to be unmanageable? Before attempting to answer this question, let us look at a few observations from the literature on political appointees in general.

As a group, political appointees to the federal bureaucracy exhibit certain systemic tendencies. Most notable, perhaps, is the growing emphasis on intellect; partisan political experience may be of declining importance in the selection process. This is not to say that partisan sympathies and a willingness to be a team player are not important considerations in the appointment process; but it appears to be increasingly recognized that, in the words of President Kennedy, "you can't beat brains." At the assistant secretary and deputy agency administrator levels, two researchers found that during the Kennedy administration, 90 percent of this group were college graduates, a figure that has risen with every administration since that of Franklin Roosevelt.[13]

At the federal-administration level, just below that of assistant secretary, another study reveals that political appointees had more formal education than their counterparts in the military, civil service, or Foreign Service.[14] A high level of education in the social services increasingly is evident among political executives, whereas the proportion of lawyers in this group (at least in the lower echelons) is only about 25 percent and is declining. Other studies show that of 108 assistant secretaries, only 30 percent were appointed on the basis of a specialization and the remainder because of generalized experience.[15]

There is declining emphasis on partisanship in selecting political appointees as well. One indication of the state of affairs in this area is that even when a presidential appointee is a member of the President's party, common political loyalty appears to have accounted for little in securing the appointment. One study concludes that a mere 10 percent of its sample of 108 assistant secretaries were appointed primarily by dint of "service to party."[16] A study made in 1981 found that the proportion of top-level presidential appointees affiliated with the President's party has never exceeded 70 percent since 1960 and has dipped as low as 56 percent.[17]

If partisanship is in decline in making presidential appointments, so is the practice of appointing to top-level federal jobs people with experience in government. Between 1933 and 1961, 80 percent of the cabinet and subcabinet political appointees had some professional experience at the national level, and one-third had devoted a major portion of their careers to federal service.[18] Studies of more recent presidential appointees, however, indicate that these ratios are sharply declining. For example, at the close of Reagan's first term, only three of his thirteen original cabinet appointees remained; the others had resigned voluntarily or had been pressured to do so.

In examining lower-level appointees, another study (conducted in 1970) found that 69 percent of presidential appointees and 40 percent of noncareer supergrade appointees had less than two years of government experience when in office.[19] Between 1960 and 1973, nearly two-thirds of the cabinet's undersecretaries and almost four-fifths of the assistant secretaries had worked fewer than two years for the same supervisor.[20] Fewer than half of the federal executives occupying these two echelons served more than two years, and one-fifth served less than a year.[21] Rapid turnover of political appointees at VISTA and the Peace Corps was common; over three years (1981–83), VISTA had three directors.

Realistically, victorious politicians will continue to appoint campaign workers as administrative heads of government agencies, regardless of their managerial experience or qualifications. Party workers may be individuals with great integrity and strong moral convictions, but these qualities do not necessarily prepare one for administrative life. The underlying fact is that few of these "transitory amateurs" have substantive knowledge of public programs or experience in government. Most political appointees have been lifelong political activists; this situation is one that Howard Rosen believes contributes to the demoralization of the federal work force.[22]

By comparison with the majority of presidential appointees, party loyalists appointed to the Peace Corps and VISTA apparently have even less administrative experience and more strongly held ideological views than other appointees from 1961 to 1985. Not to single anyone out but selecting one case that is typical, let us consider the background of Betty Brake, appointed deputy director of ACTION in 1982. Brake submitted the following data to her Senate confirmation hearings:

> Betty Brake was deputy associate director of ACTION for Older American Programs in 1981–82 and was executive director of [the] White House Conference on Aging (1981). She was a member of Oklahoma's State Republican Party from '67–'71. She was co-chairman and executive director of Ronald Reagan's state election committee in both 1976 and 1980. Ms. Brake, a 61 year old widow, also served as executive director of [the] Oklahoma Politi-

cal Action Committee during '70's. She has [a] bachelor's degree in English.[23]

Brake's personal background and character are not at issue; what is at issue is her lack of management education. Her experience is typical of many political appointees, from both major political parties, to the Peace Corps, VISTA, and ACTION.

Analysis of official biographical materials submitted for Senate confirmation of upper-level appointees to the Peace Corps, VISTA, and ACTION over the past twenty-five years is revealing.[24] Biographical data were selected randomly and included appointees from both Democratic and Republican administrations. Based on these data, only 5 percent of the appointees had prior government administrative experience. Half were defeated congressional candidates (all listed extensive campaign experience). As noted, none were former Peace Corps or VISTA volunteers.

To an even greater extent than with other partisan appointees, Peace Corps and VISTA appointees are picked because they are viewed as concurring with and committed to carrying out what they believe to be the policy preferences and ideological values of the current administration. They usually lack direct knowledge about agency programs. Their average tenure is so brief and their rate of turnover so high that they have aptly been characterized by Hugh Heclo as participants in a "government of enemies."[25]

Coalition Management at the Peace Corps and VISTA

In part, the art of administration depends on how well an administrator understands the dynamics of coalition management. No doubt, every organization, both public and private, is a churning cauldron of political coalitions. Although presidential administrations, ideologies, and organizational cultures change, politically motivated coalitions will remain common in organizations headed by political appointees. To be effective, the political appointee must quickly learn how coalitions contend, cooperate, and coalesce within a particular agency. If the appointee does not do this, he or she may end up attempting to dominate coalitions rather than manage them. The results, as the Peace Corps and VISTA make all too plain, will likely be unrelenting conflict between ideology and organizational culture, between appointees and careerists.

Other structural reforms may encourage cooperation between appointees and bureaucrats in VISTA and the Peace Corps, but none compares in importance with the sagacious appointee who accepts and manages coalitions within his or her agency. For example, potential conflict would probably be reduced by implementing more rigorous standards for selecting presidential appointees, such as those recommended by the National Academy of Public Administration. In particular, a presidential requirement that appointees serve a full term or until a change in presidents might impart continuity and improve employee morale.[26] Even a commitment by successful candidates to stress experience and qualifications over partisan loyalty would help.

It would help as well to avoid conflict if something like a commission for national voluntary service, with commissioners appointed for six-year terms, could be formed to set the mission and direction of national voluntary action. Given the climate of conflict in both programs, however, it has proved impossible thus far to establish objectives or evaluate program results. Voluntary-action organizations need to protect a strong organizational culture that encourages volunteer and employee commitment—something that simply does not happen in the current milieu of a partisan Peace Corps and VISTA. In its recommendations for reform, the Returned Peace Corps Volunteers of Washington, D.C., listed five recommendations for the Peace Corps to carry out in 1985:

—Set a goal of 10,000 volunteers, with increased representation in Latin America and Asia.

—Devote more attention to the agency's Goal III (educating Americans about other cultures).

—Remove appointment of Peace Corps country directors from the political patronage system.

—Appoint a qualified, former Peace Corps volunteer as the next agency director.

—Create a special committee of returned volunteers to advise the Peace Corps director on improving the agency.[27]

In the final analysis, these structural reforms probably are only cosmetic. Those appointees to government organizations who appreciate and practice coalition management will be the most effective in nourishing a strong organizational culture, high employee morale, and clarity of mission. As Schmidt and Tannenbaum stress, difference in values or opinions among agency employees is not a disease to be eradicated; these differences can be a source of consensus-building and organizational development.[28] All too frequently, political appointees cannot endure differences of opinion; their partisan backgrounds have prepared them in terms of loyalty and singlemindedness rather than management of human resources. They, indeed, assume a government of enemies, that the other side's organizational culture must be destroyed or at least rendered impotent.

By now it should be obvious that Peace Corps and VISTA employees hardly fit the ultraconservative mold of an "entrenched political bloc intent on preserving the status quo and protecting special interests."[29] Nor are they, as some conservatives have charged, "an elite, influenced through an interlocking network with professional schools and the professional associations, exercising substantial control over policy decision-making in the agency."[30] Partly because of their small size, the up-and-out rule for employees, and the large percentage of former volunteers among the staff, the Peace Corps and VISTA do not fit the stereotypical mold of the entrenched bureaucracy.

Organizational culture in both the Peace Corps and VISTA has lost its activist mission and purpose. Years of ideological conflict have clouded the activist vision. The Peace Corps in particular is a composite of ideologies and subcultures. Though perhaps not so vocal or dogmatic as they once were, numerous career employees are still around who began their careers during the Great Society, Nixon, or Ford years. They may have mellowed, changed, even become young urban professionals; but they remain career employees in both the Peace Corps and VISTA.[31]

Political appointees to both voluntary action agencies, the Peace Corps and VISTA, make an egregious error if they assume that a homogeneous bureaucracy exists in either agency; homogeneity of activist or radical-activist values is more likely to be found among former volunteers and volunteer groups than within the bureaucracy.[32] Political appointees to the Peace Corps and VISTA have an unusual opportunity to shape a new organizational culture, one without ideological underpinnings, committed to a nonideological desire for voluntary action in alleviating human misery, regardless of its perceived causes or cures.

Notes

Chapter One

1. Joanne Martin and Caren Siehl, "Organizational Culture and Counterculture: An Uneasy Symbiosis," *Organizational Dynamics* (August 1983): 52–64.

2. James L. Sundquist, *Politics and Policy: The Eisenhower, Kennedy and Johnson Years* (Washington: Brookings Institution, 1968).

3. David Jacob Pass, "The Politics of VISTA in the War on Poverty: A Study of Ideological Conflict" (Ph.D. diss., Columbia University, 1976).

4. David Gottlieb, *VISTA and Its Volunteers* (University Park, Pa.: Pennsylvania State University, 1971).

5. Anthony Downs, *Inside Bureaucracy* (Boston: Little, Brown, 1967).

6. Pass, "Politics of VISTA."

7. Gerald William Bush, "The Peace Corps, 1961–1965: A Study in Open Organization" (Ph.D. diss., Northern Illinois University, De Kalb, Ill., 1968).

8. Thomas J. Peters and Robert H. Waterman, Jr., *In Search of Excellence: Lessons from America's Best-Run Companies* (New York: Harper & Row, 1982).

9. Terrance Deal and Allan Kennedy, *Corporate Cultures: The Rites and Rituals of Corporate Life* (Reading, Mass.: Addison-Wesley, 1982).

10. "Managing Corporate Cultures," unpub. brochure describing the conference announcement and call for papers by the Program in Corporate Culture (Graduate School of Business, University of Pittsburgh, n.d.).

11. Sundquist, *Politics and Policy;* Daniel P. Moynihan, *Maximum Feasible Misunderstanding* (New York: Free Press, 1969); Louis A. Zurcher, Jr., *Poverty Warriors: The Human Experience of Planned Social Intervention* (Austin: University of Texas Press, 1970).

12. Deal and Kennedy, *Corporate Cultures.*

13. James W. Driscoll, Gary L. Cowger, and Robert J. Egan, "SMR Forum: Private Managers and Public Myths—Public Managers and Private Myths," *Sloan Management Review* 21 (Fall 1979): 53–57.

14. Peters and Waterman, *In Search of Excellence.*

15. See Philip Selznick, *T.V.A. and the Grassroots: A Study in the Sociology of Formal Organization* (Berkeley: University of California Press, 1980); Joseph Barbato, "America Imagines the FBI," *The Chronicle of Higher Education* (Jan. 25, 1984): 5–6; Tom Wolfe, *The Right Stuff* (New York: Farrar, Straus & Giroux, 1979); Edgar H. Schein, "The Role of the Founder in Creating Organizational Culture," *Organizational Dynamics* (Summer 1983): 13–28.

16. Hugh Heclo, *A Government of Strangers: Executive Politics in Washington* (Washington: Brookings Institution, 1977).

17. Sundquist, *Politics and Policy,* p. 385.

18. John W. Macy, Bruce Adams, and J. Jackson Walter, eds., *America's Unelected Government: Appointing the President's Team* (Cambridge, Mass.: Ballinger, 1983), p. 17.

19. Guy B. Peters, *The Politics of Bureaucracy: A Comparative Perspective* (New York: Longman, 1978).

20. Jerry Shaw, quoted in "Bridging the Gap: A Dialogue," *Management* 3 (Fall 1982): 2.

21. Dick Kirschten, "Administration Using Carter-Era Reform to Manipulate the Levers of Government," *National Journal* (Apr. 9, 1983): 732–36.

22. Weber, "Bureaucracy," in *From Max Weber: Essays in Sociology,* ed. H. H. Gerth and C. Wright Mills (New York: Oxford University Press, 1970).

23. American Society for Public Administration, "Centennial Agendas Projects," Newsletter #6 (December 1983).

24. Donald J. Devine, quoted in Kirschten, "Administration Using Carter-Era Reform to Manipulate the Levers of Government," *National Journal* (Apr. 9, 1983), p. 733.

25. Douglas Yates, *Bureaucratic Democracy* (Cambridge, Mass.: Harvard University Press, 1982).

26. Heclo, *Government of Strangers,* p. 12.

27. Michael Balzano, Jr., *Reorganizing the Federal Bureaucracy: The Rhetoric and the Reality* (Washington: American Enterprise Institute for Public Policy Research, 1977), p. 41.

28. Donald J. Devine, quoted in Shaw, "Bridging the Gap," p. 3.

29. Macy et al., *America's Unelected Government,* p. 12.

30. Kirschten, "Administration Using Carter-Era Reform," p. 736.

31. Richard P. Nathan, *The Administrative Presidency* (New York: John Wiley, 1983).

32. Michael Sanera, quoted in Eric Wiesenthal, "Top Reagan Aide Opposes Policy Role Freeze," *Public Administration Times* (Jan. 1, 1985): 12.

33. Chester Barnard, *The Function of the Executive* (Cambridge, Mass.: Harvard University Press, 1968).

34. Martin and Siehl, "Organizational Culture," p. 52.

Chapter Two

1. Herbert S. Parmet, *J. F. K.—The Presidency of John F. Kennedy* (New York: Dial Press, 1983).

2. Louis A. Zurcher, Jr., *Poverty Warriors: The Human Experience of Planned Social Intervention* (Austin: University of Texas Press, 1970).

3. Thomas Zane Reeves, "The Influence of Partisan Orientations on the Role of Voluntary Action in Anti-Poverty Agencies," *Journal of Voluntary Action Research* 3 (Winter 1974): 75–81.

4. James T. Patterson, *America's Struggle Against Poverty, 1900–1980* (Cambridge, Mass.: Harvard University Press, 1981).

5. David McClelland, *The Achieving Society* (New York: Free Press, 1961).

6. See, for example, Sigmund Freud, *Civilization and Its Discontents* (New York: W. W. Norton, 1961).

7. Theodore Roszak, *The Making of a Counter Culture: Reflections on the Technocratic Society and Its Youthful Opposition* (New York: Doubleday, 1969); George Gilder, *Wealth and Poverty* (New York: Basic Books, 1981).

8. Zurcher, *Poverty Warriors,* p. viii.

9. Saul D. Alinsky, "The War on Poverty—Political Pornography," in *Poverty, Power, Politics,* ed. Chaim Waxman (New York: Grosset & Dunlap, 1968), pp. 171–79.

10. Parmet, *J.F.K.;* Jim Miller, "Camelot Revisited," *Newsweek* (Apr. 3, 1983): 75–76; Gerald T. Rice, *The Bold Experiment: JFK's Peace Corps* (Notre Dame, Ind.: University of Notre Dame Press, 1985).

11. President John F. Kennedy, quoted in "Address by the Honorable Sargent Shriver, Twenty-fifth Anniversary of the Peace Corps," Ann Arbor, Oct. 7, 1985, speech.

12. Robert B. Textor, *Cultural Frontiers of the Peace Corps* (Cambridge, Mass.: MIT Press, 1966), p. 342.

13. Edmund Muskie, "The Frontier of Development," *Department of State Bulletin* (December 1980), p. 4.

14. Arthur M. Schlesinger, Jr., *A Thousand Days: John F. Kennedy in the White House* (Boston: Houghton Mifflin, 1965), p. 606.

15. Hubert Humphrey, *The Education of a Public Man: My Life and Politics* (Garden City, N.Y.: Doubleday, 1976), p. 229; Carl Solberg, *Hubert Humphrey* (New York: W. W. Norton, 1984).

16. Schlesinger, *A Thousand Days,* p. 606.

17. Ibid., p. 740.

18. Mead, "Foreword," *Cultural Frontiers of the Peace Corps,* ed. Robert B. Textor (Cambridge, Mass.: MIT Press, 1966), p. ix.

19. Schlesinger, *A Thousand Days,* p. 605.

20. Ibid., p. 604.

21. Textor, *Cultural Frontiers,* p. 3.

22. Gerald T. Rice, "The Bold Experiment: Remarks on the Occasion of the 25th Anniversary of John F. Kennedy's First Announcement of the Peace Corps," Ann Arbor, Nov. 2, 1985, unpub. speech.

23. Rice, *Bold Experiment,* Foreword.

24. Judith A. Clute, "Personnel Management in the Peace Corps," *Public Personnel Review* (July 23, 1962): 163–65.

25. Textor, *Cultural Frontiers,* p. 323.

26. Michael Harrington, *The Other America* (New York: Macmillan, 1962); Dwight McDonald, "Our Invisible Poor," *New Yorker* (Jan. 19, 1963): 82–132; Leon Keyserling, *Poverty and Deprivation in the United States* (Washington: Conference on Economic Progress, April 1962); Harry Caudill, *Night Comes to the Cumberlands* (Boston: Little, Brown, 1962).

27. Carl M. Brauer, "Kennedy, Johnson and the War on Poverty," *Journal of American History* 69 (June 1982): 98–119.

28. Charles S. Bullock III, James E. Anderson, and David W. Brady, *Public Policy in the Eighties* (Monterey, Calif.: Brooks/Cole, 1983), p. 147.

29. John Biddy and Roger Davidson, *On Capitol Hill: Studies in the Legislative Process* (New York: Holt, Rinehart & Winston, 1967); Richard Bluementhal, "The Bureaucracy: Anti-Poverty and the Community Action Program," *American Political Institutions and Public Policy,* ed. Allan Sindler (Boston: Little, Brown, 1969).

30. Theodore H. White, *The Making of the President: 1960* (New York: Atheneum, 1961); Theodore C. Sorensen, *Kennedy* (New York: Harper & Row, 1964); Pierre Salinger, *With Kennedy* (New York: Doubleday, 1966); Schlesinger, *A Thousand Days.*

31. See *New York Times Index for Published News of 1962* (New York: New York Times Co., 1963); *Business Periodicals Index: July 1962–June 1963* (New York: H. W. Wilson Co., 1963); *Book Review Digest: 1961* (New York: H. W. Wilson Co., 1962).

32. Edmund Muskie, "The Frontier of Development," *Department of State Bulletin* (December 1980): p. 4.

33. U.S. President's Study Group on a National Service Program, *Information on a Proposed National Service Program,* S. 1321, H.R. 5625 (Washington, 1963), pp. 3–4. Emphasis added.

34. U.S. Congress, 88th Cong., 1st sess., 1963, Senate Committee on Labor and Public Welfare, *National Service Corps: Hearings, before the Senate Committee on Labor and Public Welfare,* p. 90.

35. Ibid., pp. 102–03.

36. U.S. Congress, 88th Cong., 2d sess., House Committee on Education and Labor, *Hearings before the Subcommittee on the War on Poverty Program, part I, Economic Opportunity Act of 1964* (Washington: U.S. Government Printing Office, 1965), pp. 86, 138, 307, 328, 587, 684.

37. Earl Latham, *J. F. Kennedy and Presidential Power* (Lexington, Mass.: D. C. Heath, 1972), p. 227; Cecil Osbaine, "Kennedy: The Making of a Myth," *National Review* 20 (Nov. 5, 1969): 1113–14; Tom Wicker, "Lyndon Johnson versus the Ghost of Jack Kennedy," *Esquire* 68 (November 1965).

38. Brauer, "Kennedy, Johnson," p. 119.

39. Lyndon Baines Johnson, *Public Papers of the President of the United States: 1964* (Washington: U.S. Government Printing Office, 1964), p. 114.

40. John C. Donovan, *The Politics of Poverty* (New York: Pegasus, 1967), p. 29.

41. Brauer, "Kennedy, Johnson," p. 119.

42. Donovan, *Politics of Poverty,* p. 29.

43. Eric Goldman, *The Tragedy of Lyndon Johnson* (New York: Dell, 1969), p. 163.

44. Liz Carpenter, *Ruffles and Flourishes* (Garden City, N.Y.: Doubleday, 1970); and "Why I Believe LBJ Was a Winner," *Parade* (June 5, 1983): 5.

45. James L. Sundquist, *Politics and Policy: The Eisenhower, Kennedy and Johnson Years* (Washington: Brookings Institution, 1968), p. 385.

46. Merle Miller, *Lyndon: An Oral Biography* (New York: Putnam's, 1980), pp. 363, 364.

47. Daniel P. Moynihan, *Maximum Feasible Misunderstanding: Community Action and the "War on Poverty"* (New York: Free Press, 1969).

48. David Gottlieb, "The Socialization and Politicization of VISTA Volunteers: Sex and Generational Differences," *Journal of Voluntary Action Research* 3 (Winter 1974): 109.

49. Robert E. Lane, *Political Ideology: Why the American Common Man Believes What He Does* (New York: Free Press, 1962).

50. Thomas Gladwin, *Poverty, U.S.A.* (Boston: Little, Brown, 1967).

51. George Gallup, *The Gallup Poll: Public Opinion, 1935–1971,* vol. 3 (New York: Random House, 1972).

52. Everett Carll Ladd, "205 and Going Strong," *Public Opinion* (June–July 1981).

53. David M. Potter, *People of Plenty: Economic Abundance and the American Character* (Chicago: University of Chicago Press, 1954).

54. Billy Graham, "How to Face Temptation," sermon, Kemper Arena, Kansas City, Mo., Aug. 31, 1978.

55. Max Weber, *The Protestant Ethic and the Spirit of Capitalism* (London: Allen & Unwin, 1930).

56. Brauer, "Kennedy, Johnson," pp. 112–13.

57. Andrew Lloyd Webber and Tim Rice, "Everything's All Right," song from *Jesus Christ Superstar,* Leeds Music Ltd., London, 1969.

58. Richard Sennett, "Survival of the Fattest," *New York Review of Books* (Aug. 13, 1970): 23–26.

59. Thomas R. Dye and L. Harmon Ziegler, *The Irony of Democracy: An Uncommon Introduction to American Politics,* 6th ed. (Monterey, Calif.: Brooks/Cole Press, 1984).

60. Textor, *Cultural Frontiers of the Peace Corps,* p. 4.

61. Quoted in Cable Neuhaus, "Memoir of the Peace Corps: 20 Years Later, Veterans Salute Its Enduring Hope," *People* 16 (July 20, 1981): 16–19.

62. David Gottlieb, quoted in "LBJ's Job Corps: Full of Hope, Naiveté," *Los Angeles Times* (Dec. 25, 1980): I-A.

63. Humphrey, *Education of a Public Man,* p. 411.

64. Hyman H. Bookbinder, "OEO Veterans Sad, Not Bitter, about Its End," *Los Angeles Times* (Apr. 12, 1973): I-12.

65. Michael P. Balzano, Jr., "The Political and Social Ramifications of VISTA Programs: A Question of Ends and Means" (Ph.D. diss., Georgetown University, 1971), p. 98.

66. Ibid.

67. Joseph A. Kershaw, *Government Against Poverty* (Chicago: Markham Publishing, 1970), p. 39.

68. Ibid.

69. U.S. Senate, 90th Cong., 1st sess., 1967, *Economic Opportunity Amendment of 1967,* p. 70.

70. Donovan, *Politics of Poverty,* pp. 72–73.

71. Moynihan, *Maximum Feasible Misunderstanding;* and Donovan, *Politics of Poverty.*

72. Editorial, "The Poor in Their Place," *New Republic* 15 (Nov. 20, 1965): 5–6.

73. U.S. Senate, *Economic Opportunity Amendment,* 1967, p. 70.

74. Kershaw, *Government Against Poverty,* p. 39.

75. U.S. Senate, 90th Cong., 2d sess., Subcommittee on Employment, Manpower and Poverty, *Toward Economic Security for the Poor* (Washington: U.S. Government Printing Office, 1968).

76. Sargent Shriver, "Memorandum from the Director," September 1966, inserted in House Hearings (1967), pp. 886–89.

77. U.S. Office of Economic Opportunity, *A News Summary of the War on Poverty* I, no. 32 (Oct. 24, 1966): 1–3.

78. Donald T. Allensworth, *The U.S. Government in Action: Public Policy and Change* (Pacific Palisades, Calif.: Goodyear Publishing, 1972).

79. Miller, *Lyndon,* p. 364.

80. Adam Yarmolinsky, "The Beginnings of OEO," in *On Fighting Poverty: Perspectives from Experience,* ed. James Sundquist (New York: Basic Books, 1969), p. 49.

81. Brauer, "Kennedy, Johnson," p. 99.

82. Niccolò Machiavelli, *The Prince* and *Discourses* (New York: Random House, 1950), p. 91.

83. Joseph Alsop, "The Legacy of John F. Kennedy: Memories of an Uncommon Man," *Saturday Evening Post* 21 (November 1964): 15–19; William G. Carleton, "Kennedy in History," *Antioch Review* 24 (Fall 1964): 277–99.

84. David Zarefsky, *President Johnson's War on Poverty: Rhetoric and History* (University, Ala.: University of Alabama Press, 1985).

85. Lyndon Baines Johnson, *The Vantage Point* (New York: Holt, Rinehart & Winston, 1971), p. 75.

86. Miller, *Lyndon,* p. 364.

Chapter Three

1. Howard Tolley, Jr., "Five Years of the Nixon Peace Corps: Politics, Vietnam, and a Post-War Generation of Peace," *Intellect* (November 1974): 96–98.

2. Christine Rideout, "Job Corps," case study, Harvard University, Inter-Collegiate Clearing House, 1974.

3. U.S. President, Richard M. Nixon, *Public Papers of the President: 1971* (Washington: Office of the *Federal Register,* National Archives and Records Service, 1971).

4. U.S. President, Richard M. Nixon, *Public Papers of the President: 1970* (Washington: Office of the *Federal Register,* National Archives and Records Service, 1970), p. 259.

5. U.S. President, Richard M. Nixon, *Public Papers of the President: 1969* (Washington: Office of the *Federal Register,* National Archives and Records Service, 1969), p. 112.

6. U.S. Office of Economic Opportunity, *National Anti-Poverty Plan FY1968–FY1972* (Washington: U.S. Government Printing Office, June 1966).

7. Ibid., p. 3.

8. Nixon, *Public Papers of the President: 1969,* p. 655.

9. U.S. President, National Advisory Council on Economic Opportunity, *Third Annual Report, March 1970* (Washington: U.S. Government Printing Office, 1970), p. 1.

10. U.S. Office of Economic Opportunity, *VISTA Volunteer Handbook,* OEO/VISTA Manual 4010–1 (Washington, June 1968), p. 1.

11. U.S. Office of Economic Opportunity, *VISTA Serves* (Washington: Community Relations Division, VISTA, 1967).

12. Elmer B. Staats, *Needs for More Effective Audit Activities* (Washington: U.S. General Accounting Office, April 1973): 328.

13. Fred D. Baldwin, *Evaluating the OEO Legal Services Program: Working Papers* (Washington: Office of Economic Opportunity, July 1972); Patricia Koshel, *Working Papers: Migration and the Poor* (Washington: Office of Economic Opportunity, July 1972); W. R. Prossner, *Working Papers: Day Care in the Seventies, Some Thoughts* (Washington: Office of Economic Opportunity, May 1972); David Gottlieb, *VISTA and Its Volunteers* (University Park, Pa.: Pennsylvania State University, March 1971); U.S. Office of Economic Opportunity, *An Evaluation of the Neighborhood Health Center Program* (Washington: Office of Economic Opportunity, May 1972).

14. Gottlieb, *VISTA and Its Volunteers,* p. 1.

15. Kershaw, *Government Against Poverty,* p. 40.

16. Gottlieb, *VISTA and Its Volunteers,* p. 140.

17. Ibid., p. 17.

18. Ibid., p. 140.

19. Michael P. Balzano, "The Political and Social Ramifications of VISTA Programs: A Question of Ends and Means" (Ph.D. diss., Georgetown University, 1971).

20. Ibid., p. 393.

21. Nixon, *Public Papers of the President: 1969,* pp. 653–54.

22. U.S. National Advisory Council on Economic Opportunity, *Third Annual Report, 1970* (Washington: U.S. Government Printing Office, 1970), p. 17.

23. Nixon, *Public Papers of the President: 1969,* p. 114.

24. Ibid.

25. Rideout, "Job Corps," p. 15.

26. J. Howard Phillips, "Evening Edition," transcript of tape recording (Washington, Feb. 6, 1973).

27. Edmund Muskie, "The Frontier of Development," *Department of State Bulletin* (December 1980): 4.

28. Gerald D. Berreman, "The Peace Corps: A Dream Betrayed," *The Nation* (Feb. 26, 1968), p. 264.

29. Jack Vaughn, "The Peace Corps: Now We Are Seven," *Saturday Review* (Jan. 6, 1968): 21–23.

30. "Peace Corps Aides Ask Wide Reform," *New York Times* (Nov. 19, 1967): 15:I.

31. Douglas Robinson, "800 Ex-Peace Corpsmen Protest War to President," *New York Times* (Mar. 6, 1967): II-3.

32. Richard Witkin, "24 in Peace Corps Urge Vietnam Talks," *New York Times* (Oct. 4, 1967): 15–1.

33. "We the Undersigned . . . Oppose the War in Vietnam," *Ramparts* (September 1967): 60–62.

34. Francis Polack, "Peace Corps Returnees: The New World They See," *The Nation* (July 3, 1967): 15–17.

35. Tolley, "Five Years of the Nixon Peace Corps," p. 97.

36. Sargent Shriver, quoted in *Congressional Record, House* (Dec. 8, 1971), H-11969-70.

37. Edward R. Roybal, Letter to T. Zane Reeves (Jan. 26, 1972).

38. Peace Corps, "Peace Corps 71: Becoming a Volunteer" (Washington: ACTION, 1971), 35 pages.

39. U.S. Congress, Senate, *Reorganization Plan No. 1 of 1971: Hearings before the Subcommittee on Executive Reorganization and Government Research*, Committee on Government Operations, 92nd Cong., 1st sess. (1971).

40. Ibid., p. 62.

41. U.S. Congress, Senate, *Congressional Record*, 93d Cong., 1st sess. (July 18, 1973), S. 1148.

42. U.S. President, Richard M. Nixon, Message to the House of Representatives, *Congressional Record,* 92d Cong., 1st sess. (Mar. 24, 1971).

43. Ibid., p. 62.

44. VISTA, *VISTA Volunteer* (Washington: Office of Economic Opportunity, n.d.), p. 20.

45. Neil A. Peirce, "Power to the Hispanics," *Los Angeles Times* (May 17, 1979): II-7.

46. ACTION, *ACTION: Fiscal Year 1974: Budget Domestic Programs Submission to Congress* (Washington: U.S. Government Printing Office, March 1973), appendixes 1–2.

47. Peirce, "Power to the Hispanics," p. 7.

48. ACTION, *ACTION: Fiscal Year 1974,* appendixes 1–2.

49. Balzano, "Political and Social Ramifications," pp. 476–77; emphasis added.

50. ACTION, Office of Policy and Program Development, "Planning Grant Guidelines: University Year for Action" (Washington: U.S. Government Printing Office, 1971).

51. Dick Graham, "University Year for Action," *Change: The Magazine of Higher Learning* 4 (Winter 1972–73): 7; ACTION, *ACTION: Fiscal Year 1974.*

52. Jerry Brady, "ACTION Memorandum: Resolution of the Conference. To: UYA Conference Participants," Washington (Dec. 15, 1971).

53. Joseph Blatchford, interview with T. Zane Reeves, Los Angeles (Sept. 9, 1971).

54. Ann Ventre and Russell Pratt, "Definitions and Assumptions: The Planned Impact Programming Process," San Francisco: ACTION Region IX (October 1973).

55. Arlene Krimgold, *Everything You Always Wanted to Know about UYA: University Year for ACTION: An Evaluation* (Washington: ACTION/University Year for ACTION, February 1973).

56. General Learning Corporation, *Proposal to ACTION to Prepare Volunteers for the University Year for ACTION* (Washington: General Learning Corporation, 1971).

57. Jerry Brady, "University Year for ACTION: A Report," presentation to the National Conference on Higher Education, 27th Annual Conference, Chicago (Mar. 6, 1972), p. 3.

58. Frank Thompson, Jr., quoted in U.S. Congress, Senate, Committee on Labor and Public Welfare, and the Special Committee on Human Resources, *ACTION Act of 1972 and ACTION Domestic Programs: Hearings* (Washington, April 1972), p. 308.

59. Michael P. Balzano, Jr., *Reorganizing the Federal Bureaucracy: The Rhetoric and the Reality* (Washington: American Enterprise Institute for Public Policy Research, 1977), p. 8.

60. Ibid.

61. ACTION, University Year for ACTION, *Programmatic Terms and Conditions* (Washington: University Year for ACTION, Jan. 1, 1972), p. 1.

62. Steve Skinner, "The Ghetto, the University, the Suburbs," *VISTA Volunteer* (September 1968): 12–15.

63. Ibid., pp. 13–14.

64. Marshall Windmiller, *The Peace Corps and Pax Americana* (Washington: Public Affairs Press, 1970), p. 162.

65. Tolley, "Five Years of the Nixon Peace Corps."

66. Joseph Blatchford, "The Peace Corps in Today's World" (Washington: ACTION, 1971), p. 7.

67. Christina Kenrick, "The New Face of the Peace Corps," *Christian Science Monitor* (Nov. 14, 1977), pp. 16–17.

68. Kenrick, "New Face," p. 16.

69. "Peace Corps 71: Becoming a Volunteer."

70. George C. Lodge, "The Case for the Generalist in Rural Development," Peace Corps faculty paper, no. 4 (Washington: Peace Corps, May 1969).

71. Tolley, "Five Years of the Nixon Peace Corps," p. 98.

72. Blatchford, "The Peace Corps in Today's World," p. 6.

73. Marlene Cimons, "Project Eases the Road Back: Peace Corps Volunteers Reoriented," *Los Angeles Times* (Aug. 23, 1970): E-10.

74. Joseph Blatchford, *The Peace Corps of the 1970s* (Washington: Peace Corps, 1969), p. 1.

75. Windmiller, *Peace Corps and Pax Americana,* pp. 140–41.

76. Ibid., p. 141.

Chapter Four

1. John W. Macy, Jr., "Candidates Discuss Appointees Now," *Institute of Public Affairs Report* 1 (Spring 1984): 12.

2. John W. Macy, Bruce Adams, and J. Jackson Walter, eds., *America's Unelected Government: Appointing the President's Team,* National Academy of Public Administration (Cambridge, Mass.: Ballinger, 1983), p. 17.

3. William M. Timmins, "Relations between Political Appointees, Careerists," *Public Administration Times* (Mar. 15, 1984): 8.

4. David S. Broder, *Changing of the Guard: Power and Leadership in America* (New York: Simon and Schuster, 1980), p. 185.

5. "Balzano Places Community First," *Inter-ACTION* (Apr. 1, 1973): 1.

6. Charles Murray, *Losing Ground: American Social Policy, 1950–1980* (New York: Basic Books, 1984).

7. Jeffrey St. John, "War on Poverty: It Cheated the Poor," *Los Angeles Times* (Apr. 15, 1973): 3–7.

8. Victor R. Fuchs, "Redefining Poverty and Redistributing Income," *The Public Interest* 4 (Summer 1967), p. 91.

9. "Poverty Agency's Birth Tied to 'Marxist' Idea," *Los Angeles Times* (Feb. 4, 1973): 4.

10. "White House Aides Ordered to Cut Staffs," *Los Angeles Times* (Sept. 9, 1973): 4.

11. J. Howard Phillips, "Annual Banquet: Middlesex Bar Association," transcribed remarks (Boston, Mar. 21, 1973).

12. U.S. Congress, Senate, *Congressional Record,* 93rd Cong., 1st sess. (July 18, 1973) S. 1148.

13. J. Howard Phillips, "General Principles," handout, no. 4 (Washington, 1973).

14. Michael Balzano, interview with T. Zane Reeves, Washington (Apr. 13, 1972).

15. Frederick V. Malek, "The Development of Public Executives: Neglect and Reform," *Public Administration Review* 34, no. 3 (May–June 1974): 230–33.

16. U.S. Congress, 2d sess., Select Committee on Presidential Campaign Activities, Book 19, "Federal Political Personnel Manual" (1974).

17. *Federal Times* (Oct. 16, 1974): 12.

18. U.S. Congress, "Federal Political Personnel Manual" (1974).

19. *Federal Times* (Dec. 18, 1974).

20. David N. Henderson, statement by chairman of the Subcommittee on Manpower and Civil Service, handout (Dec. 16, 1974); U.S. Congress, House Committee on Post Office and Civil Service, *Statement Regarding Alleged Political Influence in Personnel Actions at the General Services Administration,* handout (Oct. 10, 1974); U.S. Congress, House Committee on Post Office and Civil Service, *Documents Relating to Political Influence in Personnel Actions at the General Service Administration, Hearings before the Subcommittee on Manpower and Civil Service,* 93d Cong., 2d sess. (Oct. 7, 1974); Subcommittee on Manpower and Civil Service, *Documents Relating to Political Influence in Personnel Actions at the Department of Housing and Urban Development,* 93d Cong., 2d sess., Dec. 12, 1974.

21. Inderjit Badhwar, "More on GSA Referrals," *Federal Times* 10 (Jan. 19, 1976): 2; R. W. Apple, Jr., "U.S. Agency Held Political Target," *New York Times* (Jan. 13, 1975): 20; Jule Sugarman, "What the Administration Wanted," *The Bureaucrat* 6 (Summer 1978): 5–9.

22. The Malek Manual was first published in the official record of the Watergate hearings. See U.S. Congress, Senate Select Committee on Presidential Campaign Activities, *Watergate and Related Activities,* Book 19 (Washington: U.S. Government Printing Office, 1974).

23. Badhwar, "More on GSA Referrals," p. 2; George C. Koch, testimony submitted to U.S. Congress, Senate, *Nomination: Joseph H.*

Blatchford, Hearings before the Senate Committee on Labor and Public Welfare, 92d Cong., 1st sess., 1971.

24. Apple, "U.S. Agency," p. 2.

25. U.S. Congress, Senate, *Nomination: Christopher M. Mould, Hearings before the Senate Committee on Labor and Public Welfare,* 92d Cong., 2d sess., September 1972, p. 10.

26. Ibid., p. 23.

27. Ibid., p. 10.

28. Apple, "U.S. Agency," p. 20; Badhwar, "More on GSA Referrals," p. 2.

29. Rosetta Gainey, "Letter to A. T. Briley," testimony submitted, *ACTION Act of 1972 and ACTION Domestic Programs,* pp. 106–11.

30. John A. Butler, "Personnel Changes in Region IX," ACTION Region IX memorandum to Christopher M. Mould, reprinted in *ACTION Act of 1972 and ACTION Domestic Programs,* part I, p. 100.

31. Ibid., pp. 94, 102.

32. Michael A. Lerner, "Peace Corps Imperiled," *New Republic* 185 (Nov. 25, 1981): 7.

33. Inderjit Badhwar, "Use of ACTION Employees Alleged in Nixon Campaign," *Federal Times* (Oct. 18, 1972); Alan Cranston, in U.S. Congress, Senate, *Nomination: Charles W. Ervin, Hearings before the Committee on Labor and Public Welfare,* 92d Cong., 2d sess., Oct. 12, 1972, p. 8.

34. "ACTION: How Government Should Operate," *Government Executive* 8 (August 1976), p. 36.

35. "Balzano Places Community First," *Inter-ACTION* (April 1, 1973): 1.

36. John Ehrlichman, *Witness to Power: The Nixon Years* (New York: Simon and Schuster, 1982), p. 207.

37. Michael P. Balzano, Jr., "The Political and Social Ramifications of VISTA Programs: A Question of Ends and Means" (Ph.D. diss., Georgetown University, 1971).

38. "ACTION: How Government Should Operate," p. 36.

39. Michael P. Balzano, Jr., "ACTION," lecture given at ACTION Institute, New Orleans (Aug. 26, 1973).

40. U.S. President, Richard M. Nixon, *Public Papers of the President: 1971* (Washington: U.S. Government Printing Office, 1972), pp. 436, 911.

41. "Balzano Places Community First," p. 1.

42. Howard Higman, *ACTION Institutes: Summary of the Report, July 1973–January 1974,* CAR-DOC, #42 (Boulder: University of Colorado, Bureau of Sociological Research, 1974), p. 262.

43. Ibid.

44. "ACTION: How Government Should Operate," p. 36.

45. Balzano, "Political and Social Ramifications," p. 467.

46. Ibid.

47. "Balzano Places Community First," p. 1; "ACTION: How Government Should Operate," p. 36.

48. "Balzano Places Community First," p. 1.

49. Eric Moskowitz and Dick Simpson, "Experiments in Neighborhood Empowerment: Chicago as a Laboratory," *Urban Resources* 1 (Winter 1984): 33.

50. Michael P. Balzano, Jr., *Reorganizing the Federal Bureaucracy: The Rhetoric and the Reality* (Washington: American Enterprise Institute for Public Policy Research, 1977), p. 7.

51. Balzano, "Political and Social Ramifications," p. 474.

52. Higman, *ACTION Institutes,* p. 261.

53. Balzano, "Political and Social Ramifications," p. 473.

54. Balzano, interview with T. Zane Reeves.

55. Balzano, *Reorganizing the Federal Bureaucracy,* pp. 10, 28.

56. Ibid., p. 12.

57. Ibid., p. 10.

58. Ibid., p. 28.

59. T. Zane Reeves, "The Influence of Anti-Poverty Policymaking on Poverty Decision-Making: 1964–1974" (Ph.D. diss., University of Southern California, 1974).

60. Balzano, *Reorganizing the Federal Bureaucracy,* p. 41.

61. Arnold R. Kanarick and David L. Dotlich, "Honeywell's Agenda for Organizational Change" (Minneapolis: Honeywell, Inc., unpub., n.d.), p. 14.

62. *Management Development System Study Team Report on Developing Honeywell Managers in the 80's, Final Report* (Minneapolis: Honeywell, Inc., November 1980).

63. Kanarick and Dotlich, "Honeywell's Agenda," pp. 1–2.

64. Ibid.

65. Ibid., p. 14.

66. "ACTION: How Government Should Operate," p. 36.

Chapter Five

1. Jules Witcover, *Marathon: The Pursuit of the Presidency, 1972–1976* (New York: Viking Press, 1977), p. 630.

2. John Ehrlichman, *Witness to Power: The Nixon Years* (New York: Simon and Schuster, 1982), p. 245; Theodore H. White, *America in*

Search of Itself: The Making of the President, 1956–1980 (New York: Harper & Row, 1982), p. 112.

3. Robert Howard, "Sam Brown at ACTION," *New Republic* 180 (Feb. 10, 1979): 17; "Sam Brown: The Graying of an Activist," *Newsweek* (May 16, 1983): 15.

4. "Biography of Sam Brown," circulated by State of Colorado, Department of the Treasury, 303, 1973.

5. Sam Brown, *Storefront Organizing* (New York: Pyramid Press, 1972).

6. "Sam Brown: The Graying of an Activist," p. 15.

7. White, *America in Search of Itself,* p. 112.

8. Witcover, *Marathon,* p. 630.

9. Joseph Nocera, "Sam Brown and the Peace Corps—All Talk, No ACTION," *Washington Monthly* (September 1978): 28; James M. Perry, "The Peace Corps Is Far from Peaceful under Sam Brown," *Wall Street Journal* (Jan. 16, 1979): 1.

10. Christina Kenrick, "The New Face of the Peace Corps," *Christian Science Monitor* (Nov. 14, 1977): 16.

11. "*Penthouse* Interview: Sam Brown," *Penthouse* (December 1977): 218.

12. Kenrick, "New Face of the Peace Corps," p. 17.

13. "The Peace Corps: Ready for a Comeback," *U.S. News & World Report* (Oct. 17, 1977): 45.

14. Joe Blatchford, quoted by Kenrick, "New Face of the Peace Corps," p. 17.

15. Ibid.

16. "A Very Special Volunteer," *Ebony* (September 1978): 65.

17. Perry, "Peace Corps Far from Peaceful," p. 1.

18. Ibid.

19. "*Penthouse* Interview," p. 218.

20. Karen DeWitt, "Peace Corps Ideals Get Badly Mired in Politics," *New York Times* (May 6, 1979): E-4.

21. "*Penthouse* Interview," p. 218.

22. Kenrick, "New Face of Peace Corps," p. 16.

23. "*Penthouse* Interview," p. 226.

24. Kenrick, "New Face of Peace Corps," p. 4

25. Terrence Smith, "Peace Corps: Alive But Not So Well," *New York Times Magazine* (Dec. 25, 1977).

26. Howard, "Sam Brown at ACTION," p. 19.

27. Ibid.

28. Perry, "Peace Corps Far from Peaceful," p. 1.

29. DeWitt, "Peace Corps Ideals," p. E-4.

30. Perry, "Peace Corps Far from Peaceful," p. 1.

31. DeWitt, "Peace Corps Ideals," p. E-4.

32. "Peace Corps Chief Resigns in Dispute," *New York Times* (Nov. 26, 1978): E-5.

33. Howard, "Sam Brown at ACTION," p. 17.

34. Peace Corps lectures delivered to Peace Corps Training Project of the School for International Training of the Experiment in International Living, Brattleboro, Vt., July 7–Sept. 29, 1967.

35. "Why Critics Lambaste Sam Brown's Agency," *U.S. News & World Report* 86 (Jan. 15, 1979).

36. Kenrick, "New Face of Peace Corps," p. 16.

37. Perry, "Peace Corps Far from Peaceful," p. 1.

38. Ibid.

39. Nocera, "Brown and the Peace Corps," p. 36.

40. Georgie Anne Geyer, "A '60s Activist Comes Under Fire," *Los Angeles Times* (Apr. 1, 1979): II-2.

41. Smith, "Peace Corps," p. 9.

42. Ibid.

43. Don Bonker, "For a Go-Get'm Peace Corps," *Christian Science Monitor* (June 15, 1979): 23.

44. Marjorie Miller, "Peace Corps Returning to Its Origins: People-to-People Programs," *Los Angeles Times* (Sept. 12, 1977): 20.

45. "The Peace Corps: Out of ACTION?" *Newsweek* (Jan. 22, 1979): 5; "Balzano Identifies Trends in Peace Corps Decline," *American Enterprise Institute Memorandum* (Winter/Spring 1978): 6.

46. Marta McCave, "Activist Turns to Real Estate," *USA Today* (Nov. 15, 1983): 2A.

47. Jan Worth, "And a Battle-Weary Peace Corps Volunteer Comes in from the Heat," *Los Angeles Times* (Apr. 1, 1979): V-5; "How People in the Third World View U.S.," *U.S. News & World Report* (Nov. 26, 1979): 49–51; Landrum Bolling, "The Peace Corps: Making Friends for America," *Saturday Evening Post* 254 (September 1982): 66–67; Cable Neuhaus, "Memoir of the Peace Corps: 20 Years Later, Veterans Salute Its Enduring Hope," *People* 16 (July 20, 1981): 16–19.

48. Adele Visel, *Of Brahmins and Lesser Folk: The Tale of Another Peace Corps Grandmother in India* (New York: Vantage Press, 1979); David P. Visel, Introduction, *Of Brahmins and Lesser Folk*, p. ii.

49. Gerald T. Rice, *The Bold Experiment: JFK's Peace Corps* (Notre Dame, Ind.: Notre Dame University Press, 1985).

50. Eugene J. Koprowski, "Cultural Myths: Clues to Effective Management," *Organizational Dynamics* (Autumn 1983): 39–51.

51. "The Peace Corps: Ready," p. 45; "Protect the Peace Corps," editorial, *Boston Sunday Globe* (May 2, 1979): 24.

52. Bonker, "Go-Get'm Peace Corps," p. 23.

53. Smith, "Peace Corps," p. 10.

54. Kenrick, "New Face of the Peace Corps," p. 4.

55. Smith, "Peace Corps," p. 10.

56. Bonker, "Go-Get'm Peace Corps," p. 23.

57. Smith, "Peace Corps," p. 10.

58. U.S. General Accounting Office, *Changes Needed for a Better Peace Corps* (Feb. 6, 1979).

59. "Peace Corps Hit on Its Recruiting," *Los Angeles Times* (Feb. 13, 1979): pt. 1, p. 13.

60. Ibid.

61. "New Peace Corps Director," *Newsweek* (Mar. 26, 1979): 27.

62. Don Bonker, "To Brighten a Beacon of Overseas Aid," *New York Times* (Aug. 4, 1979): 18.

63. Donald Thorsen, "The Proper Parent for the Peace Corps," *New York Times* (Nov. 27, 1981): A-26.

64. DeWitt, "Peace Corps Ideals," p. E-4.

65. Paul Tsongas, quoted in "Peace Corps," in *Higher Education and National Affairs* 28, 24 (June 15, 1979): 3.

66. Geyer, "'60s Activist," p. II-2.

67. "Homing in on the Peace Corps," *New York Times* (July 6, 1979): A-20.

68. Kenrick, "New Face of Peace Corps," p. 16.

69. Neuhaus, "Memoir of the Peace Corps," p. 16.

70. Worth, "Battle-Weary Peace Corps Volunteer."

71. Joanne Omang, "Esprit de Corps: The Importance of Being Earnest," *Washington Post National Weekly Edition* (Nov. 11, 1985): 36.

72. Neal R. Peirce, "A '60s Activist in the '70s Street Corner War," *Los Angeles Times* (Sept. 10, 1978): IV-5.

73. "Sam Brown and Self-Help," editorial, *Christian Science Monitor* (June 19, 1980): 24.

74. ACTION, "VISTA: A Louder Voice for the Nation's Poor," ACTION pamphlet 4300.6, January 1978.

75. Ibid.

76. Ibid., p. 3.

77. Pierce, "'60s Activist in the '70s," p. IV-5.

78. ACTION, "VISTA," p. IV-9.

79. Peirce, "'60s Activist in the '70s," p. IV-5.

80. "*Penthouse* Interview," p. 222.

81. Jack Germond and Julie Witcover, "Sam Brown, A Man of AC-TION," *Los Angeles Herald-Examiner* (Jan. 18, 1979): II-3.

82. Ibid.

83. *"Penthouse* Interview," p. 222.

84. Peirce, "'60s Activist in the '70s," p. IV-5.

85. ACTION, "VISTA," p. 11.

86. Geyer, "'60s Activist Comes Under Fire," p. II-2.

87. Germond and Witcover, "Sam Brown," p. II-3.

88. Howard, "Sam Brown at ACTION," p. 19.

89. "ACTION: A Case of Mismanagement Hard at Work," *Government Executive* 12 (October 1980): 34–35.

Chapter Six

1. "The New Left in Government: From Protest to Policymaking," *Institution Analysis* (November 1978).

2. Harry C. Boyte, "Ronald Reagan and America's Neighborhoods: Undermining Community Initiative," in Alan Gartner, Colin Greer, and Frank Riesnan, *What Reagan Is Doing to Us* (New York: Harper & Row, 1982), pp. 109–24.

3. "Trench War over VISTA," *Wall Street Journal* (Aug. 17, 1982): 28; "Helping Others—It's Still in Style," *U.S. News & World Report* 88 (Feb. 18, 1980): 77–78.

4. Ann Hulbert, "VISTA's Lost Horizons," *New Republic* 187 (Aug. 30, 1982): 18–20.

5. David S. Broder, *Changing the Guard: Power and Leadership in America* (New York: Simon and Schuster), p. 1.

6. Burnley, "Take My Agency—Please!" *Conservative Digest* (April 1982): 34–45.

7. Robert J. McClory, "Self-help Funds Chopped," *National Catholic Reporter* (Feb. 11, 1983): 8–9.

8. Burnley, "Take My Agency," p. 34.

9. Ibid., p. 35.

10. Cass Peterson, "ACTION under Fire from Inside and Out," *Federal Report* 106 (Dec. 28, 1982): All.

11. "VISTA Faces Budget Cuts and Eventual Elimination," *Jet* (Apr. 30, 1981): 8.

12. "Trench War over VISTA," p. 28.

13. Charles Heatherley, ed., Heritage Foundation, *Mandate for Leadership: Policy Management in a Conservative Administration* (Washington, D.C., 1981), p. 1071.

14. "The VISTA Hit List," *Mother Jones* (April 1982): 11–12.

15. Heatherley, ed., *Mandate*, p. 1059.

16. U.S. Congress, House of Representatives, 97th Cong., 2d sess. (1983), Joint Hearing before Certain Subcommittees of the Committee on Government Operations and the Committee on Education and Labor. *VISTA and Management of the ACTION Agency.* Manpower and Housing Subcommittee of Committee on Government Operations, and Subcommittee on Select Education of the Committee on Education and Labor.

17. Ibid., p. 165.

18. Heatherley, *Mandate,* p. 1061.

19. Hulbert, "VISTA's Lost Horizons," p. 18.

20. Boyte, "Reagan and America's Neighborhoods," p. 119.

21. Mimi Mager, "Friends of VISTA" mailing (June 5, 1981).

22. "VISTA Hit List," p. 12.

23. Heritage Foundation, "New Left in Government," p. 23.

24. "Congress Watch," *National Review* 33 (May 29, 1981): 596–97.

25. Heritage Foundation, "New Left in Government," p. ii.

26. Article in the *National Review* (May 29, 1981): 596.

27. "Leftist Causes Aided by VISTA," *Conservative Digest* (April 1982): 35.

28. Heatherley, *Mandate,* p. 1059.

29. Hulbert, "VISTA's Lost Horizons," p. 19.

30. Boyte, "Reagan and America's Neighborhoods," p. 121.

31. McClory, "Self-help Funds," pp. 8–9.

32. Heatherley, *Mandate,* p. 1059.

33. McClory, "Self-help Funds," p. 9.

34. Heatherley, *Mandate,* p. 1059.

35. McClory, "Self-help Funds," p. 9.

36. Heritage Foundation, *The New Left in Government,* part II, "The VISTA Program as 'Institution-Building'" (Washington, 1981).

37. Hulbert, "VISTA's Lost Horizons," p. 20.

38. Ibid.

39. Ibid.

40. Peterson, "ACTION Under Fire."

41. Hulbert, "VISTA's Lost Horizons," p. 20.

42. *VISTA and Management of the ACTION Agency,* p. 18.

43. "Trench War over VISTA," p. 28.

44. *VISTA and Management of the ACTION Agency,* p. 10.

45. Ibid., p. 39.

46. Ibid., p. 120.

47. U.S. House of Representatives, 98th Cong. 1st sess., 1983, hearings before a subcommittee of the Committee on Appropriations, *Departments of Labor, Health and Human Services, Education and Related Agencies: Appropriations for 1984* (Washington: U.S. Government Printing Office, 1983), p. 384.

48. *VISTA and Management of the ACTION Agency,* p. 6.

49. Ibid., p. 16.

50. Hearings before subcommittee of Committee on Appropriations, *Appropriations for 1984,* 1986.

51. Ibid., p. 397.

52. Ibid., p. 399.

53. Ibid., p. 401.

54. Michael A. Lerner, "Peace Corps Imperiled," *New Republic* 185 (Nov. 25, 1981): 8.

55. David G. Wilck, "Congress Gives Struggling Peace Corps Another Chance," *Christian Science Monitor* (Dec. 22, 1981): 14.

56. Richard Scobey, "The Corps at Heart," *New York Times* (Feb. 26, 1981): A-19.

57. Wilck, "Congress Gives Peace Corps Another Chance," p. 14.

58. Lerner, "Peace Corps Imperiled," p. 8.

59. Philip Geyelin, "Peace Corps Is Caught Up in Unpeaceful Senselessness," *Los Angeles Times* (May 7, 1981): II-15; Gerald T. Rice, *The Bold Experiment: JFK's Peace Corps* (Notre Dame, Ind.: Notre Dame University Press, 1985).

60. Marshall Ingwerson, "Peace Corps Adapts to GOP Rule with 'Up by the Bootstraps' Theme," *Christian Science Monitor* (Apr. 21, 1981): 5.

61. Francis X. Clines and Bernard Weinraub, "Briefing," *New York Times* (Oct. 29, 1981): A-24.

62. David Broder, "Harassing the Peace Corps Chief," *Albuquerque Journal* (Jan. 18, 1982): A-6.

63. Ibid.

64. Rowland Evans and Robert Novak, "Liberal to the Corps," *Washington Post* (Jan. 1, 1982): A-23.

65. Broder, "Harassing the Peace Corps Chief," p. A-6.

66. Clines and Weinraub, "Briefing," p. A-10.

67. Ibid.; emphasis added.

68. "Peace Corps Conceded Taping of Conversation," *New York Times* (Jan. 9, 1984): 2.

69. Howard Kurtz, "Peace Corps Director Taped Talk with Her Deputy Last Summer," *Washington Post* (Jan. 7, 1984): A-3.

70. Ibid.

71. Ibid.

72. "Executive Notes," *Washington Post* (Oct. 7, 1982): A-25.

73. Ibid. (Nov. 11, 1982): A-25.

74. Ingwerson, "Peace Corps Adapts," p. 5.

75. Daniel Barry, "Brainwashing the Peace Corps," *The Nation* (May 7, 1983): 572–73.

76. Ibid., p. 572.

77. Ibid., p. 573.

78. Ibid.

79. "Peace Corps: Some Ex-Volunteers Uneasy over Central American Role," *New York Times* (Sept. 24, 1984): A-16.

80. Ibid.

81. Thomas J. McGrew, "For the Peace Corps, A Worthy Gamble," *Los Angeles Times* (Mar. 6, 1984): II-5.

82. "Peace Corps: Some Ex-Volunteers Uneasy."

83. McGrew, "For the Peace Corps," p. 5.

84. "Peace Corps: Some Ex-Volunteers Uneasy."

85. McGrew, "For the Peace Corps," p. 5.

86. "Peace Corps: Some Ex-Volunteers Uneasy."

87. Edith Evans Asbury, "The Peace Corps in Honduras: Practical and Basic," *New York Times* (Dec. 26, 1983): A-10.

88. "Grenada: Now the Peace Corps," *Christian Science Monitor* (Jan. 3, 1984): 23.

89. Wilck, "Congress Gives Peace Corps Another Chance," p. 14.

90. Ibid.

91. Barbara Crossette, "Peace Corps Seeks a Review of Cuts," *New York Times* (Nov. 1, 1981): I-9.

92. Heritage Foundation, "The Peace Corps: Out of Step with Reagan," *Institution Analysis* 33 (Dec. 5, 1984).

93. Robert M. Press, "Useful or Not, Anti-Poverty Programs Are Still Being Trimmed," *Christian Science Monitor* (Apr. 4, 1985): 6.

Chapter Seven

1. Daniel Barry, "Brainwashing the Peace Corps," *The Nation* (May 7, 1983): 572; Edmund Muskie, "The Frontier of Development," *Department of State Bulletin* (December 1980): pp. 4–6.

2. Heritage Foundation, "The Peace Corps: Out of Step with Reagan," p. 4.

3. Ibid., p. 8.

4. Kenneth E. Johnson, "How Liberal Are Bureaucrats?" *Washington Post National Weekly Edition* (Feb. 13, 1984): 38.

5. "Poll Indicates Baby-Boom Generation Prefers Reagan," *Albuquerque Journal* (May 12, 1984): A-3.

6. Barry Sussman, "Reagan's Policies Are the Key—Not His Personality," *Washington Post National Weekly Edition* (Feb. 13, 1984): 37.

7. *Albuquerque Journal* (July 12, 1984): A-1.

8. Thomas R. Dye and Harmon Ziegler, *The Irony of Democracy,* 6th ed. (Monterey, Calif.: Brooks/Cole, 1984).

9. Timothy McQuay, "Thousands Answer Peace Corps Call," *USA Today* (Feb. 8, 1985); Elizabeth Greene, "Applications for Peace Corps Rise Dramatically; Recruiting Tactics, Altruism, Anniversary Cited," *Chronicle of Higher Education* (Jan. 15, 1986): 29–32.

10. Howard Smith, *The Three Biggest Lies of a Politician Who Has Just Won* (Secaucus, N.J.: Castle Books, 1979), p. 29.

11. James W. Fesler, "Politics, Policy, and Bureaucracy at the Top," *Annals of the American Academy of Political and Social Science* 466 (March 1983): 23–41.

12. James W. Fesler, *Public Administration: Theory and Practice* (Englewood Cliffs, N.J.: Prentice-Hall, 1980), p. 134.

13. Dean E. Mann, with Jameson W. Doig, *The Assistant Secretaries: Problems and Processes of Appointment* (Washington: Brookings Institution, 1985).

14. Lloyd W. Warner et al., *The American Federal Executive* (New Haven: Yale University Press, 1963).

15. Thomas P. Murphy, Donald E. Neuchterlein, and Ronald J. Stupak, *Inside the Bureaucracy: The View from the Assistant Secretary's Desk* (Boulder: Westview Press, 1978).

16. Frederick C. Mosher, *Democracy and the Public Service,* 2d ed. (New York: Oxford University Press, 1982), p. 179.

17. Roger G. Brown, "Party and Bureaucracy: The Presidents since JFK," paper prepared for the 1981 annual meeting of the American Political Science Association (New York, Sept. 3–6, 1982), tables 1–10.

18. Mann and Doig, *Assistant Secretaries.*

19. Joel D. Aberbach, James D. Chesney, and Burt A. Rockman, "Exploring Elite Political Attitudes," *Political Methodology* 2, no. 1 (1975): 1–28.

20. Arch Patton, "Government's Revolving Door," *Business Week* (Sept. 22, 1973): 13.

21. National Academy of Public Administration, *Watergate: Its Implications for Responsible Government* (New York: National Academy of Public Administration, 1974), p. 107.

22. Howard Rosen, *Servants of the People: The Uncertain Future of the Federal Civil Service* (Salt Lake City: Olympus Publishing, 1985).

23. U.S. House of Representatives, *Department of Labor, Health and Human Services, Education, and Related Agencies Appropriations for 1984,* part VII, Hearings before subcommittee of the Committee Appropriations, 98th Cong., 1st sess. (Washington: U.S. Government Printing Office, 1983), p. 377.

24. T. Zane Reeves, "An Analysis of Appointee Backgrounds to ACTION, Peace Corps and VISTA: 1961–1985," unpub. paper, 1985.

25. Hugh Heclo, "A Government of Enemies," *The Bureaucrat* (Fall 1984): 12–15.

26. John W. Macy, Jr., "Candidates Discuss Appointees Now," *IPA Report* (Spring 1984): 12; Jeffrey A. Bragg, "Accountability without More Political Appointments," *Management* 4, 3 (1984): 29.

27. Returned Peace Corps Volunteers of Washington, D.C., "Peace Corps 1985: Meeting the Challenge" (Washington, 1985).

28. Warren G. Schmidt and Robert Tannenbaum, "Management of Differences," *Harvard Business Review* (November–December 1960): 107–15.

29. Heritage Foundation, *Mandate for Leadership II: Continuing the Conservative Revolution* (Washington, 1984).

30. Michael Senera, quoted in Eric Wiesenthal, "Top Reagan Aide Opposes Policy Role Freeze," *Public Administration Times* (Jan. 1, 1985): 12.

31. Sandy Grady, "Yes, There Is Idealism in Yuppieland," *Albuquerque Journal* (Jan. 24, 1985).

32. Nancy Shute, "After a Turbulent Youth, the Peace Corps Comes of Age," *Smithsonian* 16 (February 1986): 81–89.

Bibliography

Aberbach, Joel D., James D. Chesney, and Burt A. Rockman, "Exploring Elite Political Attitudes." *Political Methodology* 2 (1975): 1–28.

ACTION. *ACTION: Fiscal Year 1974: Budget Domestic Programs, Submission to Congress.* Washington: U.S. Government Printing Office, March 1973.

———. Office of Policy and Program Development. "Planning Grant Guidelines: University Year for Action." Washington: U.S. Government Printing Office, 1971.

———. University Year for Action. *Programmatic Terms and Conditions.* Washington: University Year for ACTION, January 1, 1972.

———. "VISTA: A Louder Voice for the Nation's Poor." ACTION pamphlet, no. 4300, 6. Washington, January 1978.

"ACTION: A Case of Mismanagement at Work." *Government Executive* 12 (October 1980): 34–36.

"ACTION: How Government Should Operate." *Government Executive* 8 (August 1976): 36–40.

Alinsky, Saul D. "The War on Poverty—Political Pornography." In *Poverty, Power, Politics,* edited by Chaim Waxman, 171–79. New York: Grosset & Dunlap, 1968.

Allensworth, Donald T. *The U.S. Government in Action: Public Policy and Change.* Pacific Palisades, Calif.: Goodyear Publishing, 1972.

Alsop, Joseph. "The Legacy of John F. Kennedy: Memories of an Uncommon Man." *Saturday Evening Post* 21 (November 1964): 15–19.

American Society for Public Administration. "Centennial Agendas Projects." Newsletter #6 (December 1983).

Apple, R. W., Jr. "U.S. Agency Held Political Target." *New York Times* (January 13, 1975).

Badhwar, Inderjit. "More on GSA Referrals." *Federal Times* 10 (January 19, 1976): 2:16.

———. "Use of ACTION Employees Alleged in Nixon Campaign." *Federal Times* (October 18, 1972).

Baldwin, Fred D. *Evaluating the OEO Legal Services Program: Working Papers.* Washington: Office of Economic Opportunity (July 1972).

Balzano, Michael P., Jr. "ACTION." Lecture given at the ACTION Institute, New Orleans (August 26, 1973).

————. ACTION Director, Washington. Interview, April 13, 1972.

————. "The Political and Social Ramifications of VISTA Programs: A Question of Ends and Means." Ph.D. diss., Georgetown University, 1971.

————. *Reorganizing the Federal Bureaucracy: The Rhetoric and the Reality.* Washington: American Enterprise Institute for Public Policy Research (1977).

"Balzano Identifies Trends in Peace Corps Decline." *American Enterprise Institute Memorandum* (Winter/Spring 1978): 6.

"Balzano Places Community First." *Inter-ACTION* (April 1, 1973): 1–3.

Barbato, Joseph. "America Imagines the FBI." *Chronicle of Higher Education* (January 25, 1984): 5–6.

Barnard, Chester. *The Function of the Executive.* Cambridge, Mass.: Harvard University Press, 1968.

Barry, Daniel. "Brainwashing the Peace Corps." *The Nation* (May 7, 1983): 572–73.

Berreman, Gerald D. "The Peace Corps: A Dream Betrayed." *The Nation* (February 26, 1968): 263–68.

Biddy, John, and Roger Davidson. *On Capitol Hill: Studies in the Legislative Process.* New York: Holt, Rinehart & Winston, 1967.

"Biography of Sam Brown." Circulated by the Department of the Treasury, State of Colorado, 1973.

Blatchford, Joseph. Interview, Los Angeles, September 9, 1971.

————. "The Peace Corps in Today's World." Washington: ACTION, 1971.

————. *The Peace Corps of the 1970s.* Washington: Peace Corps, 1969.

Bluementhal, Richard. "The Bureaucracy: Anti-Poverty and the Community Action Program." In *American Political Institutions and Public Policy,* edited by Allan Sindler, 128–70. Boston: Little, Brown, 1969.

Bolling, Landrum. "The Peace Corps: Making Friends for America." *Saturday Evening Post* 254 (September 1982): 66–67.

Bonker, Don. "For a Go-Get'm Peace Corps." *Christian Science Monitor* (June 15, 1979): 23.

————. "To Brighten a Beacon of Overseas Aid." *New York Times* (August 4, 1979): 18.

Bookbinder, Hyman H. "OEO Veterans Sad, Not Bitter, about Its End." *Los Angeles Times* (April 12, 1973): I:12.

Book Review Digest: 1961. New York: H. W. Wilson Co., 1962.

Boyte, Harry C. "Ronald Reagan and America's Neighborhoods: Undermining Community Initiative." In *What Reagan Is Doing to Us,* edited by Alan Gartner, Colin Greer, and Frank Riesnan, 109–24. New York: Harper & Row, 1982.

Brady, Jerry. "ACTION Memorandum: Resolution of the Conference. To: UYA Conference Participants." Washington, December 15, 1971.

———. "University Year for Action: A Report." Presentation to the National Conference on Higher Education, 27th Annual Conference, Chicago, March 6, 1972.

Bragg, Jeffrey A. "Accountability without More Political Appointments." *Management* 4 (1984): 29.

Brauer, Carl M. "Kennedy, Johnson and the War on Poverty." *Journal of American History* 69 (June 1982): 98–119.

"Bridging the Gap: A Dialogue." *Management* 3 (Fall 1982): 2–9.

Broder, David S. *Changing of the Guard: Power and Leadership in America.* New York: Simon and Schuster, 1980.

———. "Harassing the Peace Corps Chief." *Albuquerque Journal* 18, (January 18, 1982): A-6.

Brown, Roger G. "Party and Bureaucracy: The Presidents since JFK." Paper prepared for the 1981 annual meeting of the American Political Science Association, New York, September 3–6, 1982.

Brown, Sam. *Storefront Organizing.* New York: Pyramid Press, 1972.

Bullock, Charles S. III, James E. Anderson, and David W. Brady. *Public Policy in the Eighties.* Monterey, Calif.: Brooks/Cole, 1983.

Burnley, James. "Take My Agency—Please!" *Conservative Digest* (April 1982): 34–45.

Bush, Gerald William. "The Peace Corps, 1961–1965: A Study in Open Organization." Ph.D. diss., Northern Illinois University, 1968.

Business Periodicals Index: July 1962–June 1963. New York: H. W. Wilson Co., 1963.

Butler, John A. "Personnel Changes in Region IX." ACTION Region IX memorandum to Christopher M. Mould. Reprinted in *ACTION Act of 1972 and ACTION Domestic Programs,* part I, pp. 94, 100, 102.

Carleton, William G. "Kennedy in History." *Antioch Review* 24 (Fall 1964): 277–99.

Carpenter, Liz. *Ruffles and Flourishes.* Garden City, N.Y.: Doubleday, 1970.

———. "Why I Believe LBJ Was a Winner." *Parade* (June 5, 1983).

Caudill, Harry. *Night Comes to the Cumberlands.* Boston: Little, Brown, 1962.

Cimons, Marlene. "Project Eases the Road Back: Peace Corps Volunteers Reoriented." *Los Angeles Times* (August 23, 1970): E-10.

Clines, Francis X., and Bernard Weinraub. "Briefing." *New York Times* (October 29, December 5, 1981).

Clute, Judith A. "Personnel Management in the Peace Corps." *Public Personnel Review* (July 23, 1962): 163–65.

"Congress Watch." *National Review* 33 (May 29, 1981): 596–97.

Crossette, Barbara. "Peace Corps Seeks a Review of Cuts." *New York Times* (November 1, 1981): I-9.

Deal, Terrance, and Allan Kennedy. *Corporate Cultures: The Rites and Rituals of Corporate Life.* Reading, Mass.: Addison-Wesley, 1982.

DeWitt, Karen. "Peace Corps Ideals Get Badly Mired in Politics." *New York Times* (May 6, 1979): E-4.

Donovan, John C. *The Politics of Poverty.* New York: Pegasus, 1967.

Downs, Anthony. *Inside Bureaucracy.* Boston: Little, Brown, 1967.

Driscoll, James W., Gary L. Cowger, and Robert J. Egan. "SMR Forum: Private Managers and Public Myths—Public Managers and Private Myths." *Sloan Management Review* 21 (Fall 1979): 53–57.

Dye, Thomas R., and L. Harmon Ziegler. *The Irony of Democracy: An Uncommon Introduction to American Politics,* 6th ed. Monterey, Calif.: Brooks/Cole Press, 1984.

Ehrlichman, John. *Witness to Power: The Nixon Years.* New York: Simon and Schuster, 1982.

Evans Asbury, Edith. "The Peace Corps in Honduras: Practical and Basic." *New York Times* (December 26, 1983): A-10.

Evans, Rowland, and Robert Novak. "Liberal to the Corps." *Washington Post* (January 1, 1982): A-23.

"Executive Notes." *Washington Post* (October 7, November 11, 1982): A-25.

Fesler, James W. "Politics, Policy and Bureaucracy at the Top." *Annals of the American Academy of Political and Social Science* 466 (March 1983): 23–41.

———. *Public Administration: Theory and Practice.* Englewood Cliffs, N.J.: Prentice-Hall, 1980.

Freud, Sigmund. *Civilization and Its Discontents.* New York: W. W. Norton, 1961.

Fuchs, Victor R. "Redefining Poverty and Redistributing Income." *The Public Interest* 4 (Summer 1967): 91.

Gainey, Rosetta. "Letter to A. T. Briley." Testimony submitted to Senate Committee of Labor and Public Welfare and the Special Committee on Human Resources, Subcommittee on Aging. *ACTION Act of 1972 and ACTION Domestic Programs,* part I. Washington, April 1972, pp. 106–11.

Gallup, George. *The Gallup Poll: Public Opinion, 1935–1971.* Vol. 3. New York: Random House, 1972.

General Learning Corporation. *Proposal to ACTION to Prepare Volunteers for the University Year for ACTION.* Washington: General Learning Corporation, 1971.

Germond, Jack, and Julie Witcover. "Sam Brown, A Man of ACTION." *Los Angeles Herald Examiner* (January 18, 1979): II-3.

Geyelin, Philip. "Peace Corps Is Caught Up in Unpeaceful Senselessness." *Los Angeles Times* (May 7, 1981): II-15.

Geyer, Georgie Anne. "A '60s Activist Comes Under Fire." *Los Angeles Times* (April 1, 1979): V-5.

Gilder, George. *Wealth and Poverty.* New York: Basic Books, 1981.

Gladwin, Thomas. *Poverty, U.S.A.* Boston: Little, Brown, 1967.

Goldman, Eric. *The Tragedy of Lyndon Johnson.* New York: Dell Publishing, 1969.

Gottlieb, David. "The Socialization and Politicization of VISTA Volunteers: Sex and Generational Differences." *Journal of Voluntary Action Research* 3 (Winter 1974): 109.

――――. *VISTA and Its Volunteers.* University Park, Pa.: Pennsylvania State University (March 1971).

Grady, Sandy. "Yes, There Is Idealism in Yuppieland." *Albuquerque Journal* (January 24, 1985).

Graham, Billy. "How To Face Temptation," sermon, Kemper Arena, Kansas City, Mo., August 31, 1978.

Graham, Dick. "University Year for Action." *Change: The Magazine of Higher Learning* 4 (Winter 1972–73): 7.

Greene, Elizabeth. "Applications for Peace Corps Rise Dramatically; Recruiting Tactics, Altruism, Anniversary Cited." *Chronicle of Higher Education* (January 15, 1986): 29–32.

"Grenada: Now the Peace Corps." *Christian Science Monitor* (January 3, 1984): 23.

Harrington, Michael. *The Other America.* New York: Macmillan, 1962.

Heclo, Hugh. "A Government of Enemies." *The Bureaucrat* (Fall 1984): 12–15.

――――. *A Government of Strangers: Executive Politics in Washington.* Washington: Brookings Institution, 1977.

"Helping Others—It's Still in Style." *U.S. News & World Report* 88 (February 18, 1980): 77–78.

Henderson, David N. Subcommittee on Manpower and Civil Service, statement by chairman, handout, December 16, 1974.

Heritage Foundation. *Mandate for Leadership: Policy Management in a Conservative Administration.* Edited by Charles Heatherley. Washington, 1981.

———. *Mandate for Leadership II: Continuing the Conservative Revolution.* Washington, 1984.

———. "The New Left in Government: From Protest to Policymaking." *Institution Analysis* 9 (November 1978).

———. "The New Left in Government, Part II: The VISTA Program as 'Institution Building.'" Washington, 1981.

———. "The Peace Corps: Out of Step with Reagan." *Institution Analysis* 33 (December 1984).

Higman, Howard. *ACTION Institutes: Summary of the Report, July 1973–January 1974,* CAR-DOC, #42. Boulder: University of Colorado: Bureau of Sociological Research, 1974.

"Homing in on the Peace Corps." *New York Times* (July 6, 1979): A-20.

"How People in the Third World View U.S." *U.S. News & World Report* (November 26, 1979): 49–51.

Howard, Robert. "Sam Brown at ACTION." *New Republic* 180 (February 10, 1979): 17–21.

Hulbert, Ann. "VISTA's Lost Horizons." *New Republic* 187 (August 30, 1982): 18–20.

Humphrey, Hubert. *The Education of a Public Man: My Life and Politics.* Garden City, N.Y.: Doubleday, 1976.

Ingwerson, Marshall. "Peace Corps Adapts to GOP Rule with 'Up by the Bootstraps' Theme." *Christian Science Monitor* (April 21, 1981): 5.

Johnson, Kenneth E. "How Liberal Are Bureaucrats?" *Washington Post National Weekly Edition* (February 13, 1984): 38.

Johnson, Lyndon Baines. *Public Papers of the President of the United States: 1964.* Washington: U.S. Government Printing Office, 1964.

———. *The Vantage Point.* New York: Holt, Rinehart & Winston, 1971.

Kanarick, Arnold R., and David L. Dotlich. "Honeywell's Agenda for Organizational Change." Minneapolis: Honeywell, Inc., unpub., n.d.

Kenrick, Christina. "New Attempts to Reorganize the Peace Corps." *Christian Science Monitor* (March 12, 1979): 4.

———. "New Face of the Peace Corps." *Christian Science Monitor* (November 14, 1977): 16–17.

Kershaw, Joseph A. *Government Against Poverty.* Chicago: Markham Publishing, 1970.

Keyserling, Leon. *Poverty and Deprivation in the United States.* Washington: Conference on Economic Progress (April 1962).

Kirschten, Dick. "Administration Using Carter-Era Reform to Manipulate the Levers of Government." *National Journal* (April 9, 1983): 732–36.

Koprowski, Eugene J. "Cultural Myths: Clues to Effective Management." *Organizational Dynamics* (Autumn 1983): 39–51.

Koshel, Patricia. *Working Papers: Migration and the Poor.* Office of Economic Opportunity, Washington (July 1972).

Krimgold, Arlene. *Everything You Always Wanted to Know about UYA: University Year for ACTION: An Evaluation.* Washington: ACTION/ University Year for ACTION (February 1973).

Kurtz, Howard. "Peace Corps Director Taped Talk with Her Deputy Last Summer." *Washington Post* (January 7, 1984): A-3.

Lane, Robert E. *Political Ideology: Why the American Common Man Believes What He Does.* New York: Free Press, 1962.

Latham, Earl. *J. F. Kennedy and Presidential Power.* Lexington, Mass.: D. C. Heath, 1972.

"LBJ's Job Corps: Full of Hope, Naiveté." *Los Angeles Times* (December 25, 1980): I-A.

"Leftist Causes Aided by VISTA." *Conservative Digest* (April 1982): 35.

Lerner, Michael A. "Peace Corps Imperiled." *New Republic* 185 (November 25, 1981): 7–8.

Lodge, George C. "The Case for the Generalist in Rural Development." Peace Corps faculty paper no. 4. Washington: Peace Corps, May 1969.

McCave, Marta. "Activist Turns to Real Estate." *USA TODAY* (November 15, 1983): 2-A.

McClelland, David. *The Achieving Society.* New York: Free Press, 1961.

McClory, Robert J. "Self-Help Funds Chopped." *National Catholic Reporter* (February 11, 1983): 8–9.

McDonald, Dwight. "Our Invisible Poor." *New Yorker* (January 19, 1963).

McGrew, Thomas J. "For the Peace Corps, A Worthy Gamble." *Los Angeles Times* (March 6, 1984): II-5.

McNaspy, C. J. "Whatever Happened to the Peace Corps?" *America* 31 (January 15, 1983): 29–31.

McQuay, Timothy. "Thousands Answer Peace Corps Call." *USA Today* (February 8, 1985): 3–4.

Machiavelli, Niccolò. *The Prince* and *Discourses.* New York: Random House, 1950.

Macy, John W., Jr. "Candidates Discuss Appointees Now." *Institute of Public Affairs Report* 1 (Spring 1984): 12.

Macy, John W., Bruce Adams, and J. Jackson Walter, eds. *America's Unelected Government: Appointing the President's Team.* National Academy of Public Administration. Cambridge, Mass.: Ballinger, 1983.

Mager, Mimi. "Friends of VISTA" mailing (June 5, 1981).

Malek, Frederick V. "The Development of Public Executives: Neglect and Reform." *Public Administration Review* 34, no. 3 (May–June 1974): 230–33.

Management Development System Study Team Report on Developing Honeywell Managers in the 80's, Final Report. Minneapolis: Honeywell, Inc., November 1980.

"Managing Corporate Cultures." Brochure describing the conference announcement and call for papers by the Program in Corporate Culture, University of Pittsburgh, Graduate School of Business, n.d.

Mann, Dean E., and Jameson W. Doig. *The Assistant Secretaries: Problems and Processes of Appointment.* Washington: Brookings Institution, 1985.

Martin, Joanne, and Caren Siehl. "Organizational Culture and Counterculture: An Uneasy Symbiosis." *Organizational Dynamics* (August 1983): 52–64.

Miller, Jim. "Camelot Revisited." *Newsweek* (April 3, 1983): 75–76.

Miller, Marjorie. "Peace Corps Returning to Its Origins: People-to-People Programs." *Los Angeles Times* (September 12, 1977): 20.

Miller, Merle. *Lyndon: An Oral Biography.* New York: G. P. Putnam's Sons, 1980.

Mosher, Frederick C. *Democracy and the Public Service.* 2d ed. New York: Oxford University Press, 1982.

Moskowitz, Eric, and Dick Simpson. "Experiments in Neighborhood Empowerment: Chicago as a Laboratory." *Urban Resources* 1 (Winter 1984): 33.

Moynihan, Daniel P. *Maximum Feasible Misunderstanding: Community Action and the "War on Poverty."* New York: Free Press, 1969.

Murphy, Thomas P., Donald E. Neuchterlein, and Ronald J. Stupak. *Inside the Bureaucracy: The View from the Assistant Secretary's Desk.* Boulder: Westview Press, 1978.

Murray, Charles. *Losing Ground: American Social Policy, 1950–1980.* New York: Basic Books, 1984.

Muskie, Edmund. "The Frontier of Development." *Department of State Bulletin* (December 1980): 4–6.

Nathan, Richard P. *The Administrative Presidency.* New York: John Wiley, 1983.

National Academy of Public Administration. *Watergate: Its Implications for Responsible Government.* New York: National Academy of Public Administration, 1974.

Neuhaus, Cable. "Memoir of the Peace Corps: 20 Years Later, Veterans Salute Its Enduring Hope." *People* 16 (July 20, 1981): 16–19.

"New Peace Corps Director." *Newsweek* (March 26, 1979): 27.

New York Times Index for Published News of 1962. New York: New York Times Co., 1963.

Nocera, Joseph. "Sam Brown and the Peace Corps—All Talk, No ACTION." *Washington Monthly* (September 1978): 28–40.

Omang, Joanne. "Esprit de Corps: The Importance of Being Earnest." *Washington Post National Weekly Edition* (November 11, 1985): 36.

Osbaine, Cecil. "Kennedy: The Making of a Myth." *National Review* 20 (November 5, 1969): 1113–14.

Parmet, Herbert S. *J. F. K.—The Presidency of John F. Kennedy.* New York: Dial, 1983.

Pass, David Jacob. "The Politics of VISTA in the War on Poverty: A Study of Ideological Conflict." Ph.D. diss., Columbia University, 1976.

Patterson, James T. *America's Struggle Against Poverty 1900–1980.* Cambridge, Mass.: Harvard University Press, 1981.

Patton, Arch. "Government's Revolving Door." *Business Week* (September 22, 1973): 13.

Peace Corps. Lectures delivered to Peace Corps Training Project of the School for International Training of the Experiment in International Living, Brattleboro, Vt., July 7–September 29, 1967.

———. "Peace Corps 71: Becoming a Volunteer." Washington: ACTION, 1971.

"Peace Corps." *Higher Education and National Affairs* 28 (June 15, 1979): 3.

"Peace Corps Aides Ask Wide Reform." *New York Times* (November 19, 1967): 15-I.

"Peace Corps Chief Resigns in Dispute." *New York Times* (November 26, 1978): E-5.

"Peace Corps Conceded Taping of Conversation." *New York Times* (January 9, 1984): 2.

"Peace Corps Hit on Its Recruiting." *Los Angeles Times* (February 13, 1979): I-13.

"The Peace Corps: Out of ACTION?" *Newsweek* (January 22, 1979): 5.

"Peace Corps: Ready for a Comeback." *U.S. News & World Report* (October 17, 1977): 45–56.

"Peace Corps: Some Ex-Volunteers Uneasy over Central American Role." *New York Times* (September 24, 1984): A-16.

Peirce, Neal A. "A '60s Activist in the '70s Street Corner War." *Los Angeles Times* (September 10, 1978): V-5.

———. "Power to the Hispanics." *Los Angeles Times* (May 17, 1979): II-7.

"Penthouse Interview: Sam Brown." *Penthouse* (December 1977): 185–232.

Perry, James M. "The Peace Corps Is Far from Peaceful under Sam Brown." *Wall Street Journal* (January 16, 1979): 1.

Peters, Guy B. *The Politics of Bureaucracy: A Comparative Perspective.* New York: Longman, 1978.

Peters, Thomas J., and Robert H. Waterman, Jr. *In Search of Excellence: Lessons from America's Best-Run Companies.* New York: Harper & Row, 1982.

Peterson, Cass. "ACTION under Fire from Inside and Out." *Federal Report* 106 (December 28, 1982).

Phillips, J. Howard. "Annual Banquet, Middlesex Bar Association," Boston, March 21, 1973. Transcribed remarks.

_____. "Evening Edition." Washington, February 6, 1973. Transcript of tape recording.

_____. "General Principles." Handout, no. 4. Washington, 1973.

Polack, Francis. "Peace Corps Returnees: The New World They See." *The Nation* (July 3, 1967): 15–17.

"Poll Indicates Baby-Boom Generation Prefers Reagan." *Albuquerque Journal* (May 12, 1984): A-3.

"The Poor in Their Place." *New Republic* 153 (November 20, 1965): 5–6.

Potter, David M. *People of Plenty: Economic Abundance and the American Character.* Chicago: University of Chicago Press, 1954.

"Poverty Agency's Birth Tied to 'Marxist' Idea." *Los Angeles Times* (February 4, 1973): 4.

Press, Robert M. "Useful or Not, Anti-Poverty Programs Are Still Being Trimmed." *Christian Science Monitor* (April 4, 1985): 5–6.

Prossner, W. R. *Working Papers: Day Care in the Seventies, Some Thoughts.* Office of Economic Opportunity, Washington, May 1972.

"Protect the Peace Corps." *Boston Sunday Globe* (May 2, 1979): 24.

Reeves, T. Zane. "An Analysis of Appointee Backgrounds to ACTION, Peace Corps and VISTA: 1961–1985." Unpub. paper, 1985.

_____. "The Influence of Anti-Poverty Policymaking on Poverty Decision-Making: 1964–1974." Ph.D. diss., University of Southern California, 1974.

_____. "The Influence of Partisan Orientations on the Role of Voluntary Action in Anti-Poverty Agencies." *Journal of Voluntary Action Research* 3 (Winter 1974): 75–81.

Returned Peace Corps Volunteers of Washington, D.C. "Peace Corps, 1985: Meeting the Challenge." Washington, 1985.

Rice, Gerald T. *The Bold Experiment: J. F. K.'s Peace Corps.* Notre Dame, Ind.: Notre Dame University Press, 1985.

_____. "The Bold Experiment: Remarks on the Occasion of the 25th Anniversary of John F. Kennedy's First Announcement of the Peace Corps." Ann Arbor, November 2, 1985. Text of speech.

Rideout, Christine. "Job Corps." Case study, Harvard University, Inter-Collegiate Clearing House, 1974.

Robinson, Douglas. "800 Ex-Peace Corpsmen Protest War to President." *New York Times* (March 6, 1967): II-3.

Rosen, Howard. *Servants of the People: The Uncertain Future of the Federal Civil Service.* Salt Lake City: Olympus Publishing, 1985.

Roszak, Theodore. *The Making of a Counter Culture: Reflections on the Technocratic Society and Its Youthful Opposition.* New York: Doubleday, 1969.

Roybal, Edward R. Letter to T. Zane Reeves, January 26, 1972.

Ruppe, Loret Miller. "A Wise Investment in Peace." *Christian Science Monitor* (October 22, 1981): 23.

———. "Why a Peace Corps in the 1980s?: The Way of Human Caring and Sharing." *Vital Speeches of the Day* 47 (September 15, 1981): 720–24.

St. John, Jeffrey. "War on Poverty: It Cheated the Poor." *Los Angeles Times* (April 15, 1973): 3–7.

Salinger, Pierre. *With Kennedy.* New York: Doubleday, 1966.

"Sam Brown: The Graying of an Activist." *Newsweek* (May 16, 1983): 15.

"Sam Brown and Self-Help." *Christian Science Monitor* (June 19, 1980): 24.

Santoli, Al. "Is the Peace Corps Obsolete?" *Parade* (March 27, 1983): 14–17.

Schein, Edgar H. "The Role of the Founder in Creating Organizational Culture." *Organizational Dynamics* (Summer 1983): 13–28.

Schlesinger, Arthur M., Jr. *A Thousand Days: John F. Kennedy in the White House.* Boston: Houghton Mifflin, 1965.

Schmidt, Warren G., and Robert Tannenbaum. "Management of Differences." *Harvard Business Review* (November–December 1960): 107–15.

Scobey, Richard. "The Corps at Heart." *New York Times* (February 26, 1981): A-19.

Seiden, Matt. "Brazil: From Dream to Despair; The Peace Corps Tries Hard But Is Ousted with Job Half-Done." *Los Angeles Times* (December 10, 1980): II-11.

Selznick, Philip. *T.V.A. and the Grassroots: A Study in the Sociology of Formal Organization.* Berkeley: University of California Press, 1980.

Sennett, Richard. "Survival of the Fattest." *New York Review of Books* (August 13, 1970): 23–26.

Shogan, Robert. "When Idealism Was in Flower." *New York Times Book Review* (February 9, 1986): ii.

Shriver, Sargent. Address, Twenty-Fifth Anniversary of the Peace Corps. Ann Arbor, University of Michigan, October 7, 1985.

———. "The Peace Corps: Free Human Services." *Vital Speeches of the Day* 47 (September 1, 1981): 700–704.

Shute, Nancy. "After a Turbulent Youth, the Peace Corps Comes of Age." *Smithsonian* 16 (February 1986): 80–89.

Skinner, Steve. "The Ghetto, the University, the Suburbs." *VISTA Volunteer* (September 1968): 12–15.

Smith, Howard K. *The Three Biggest Lies.* Secaucus, N.J.: Castle Books, 1979.

Smith, Terrence. "Peace Corps: Alive But Not So Well." *New York Times Magazine* (December 25, 1977): 7–10.

Solberg, Carl. *Hubert Humphrey.* New York: W. W. Norton, 1984.

Sorcnsen, Theodore C. *Kennedy.* New York: Harper & Row, 1964.

Staats, Elmer B. *Need for More Effective Audit Activities.* Washington: U.S. General Accounting Office, April 1973.

Stein, Morris I. *Volunteers for Peace: The First Group of Peace Corps Volunteers in a Rural Community Development Program in Colombia, South America.* New York: John Wiley, 1966.

Sugarman, Jule. "What the Administration Wanted." *The Bureaucrat* 6 (Summer 1978): 5–9.

Sundquist, James L. *Politics and Policy: The Eisenhower, Kennedy and Johnson Years.* Washington: Brookings Institution, 1968.

Sussman, Barry. "Reagan's Policies Are the Key—Not His Personality." *Washington Post National Weekly Edition* (February 13, 1984): 37.

Textor, Robert B., ed. *Cultural Frontiers of the Peace Corps.* Foreword by Margaret Mead. Cambridge, Mass.: MIT Press, 1966.

Thorson, Donald. "The Proper Parent for the Peace Corps." *New York Times* (November 27, 1981): A-26.

Timmins, William M. "Relations between Political Appointees, Careerists." *Public Administration Times* (March 15, 1984): 8.

Tolley, Howard, Jr. "Five Years of the Nixon Peace Corps: Politics, Vietnam, and a Post-War Generation of Peace." *Intellect* (November 1974): 96–98.

"Trench War over VISTA." *Wall Street Journal* (August 17, 1982): 28.

U.S. Congress, House of Representatives. Appropriations Committee. *Department of Labor, Health and Human Services, Education and Related Agencies: Appropriations for 1984. Hearings before a House Subcommittee on Appropriations.* 98th Cong., 1st sess., 1983.

———. Committee on Education and Labor. *War on Poverty Program, part I, Economic Opportunity Act of 1964. Hearings before a House Subcommittee on Education and Labor.* 88th Cong., 2d sess., 1964.

————. Committee on Government Operations and Committee on Education and Labor. *VISTA and Management of the ACTION Agency. Joint Hearings before the Manpower and Housing Subcommittee of Committee on Government Operations, and the Subcommittee on Select Education of Committee on Education and Labor.* 97th Cong., 2d sess., 1983.

————. Committee on Post Office and Civil Service. *Documents Relating to Political Influence in Personnel Actions at the Department of Housing and Urban Development. Hearings before the Subcommittee on Manpower and Civil Service.* 93d Cong., 2d sess., December 12, 1974.

————. Committee on Post Office and Civil Service. *Documents Relating to Political Influence in Personnel Actions at the General Service Administration. Hearings before the Subcommittee on Manpower and Civil Service.* 93d Cong., 2d sess., October 7, 1974.

————. Committee on Post Office and Civil Service. *Statement Regarding Alleged Political Influence in Personnel Actions at the General Services Administration.* October 10, 1974. Handout.

————. President Richard M. Nixon, Message to the House of Representatives for Reorganization Plan No. 1. 92d Cong., 1st sess., March 24, 1971. *Congressional Record,* December 14, 92–74.

U.S. Congress, Senate. Committee on Government Operations, *Reorganization Plan No. 1 of 1971: Hearings before the Subcommittee on Executive Reorganization and Government Research.* 92d Cong., 1st sess., 1971.

————. Committee on Labor and Public Welfare. *National Service Corps: Hearings before the Senate Committee on Labor and Public Welfare.* 88th Cong., 1st sess., 1963.

————. Committee on Labor and Public Welfare. *Nomination: Charles W. Ervin, Hearings before the Senate Committee on Labor and Public Welfare.* 92d Cong., 2d sess., October 12, 1972.

————. Committee on Labor and Public Welfare. *Nomination: Christopher M. Mould, Hearings before the Senate Committee on Labor and Public Welfare.* 92d Cong., 2d sess., September 1972.

————. Committee on Labor and Public Welfare. *Nomination: Joseph H. Blatchford, Hearings before the Senate Committee on Labor and Public Welfare.* 92d Cong., 1st sess., 1971.

————. Committee on Labor and Public Welfare and the Special Committee on Human Resources. *ACTION Act of 1972 and ACTION Domestic Programs: Hearings.* Subcommittee on Aging, April 1972.

————. *Congressional Record.* 93d Cong., 1st sess., July 18, 1973, S. 1148.

———. *Economic Opportunity Amendment of 1967*. 90th Cong., 1st sess., 1967.

———. Select Committee on Presidential Campaign Activities. *Watergate and Related Activities*, Book 19. Washington: U.S. Government Printing Office, 1974.

———. Subcommittee on Employment, Manpower and Poverty. *Toward Economic Security for the Poor*. Washington: U.S. Government Printing Office, 1968.

U.S. General Accounting Office. *Changes Needed for a Better Peace Corps*, February 6, 1979.

U.S. National Advisory Council on Economic Opportunity. *Third Annual Report, March 1970*. Washington: U.S. Government Printing Office, 1970.

U.S. Office of Economic Opportunity. *An Evaluation of the Neighborhood Health Center Program*. Washington: Office of Economic Opportunity, May 1972.

———. *National Anti-Poverty Plan FY1968–FY1972*. Washington: U.S. Government Printing Office, June 1966.

———. *A News Summary of the War on Poverty* I, no. 32, October 24, 1966.

———. *VISTA Volunteer Handbook*. OEO/VISTA Manual 4010–1, Washington, D.C., June 1968.

———, Community Relations Division. *VISTA Serves*. Washington: VISTA, 1967.

U.S. President. *Public Papers of the President of the United States: 1969*. Washington: Office of the *Federal Register*, National Archives and Records Service, Richard M. Nixon, 1969.

———. *Public Papers of the President of the United States: 1970*. Washington: Office of the *Federal Register*, National Archives and Records Service, Richard M. Nixon, 1970.

———. *Public Papers of the President of the United States: 1971*. Washington: Office of the *Federal Register*, National Archives and Records Service, Richard M. Nixon, 1971.

U.S. President's Study Group on a National Service Program. *Information on a Proposed National Service Program*, S 1321, H.R. 5625, 1963.

Vaughn, Jack. "The Peace Corps: Now We Are Seven." *Saturday Review* (January 6, 1968): 21–23.

Ventre, Ann, and Russell Pratt. "Definitions and Assumptions: The Planned Impact Programming Process." San Francisco: ACTION Region IX (October 1973).

"A Very Special Volunteer." *Ebony* (September 1978): 64–70.

Visel, Adele. *Of Brahmins and Lesser Folk: The Tale of Another Peace Corps Grandmother in India.* New York: Vantage Press, 1979.

VISTA. *VISTA Volunteer.* Washington: Office of Economic Opportunity, n.d.

"VISTA Faces Budget Cuts and Eventual Elimination." *Jet* (April 30, 1981): 8.

"The VISTA Hit List." *Mother Jones* (April 1982): 11–12.

Warner, Lloyd W. et al. *The American Federal Executive.* New Haven: Yale University Press, 1963.

"We the Undersigned . . . Oppose the War in Vietnam." *Ramparts* (September 1967): 60–62.

Webber, Andrew Lloyd, and Tim Rice. "Everything's All Right." Song from *Jesus Christ Superstar,* Leeds Music Ltd., London, 1969.

Weber, Max. "Bureaucracy." In *From Max Weber: Essays in Sociology,* edited by H. H. Gerth and C. Wright Mills, 196–244. New York: Oxford University Press, 1970.

――――. *The Protestant Ethic and the Spirit of Capitalism.* London: Allen & Unwin, 1930.

White, Theodore H. *America in Search of Itself: The Making of the President, 1956–1980.* New York: Harper & Row, 1982.

――――. *The Making of the President: 1960.* New York: Atheneum, 1961.

"White House Aides Ordered to Cut Staffs." *Los Angeles Times* (September 9, 1973): 4.

"Why Critics Lambaste Sam Brown's Agency." *U.S. News & World Report* 86 (January 15, 1979): 37–40.

Wicker, Tom. "Lyndon Johnson versus the Ghost of Jack Kennedy." *Esquire* 68 (November 1965): 87–160.

Wiesenthal, Eric. "Top Reagan Aide Opposes Policy Role Freeze." *Public Administration Times* (January 1, 1985): 12.

Wilck, David G. "Congress Gives Struggling Peace Corps Another Chance." *Christian Science Monitor* (December 22, 1981): 14.

Windmiller, Marshall. *The Peace Corps and Pax Americana.* Washington: Public Affairs Press, 1970.

Witcover, Jules. *Marathon: The Pursuit of the Presidency, 1972–1976.* New York: Viking Press, 1977.

Witkin, Richard. "24 in Peace Corps Urge Vietnam Talks." *New York Times* (October 4, 1967): 15:1.

Wolfe, Tom. *The Right Stuff.* New York: Farrar, Straus & Giroux, 1979.

Worth, Jan. "And a Battle-Weary Peace Corps Volunteer Comes in from the Heat." *Los Angeles Times* (April 1, 1979): V-5.

Yarmolinsky, Adam. "The Beginnings of OEO." In *On Fighting Poverty: Perspectives from Experience,* edited by James Sundquist, 34–51. New York: Basic Books, 1969.

Yates, Douglas. *Bureaucratic Democracy.* Cambridge, Mass.: Harvard University Press, 1982.

Zarefsky, David. *President Johnson's War on Poverty: Rhetoric and History.* University, Ala.: University of Alabama Press, 1985.

Zurcher, Louis A., Jr. *Poverty Warriors: The Human Experience of Planned Social Intervention.* Austin: University of Texas Press, 1970.

Index

About the Author

T. Zane Reeves is Professor of Public Administration and Director of the Division of Public Administration, University of New Mexico. He received his Ph.D. from the University of Southern California, his M.A. from the University of California, Los Angeles, and his B.A. from Harding College. He is author of *Public Sector Administration,* and co-author of *Personnel Management in the Public Sector, Collective Bargaining in the Public Sector,* and *Western European Governmental and Political Organization.*